The CompleteLandlord.com™

ULTIMATE
REAL ESTATE
INVESTING
HANDBOOK

The**CompleteLandlord**.com™
ULTIMATE
REAL ESTATE
INVESTING
HANDBOOK

William A. Lederer

WILEY

John Wiley & Sons, Inc.

For general information on our other products and services or for technical support, please contact our Customer Care Department within the United States at (800) 762-2974, outside the United States at (317) 572-3993 or fax (317) 572-4002.

Wiley also publishes its books in a variety of electronic formats. Some content that appears in print may not be available in electronic books. For more information about Wiley products, visit our web site at www.wiley.com.

ISBN: 978-0-470-32316-8

Printed in the United States of America.

10 9 8 7 6 5 4 3 2 1

In honor of my family: Renda, Adam, Eric, and Muriel Lederer;

To Jill, John, Robert, Sarah, and Edward Doherty; Peggy, Marc (one of America's great real estate investors and landlords), Josh, Davis, and Chloe Blum;

And in memory of Frederick Lederer, Beverly and Irwin Lippmann, and Stella Natenberg, anyone's idea of a great real estate asset and team member

CONTENTS

ACKNOWLEDGMENTS

I am pleased to acknowledge those without whose help and guidance neither this series nor my landlording odyssey would be complete:

- My copy, editorial, graphics, and marketing team of Bridget McCrea, Shannon Vargo, Linda Indig, Mohammed Ejaz Ali, Brian Neill, Beth Zipko, and Kim Dayman, who really pulled through for me and to whom I am much indebted. A big thank you and recommendation to the best non-fiction literary agent in America and my great friend, Cynthia Zigmund.
- My inspirations: the courageous, selfless and impactful John Wood of Room to Read, business leader and good friend Dean Debiase, and real estate entrepreneur/attorney/friend Dr. Arnold S. Goldstein, Esq.
- My wife Renda and mother Muriel deserve much credit for this ultimate series, our education in landlording, and the staying force to persist. Too seldom do family members get their due in these endeavors. I have been blessed beyond belief.
- My long-time colleagues Enid Becker, Jonas Hedsund, and Jay Rawlings; accountant and lawyers Harry Kramer, Stewart Schechter, Peter Lieberman, and Todd Mazur; and my former colleagues Bruce Masterson, Cindy Fitzgerald, and Paul Barrett.
- Mona Hellinga as my favorite and utterly professional residential real estate agent.
- My friends and business partners at Buildium property management software, including Michael Monteiro and Dimitri Georgakopoulos.

LIST OF ICONS

Money Savers

These sections are designed to save you money. Use the information in them to make frugal decisions regarding your cash outlay when investing in and running your properties.

Money Makers

Here's where you'll learn how to make money in real estate. Ferret out the best possible tips and advice from these sections of the book and you'll be well braced to earn a living and more from your real estate investments.

Time Savers

We know there are only so many hours in a day, so use these areas of the book to shave precious time from your schedule and maximize the time spent on your landlording and real estate investment business.

INTRODUCTION

There's nothing quite like starting a new business venture. The slate is clean, your enthusiasm is peaked, and your passion is serving as the rudder as you make your way through the learning years. This time, you're looking to get a piece of the real estate pie that many others have already come to rely on for income, and you're going to do it through a targeted investment process.

Well, you've come to the right place. This book, in combination with the landlording and real estate property management books that complete this series, will equip you to take on just about anything that comes your way as a real estate investor.

This book is designed to serve you, the reader, in several ways. You can read it from cover to cover, stick to those sections that are most applicable to your situation, and/or supplement it with the knowledge that you'll find in the other two volumes. Regardless of how you tackle it, the key is for you to come away with a broad knowledge of exactly what it means to be a successful real estate investor.

From this book, you'll take away valuable knowledge about residential real estate investment, find out which options are most appropriate for your individual situation, get the inside track on legal and asset protection strategies, and of course, learn how to source, value, negotiate, finance, and refinance properties.

If you want to know what makes us experts in this field, consider the fact that CompleteLandlord.com has already helped hundreds of thousands of property investors—who combined own millions of rental units—save time and money. We believe life is short and it's important to manage properties efficiently, easily, and profitably.

The editorial team at CompleteLandlord.com, publisher of the *Landlord Profit Letter* and numerous special reports, and books and monitors of the CompleteLandlord Forum, has more than 25 years of landlord, property investment, rental management, and overall real estate experience. We also have a dedicated staff of attorneys and advisors who review our articles and forms library to ensure their accuracy and compliance with all federal, state, and local real estate laws. Or simply put, they help us ensure all our i's are dotted and t's are crossed.

CompleteLandlord.com is for people like you: landlords and property investors. It's the online destination that thousands of savvy landlords and real estate investors go to for real-world advice on managing properties and tenants, as well as to pick up products, services, and essential forms. All our efforts are aimed at helping people run a more profitable and successful real estate business.

We've also assembled a diverse advisory team of more than a dozen landlords from places like Ohio, Texas, Georgia, and Illinois (just to name a few). This team is not afraid to mix it up and share the real scoop on what it's like to be a landlord. They review and comment on (and sometimes argue about) our product in order to share insights with us (and you) on money- and time-saving strategies and tips to help build real wealth with investment properties. The advisory team includes landlords who own, manage, and have sold both large and small multi- and single-family properties, as well as other investment real estate.

Now it's time to turn the page and start learning the ropes of real estate investing. We will guide you through the process, helping you through the hurdles, and supporting you in your quest to reach your Holy Grail: successful real estate property investing. Good luck in your venture!

About This Book

This book is written for the first-time real estate investor. Note that we did not use the word *homeowner* when describing our readers because homeowners "own" a piece of real estate as a primary residence. While they may enjoy the tax benefits they have accrued and be gratified to see their property's value increase, they should not think of a long-term residence as an investment. This is because a permanent residence often has practical and emotional components that true investments should not have.

Much like a stock or a bond, a real estate investment should be an entity that an individual or group will buy or sell as market conditions warrant. There shouldn't be any emotional ties to an investment.

And while some people make money moving into fixer-uppers, making upgrades, and then moving on, these short-term living scenarios cannot be called true homes. They are a means of making money in the short term or creating income in the long term and should be viewed as investments.

It may seem a curious mindset, but one that should be adopted by anyone who plans to successfully invest in real estate. The purpose of this book is to introduce new investors to the best manner of researching, financing, buying, and selling investment property. In doing so, we'll explore the phenomenon of *flipping*—choreographed buying, refurbishing, and selling of properties during a short period for maximum returns.

We'll also look at the kind of buy-and-hold strategies for real estate ownership that might make sense to more cautious investors. This is important since the professionals at CompleteLandlord see flipping as a full-time business. People who are truly successful at investing need to develop a strong business mindset and an infrastructure based on financing options, a support team (brokers, attorneys, tax advisors, and so forth), and an ability to gauge changing market conditions so that they can maximize profit based on minimum investment.

Those who make a living flipping property do not necessarily make large profits on every sale, which is why it is important to have a thorough understanding of market conditions before entering each transaction. This is not to say that those who decide to take advantage of a sudden opportunity in real estate cannot make a quick return. It happens every day. But taking the time to fully understand real estate investment as a business ensures that success comes from knowledge instead of favorable market conditions and pure luck.

Along with reading this book, we encourage you to read, watch, and listen to everything around you on this subject. The best skill any investor can have is the desire and ability to absorb all the information he or she can and then take the time to determine whether that advice is worthwhile. This book is one more piece of information an investor should consider before investing.

Despite the headlines and broadcasts promising quick riches, real estate investment requires individuals to become experts—experts about financing, types of properties, and, most importantly, market conditions as they change. Potential investors need to consult a wide variety of resources before they begin the process of buying and selling real estate for profit.

The best real estate investors stay abreast of current trends in the real estate market on a local and national level. They read relevant information, talk to those with information, and are able to zero in on small pockets of success in real estate. Migration patterns, particularly those of older Americans who have been homeowners for a long time, are critical to watch as the baby boomer generation moves into retirement. Combine all of this information and put it to work in your own real estate investment strategy and you're sure to come out a winner.

SECTION ONE

Becoming a Property Investor

CHAPTER 1

New Investors: Why and When to Invest in Residential Income Property

The investment psyche of many Americans has undergone a major reversal since 2000. That's because for most of the 1980s and 1990s, the place to invest money was the stock market, propelled in no small part by the creation of 401(k) plans that put ordinary investors in the driver's seat of their personal finances as never before.

Although the stock market was previously the domain of the rich, the "common man" suddenly found himself dabbling in—and making money in—uncharted territory. Investment self-determination—with or without professional advice and information—became the way to go. Online stock-trading sites helped drive the trend, allowing anyone with money to open an account and become a day trader overnight.

Enter the tech wreck of April 2000, and a subsequent market slide triggered by the September 11, 2001, terrorist attacks. Both events left investors with tattered portfolios and an uncertain view of the future. Anyone made into a day trader by the advent of E*Trade or Ameritrade was suddenly left longing for what they had in the 1990s: double-digit investment games with little or no effort.

Even as stock prices fell and once-revered dot-com businesses disappeared (taking billions of dollars of venture capital with them), the U.S. real estate market continued to soar. It would, in fact, prop up the U.S. economy for years to come, and continues to do so in spite of the residential market contraction that took hold in 2006.

Reaping the Rewards

Today, more Americans are investing in real estate to reap its financial rewards. Though owning property has historically been a sound investment, most buyers looked no further than their primary residence. That has since changed. Fueled by low interest rates, rapid appreciation, and a growing number of ways to borrow money, many Americans now view real estate as a safe financial investment—and one more lucrative than the stock market in recent years.

A 2007 analysis of U.S. Census Bureau data shows there are 6.8 million vacation homes nationwide, along with 37.4 million investment units and 74.6 million owner-occupied units.

According to the National Association of Realtors' (NAR) 2007 Investment and Vacation Home Buyers Survey, the combined total of vacation and investment home sales accounted for 33 percent of all existing and new home sales, which is close to historic norms.

NAR reports that the market share of homes purchased for investment in 2007 was 21 percent, down from 22 percent in 2006, while another 12 percent were vacation homes, compared with a 14 percent market share in 2006. Fifty-nine percent of vacation homes purchased in 2007 were detached single-family homes, 29 percent condos, 7 percent townhouses or row houses, and 5 percent other. In 2006, detached single-family homes accounted for 67 percent of vacation home sales, while condos were 21 percent.

As you can see, the real estate investment market wasn't immune to the overall fallout within the residential sector: NAR found that investment home sales fell 18.1 percent to 1.35 million in 2007, from 1.65 million in 2006. By comparison, primary residence sales declined 10.0 percent to 4.34 million in 2007 from 4.82 million in 2006. NAR reported that the median price of a vacation home was $195,000 in 2007, down 2.5 percent from $200,000 in 2006. The typical investment property cost $150,000 in 2007, a number that was unchanged compared to 2006.

Real Estate Investor Insights

You are seeing people now for whom investing in real estate is their life. They are quasi-pro and amateur investors driven by the idea of self-sufficiency. This is their way to become financially independent. It is a move taken straight from the old day traders of the stock market.

—Jay Butler, director of the Real Estate Center
at Arizona State University

Patterns to Follow

Real estate, like any investment market, consists of patterns that repeat themselves.

Some call them cycles. Knowledgeable investors continue to buy in all markets, not just good ones. In fact, some of the best make their move when the market is down.

Following market trends, and knowing when, where, and what to buy, is the key to successful real estate investing.

Do You "Get" It?

Successful real estate investors understand trends on a micro level, which means researching the local community in which you plan to invest. You need to know answers to questions such as:

- *What is the job outlook in this community?* A healthy economy (signs of new business growth and a solid job market) is a good indication that local residents are securely employed and therefore are able to meet their financial obligations.
- *Has the local cost of living changed?* That is, can older residents afford to stay and can younger ones afford to move in?
- *How much land remains undeveloped?* In a mature community, with little room for new development, there is often intense competition for property.
- *What has happened to home and commercial real estate prices in the past 5, 10, or 15 years?* Understanding when and why prices increased, decreased, or stalled in the community is crucial. Real estate markets often stall when a major employer has moved out or boom when a new one has moved in. Knowing the commercial real estate market provides important information about the local economy. Commercial real estate vacancies mean lower rates of employment in the community.
- *If job losses or gains are occurring, what industries are involved?* What type of impact is this likely to have on the local housing market? Job losses at a small, nonunion factory will affect a different real estate market than those at a large community hospital because factory employees and medical personnel may occupy different sectors of the housing market.

(continued)

Do You "Get" It? (*Continued*)

- *Where are the largest new real estate developments?* Who is responsible for them? Knowing the largest residential developers in the community, and watching their movements, may help you identify the next area of growth.
- *Is the city or township government in good financial shape?* A community in budget trouble is a community that may be forced to raise taxes or change zoning requirements to bring in more revenue. Higher taxes can scare away many potential buyers, and zoning changes (e.g., those that allow more industry or fast-food businesses) may bring in more revenue but will result in a less attractive community.

Why is this important? Well, it makes sense to have a working knowledge of what various property markets around the country are doing, even if you plan to invest only locally, because it provides an understanding about what makes a community more or less valuable.

IMPORTANT NOTE

The federal government, and particularly the U.S. Census Bureau, keeps many statistics relative to population, housing, rental property, and beyond. Visit www.census.gov for more information, or bookmark this site as an addition to your resource file.

One particularly good way to make good investment choices is by looking at market demographics, or more simply, who is buying what and where. A recent Harvard study, for example, shows that over the past two decades the number of heads of households that were foreign-born or the native-born child of an immigrant rose to one in five (*Rental Property Investing*, Minotaur Media LLC, 2006). Today, more than 25 percent of all households are headed by minorities, a statistic largely attributed to the rise in the nation's immigrant population.

The trend of nontraditional households is rising as well. As of 2000 (the most recent U.S. Census data available), single-person households—unmarried couples, single female heads of households, and singles without children—numbered 26.5 million. The never-married share of households has been on the upswing since the first group of baby boomers reached adulthood.

The study also found that 43 percent of heads of households younger than age 35 have never married, in contrast to only 26 percent of their same-age counterparts in 1980. The growth of these two groups may lead to the largest net household growth since the baby boomers entered the housing market in the 1970s. This should be food for thought as you go about purchasing and renting out investment real estate.

Minority Report

When it comes to real estate, the fastest-growing group in the market is ethnic minorities.

Though the Harvard report points out that "the minority share of home remodeling activity and trade-up home buying is up only slightly, the increase in the rental and first-time buyer markets is dramatic. With their high immigration and birth rates, Hispanics have been at the forefront of this growth, with blacks and Asians also making progress" (*Rental Property Investing*, Minotaur Media LLC, 2006).

The study also points out that minority households are making more money. "Between 1980 and 2000, over 6.2 million minority households joined the ranks of middle-income Americans—nearly matching the gains among whites," with 2.4 million minority households added to the top-income group. Sheer population numbers are one factor, but the growing number of minorities with higher degrees are another factor in their improving earnings picture, the study notes.

The Megalopolitan Era

A few years ago, Virginia Tech urban planning professor Robert Lang and researchers at the Brookings Institution took a closer look at how 10 specific groups of regional metropolitan areas are growing together as single units (*Rental Property Investing*, Minotaur Media LLC, 2006). Called megalopolitans, these areas with populations of more than 10 million are expected to define the nation's biggest population growth over the coming decades. This trend will also redefine real estate investment, many believe, as populations grow within these designated areas. Chart 1.1 defines these new megalopolitans. (Note that these results were released before Hurricane Katrina hit the Gulf Coast.)

Top 10 U.S. Megalopolitan Areas

Megalopolitan Area	Megalopolitan States	Biggest Metro	Signature Industry*	Republican versus Democratic Politics**
1. Cascadia	OR, WA	Seattle	Aerospace	Democrat
2. Gulf Coast	AL, FL, LA, MS, TX	Houston	Energy	Republican
3. I-35 Corridor	KS, MO, OK, TX	Dallas	High tech	Republican
4. Midwest	IL, IN, KY, MI, OH, PA, WI, WV	Chicago	Manufacturing	Democrat
5. NorCal	CA, NV	San Francisco	High tech	Democrat
6. Northeast	CT, DE, MA, MD, ME, NH, NJ, NY, PA, RI, VA, WV	New York	Finance	Democrat
7. Peninsula	FL	Miami	Tourism	Republican
8. Piedmont	AL, GA, NC, SC, TN, VA	Atlanta	Banking	Republican
9. Southland	CA, NV	Los Angeles	Entertainment	Democrat
10. Valley of the Sun	AZ	Phoenix	Home building	Republican

* The industry most easily identified with leading metros in the megalopolitan area.

** How a megalopolitan area leans politically, based on the 2000 and 2004 presidential elections.

Source: R.E. Lang and D. Dhavale, *Beyond Megalopolis: Exploring America's New "Megalopolitan" Geography* (Cambridge, MA: Lincoln Institute of Land Policy, 2005).

Chart 1.1 Top 10 U.S. Megalopolitan Areas.

This research helps guide today's real estate investors by providing information on areas of population growth and the growing need for infrastructure in those areas. Each of these clustered networks of cities has a population of at least 10 million. According to the study, "megalopolitan areas are expected to add 83 million people (or the current population of Germany) by 2040, accounting for 7 in every 10 new Americans" (*Rental Property Investing*, Minotaur Media LLC, 2006). It adds that by 2040, some $33 trillion will be spent on megalopolitan building construction. The figure represents over three-quarters of all the capital that will be expended nationally on private real estate development.

The study estimates that by 2040 the megalopolitans will provide 75 percent of all money spent in the United States on private real estate and create 64 million new jobs. Those projections may not only affect where you invest, but perhaps where you will live.

Getting Your Financial House in Order

Before you can achieve success in real estate investing, you'll have to prove that you can successfully handle your own financial dealings. For most people who begin by moonlighting as investors—and those who jump into the arena on a full-time basis—the process starts with a visit to an attorney, lawyer, tax advisor, bank, thrift, and/or mortgage loan officer. From those meetings, new investors come away with an idea of how well they've handled their own finances, and whether they have the capability to achieve success in real estate investing.

How Hard Can It Be?

The implosion of the subprime mortgage market in 2007 made many people aware of just how lax lending standards became during the housing boom of the late-1990s and early-2000s. In fact, much has been written about mortgage loans being awarded to people with bankruptcies, liens, and other signs of subpar credit.

While subpar credit is not the stigma it used to be, you can be sure that anyone who has a credit score of 650 or lower is paying handsomely for the chance to get financing, particularly as lenders clamp down on their standards in the wake of the subprime mortgage market fallout.

One way to ensure fewer hassles on your route to becoming a real estate investor is to pull your own credit report first, thoroughly reviewing it and cleaning up any errors that may be on it. Do this *before* you start buying properties and you'll have an easier time getting the financing and support that you need to make the move into real estate investing.

IMPORTANT NOTE

Learn more about real estate investing on CompleteLandlord.com, where you will find tips, Q&As, and a plethora of other information that will help you in your real estate investing venture.

In fact, this simple step may yield more than premier loan rates or higher credit limits. The process of creating a pristine, or near-pristine, credit report will force you to acknowledge any past financial mistakes and make the changes necessary to ensure your future financial health.

 That last point is essential: There is a need to change your personal finances for the better. That's because it can take years for people to start showing significant success in *any* business, not just real estate. Along the way, you can expect to make bad decisions, waste some money, and learn from errors in judgment. It's just part of the game, and something you'll have to accept if you want to play.

IMPORTANT NOTE

Creating a personal balance sheet that reflects smart spending, savings, and minimal debt can be a valuable asset not only on a personal basis, but also if you ever get into a jam as a real estate investor. This snapshot of your finances—which can easily be created, maintained, and accessed on a computer—will give you a good idea of exactly where you stand financially and allow you to make the wisest decisions possible.

Worst-Case Scenario

Sometimes it helps to have a "glass-is-half-empty" philosophy in business. For real estate investors, the negatives typically include cash flow crunches (created by a short-term loss of tenants, for example) and the possibility that a property will be on the market and vacant for longer than anticipated.

For a true reality check, consider the property owners whose units were located on the Gulf Coast in 2005, the year Hurricane Katrina battered both the coastal and inland areas of the region. It will take years for them to recover after that destruction. While reading the rest of this chapter, try putting yourself in their shoes, considering exactly what you would do if you were in their position.

Step 1: Figure Out Your Net Worth

Here's why you should figure out your net worth: If you took one to two years off without pay while at the same time taking on significant debt and facing an initially unpredictable array of expense, could you manage it financially?

If you're doubtful, congratulate yourself on being normal. Starting an investor program or a business *should* feel like an enormous leap of faith for everyone involved, including yourself, your family, and your lenders. If it doesn't, then you're one of the very few who can jump into a major undertaking with no doubts.

When investing in real estate, your goal should be to avoid as much debt as possible. Ideally, that means creating a balance sheet that has more money in the Assets column than in the Debts column. One way to ensure that this happens is by generating as much of the initial investment as you can without having to borrow from commercial lenders.

You can do this by:

◆ Borrowing from savings (including retirement accounts)
◆ Borrowing from family
◆ Borrowing from friends

◆ Taking on an investment partner
◆ Selling any property for cash

If those options fail, you will need a loan.

WORKSHEET FOR STEP 1: FIGURE OUT YOUR NET WORTH

There are many computerized programs that you can use to compute your net worth on a daily basis, if needed. Before you start plugging numbers into one of these programs, however, you'll want to sit down with a pencil and fill in this worksheet:

Net Worth Worksheet

Assets
Cash in savings accounts _____
Cash in checking accounts _____
Certificates of deposit (CDs) _____
Cash on hand _____
Money market accounts _____
Money owed to me (rent deposits, etc.) _____
Cash value of life insurance _____
Savings bonds (current value) _____
Stocks _____
Bonds _____
Mutual funds _____
Vested value of stock options _____
Other investments _____
Individual retirement accounts (IRAs) _____
Keogh accounts _____
401(k) or 403(b) accounts _____
Other retirement plans _____
Market value of your home _____
Market value of other real estate _____
Resale value of cars/trucks _____
Boats, planes, other vehicles _____
Jewelry _____
Collectibles _____

(continued)

Net Worth Worksheet (*Continued*)

Furnishings and other personal property _____

Other _____

Total Assets _____

Liabilities

Mortgages _____

Car loans _____

Bank loans _____

Student loans _____

Home equity loans _____

Other loans _____

Credit card balances _____

Real estate taxes owed _____

Income taxes owed _____

Other taxes owed _____

Other debts _____

Total Liabilities _____

(Total assets − Total liabilities = Net worth)

Step 2: Consider a Financial Advisor

Most people don't want to spend the day thinking about their personal finances. Chances are that if you're reading this book you are attempting to find a way to improve your finances via a potentially risky and certainly complex strategy of real estate investment. Luckily, there is a professional who can bridge the gap between that investment and your desire to think about something else other than your finances. This person is a *financial advisor.*

One way to take a comprehensive view of your past investment results and future plans is to consult a skilled financial advisor, also known as a *financial planner.* The U.S. Securities and Exchange Commission (SEC) provides the following information about this industry:

> Most financial planners are investment advisors—people who give advice about securities to clients—but not all investment advisors are financial planners. Some financial planners assess every aspect of your financial life, including savings, investments, insurance, taxes, retirement, and estate planning, and help you develop a detailed strategy or financial

plan for meeting all your personal and financial goals. Others call themselves financial planners, but they may only be able to recommend that you invest in a narrow range of products, and sometimes products that are not securities.

For a listing of financial planners who work on a fee-only basis (as opposed to working on a commission structure), check out www.napfa .org, the web site for the National Association of Fee-Only Financial Planners. Use the site's "Find an Advisor" section to find one or more options in your region.

Before hiring a financial professional, figure out exactly what services you need, what services the prospective planner can deliver, any limitations on what he or she can recommend, how much you'll have to pay for the specified services, and how the advisor or planner gets paid. Understand that the planner may handle the latter several different ways, including hourly, fixed fee, or commission.

How Do You Pay Your Advisor?

It's no secret that financial types command a hefty fee for what they do. Rather than getting a nasty surprise when the bill comes, find out upfront exactly how your stockbroker, financial planner, or investment advisor gets paid.

Investment advisors generally are paid in one of the following ways:

- A percentage of the value of the assets they manage for you
- An hourly fee for the time they spend working for you
- A fixed fee
- A commission on the securities they sell
- Some combination of the above

Each compensation method has potential benefits and possible drawbacks, depending on your individual needs. Ask the investment advisors you interview to explain the differences to you before you do business with them, and get several opinions before making your decision.

Once you've determined if the professional can do what you need him or her to do within your budget, ask the most important question: Do I like this person and can I work with him or her? Forming this type of bond is important because discussing money is extremely personal, so you'll want to find someone with whom you can be completely honest. That honesty will allow a productive relationship.

There are many ways to find financial planners, although personal recommendations from trusted sources (friends, family, colleagues, coworkers, and so forth) are probably the best option. The Financial Planners Association (www.fpanet.org) can help you find individuals by geography and focus. Some planners in your area may also carry the Certified Financial Planners™ (CFP) designation, which indicates that they have gone through rigorous training in their field.

When you find a selection of planners, interview them by phone and ask the following questions:

- What experience do you have, especially with people in my circumstances?
- Where did you go to school? What is your recent employment history?
- What licenses do you hold? Are you registered with the SEC, a state, or the National Association of Securities Dealers?
- What products and services do you offer?
- Can you only recommend a limited number of products or services to me? If so, why?
- How are you paid for your services? What is your usual hourly rate, flat fee, or commission?
- Have you ever been disciplined by any government regulator for unethical or improper conduct or been sued by a client who was not happy with the work you did?
- (This is for registered investment advisors only): Will you send me a copy of both parts of your Form ADV (the registration form investment advisors file with the SEC)?
- Can you provide me with the names and phone numbers of some people you have worked with?

After narrowing your choices to one or two advisors, arrange for a personal meeting with each one. Make it your goal to find a professional who takes a comprehensive approach to your finances—preferably one who deals with everything from taxes to insurance and investing to estate planning, and everything in between. Financial planners can develop an overall plan for you to meet your long-term goals, but not all financial planners are the same, and you must do your homework to make sure you find the one who is right for you.

A financial advisor can provide the most value by understanding how your finances interrelate and giving advice on the best course of action in regards to your whole financial picture. The overall goal should be to consider the short-term effects of your decisions, all the while keeping the end in sight. Using a system of stepping stones, you'll be able to reach your end goal while making the best possible decisions along the way.

Getting there starts with a definition of the length and scope of the relationship with your financial planner. As the client, it's up to you to determine what you want from the professional that you're working with. Once you have that nailed down, the planner will explain and put in writing what services he or she will provide as well as what your responsibilities are.

You should also decide how you will measure success with your new financial strategy. A financial planner begins with a discovery phase that involves gathering and reviewing all the relevant information about your current financial situation, including tax returns, investments, debts, wills, and insurance policies. With that information in mind, the planner should then have a discussion with you about your objectives and risk tolerance. Then, the planner will create an individualized, written financial plan that includes the following:

◆ Net worth statement
◆ Cash flow analysis
◆ Tax plan
◆ College savings plan
◆ Retirement plan
◆ Investment analysis
◆ Estate plan
◆ Liability protection
◆ Debt strategy
◆ Insurance analysis

Every plan should assume realistic rates of return and make suitable investment recommendations. Make sure you fully understand and agree with the plan before implementing it. Exactly how you and your planner will execute and monitor your financial plan is up to you (just be sure to get it all in writing).

Conflicts of Interest

Planners should always disclose the ways by which they are paid. While one compensation structure is not inherently better than another, you should be aware of any conflicts of interest. If a planner only recommends investment or insurance products that his or her company provides, make sure you understand how the planner is compensated. There may be nothing wrong with these products, but a reputable planner should be open to discussing alternatives that might better suit your needs.

Planners also should not give you advice before they have gathered all of your necessary financial information. For example, they may attempt to sell you a financial product before they fully understand your situation. To check the disciplinary history of a financial planner or other advisor, visit the Certified Financial Planner Board of Standards at www.cfp.net/search.

While it is always possible to lose money in real estate or the financial markets, you shouldn't lose money because of a dishonest or incompetent financial planner. If this does happen, you might consider filing a complaint against the planner. Your recourse in these situations lies with the Certified Financial Planner Board of Standards that investigates complaints and may censure or suspend a CFP or revoke his or her right to use the CFP marks.

Real Estate Investor Insights

If you want to go out and buy something, use a bonus. Use an inheritance. Use savings that you have built up for that purpose. Do not use earmarked savings or credit to get into this game.

In a market that has just caught steam, that might work because appreciation will take care of some of your leverage costs, but people always make mistakes, and when you are in that much debt, the mistakes always get worse.

—Phillip Cook, financial planner

Most financial planners are also registered investment advisors, which means they are registered with regulators in their state and the SEC. You can contact those agencies to make a complaint. The SEC investigates complaints and advises investors about possible remedies.

The SEC may also prosecute individuals who violate federal securities laws. The NASD investigates complaints and offers mediation and arbitration.

For a list of state securities regulators, visit www.nasaa.org/ quicklinks/ContactYourRegulator.cfm. For the SEC, visit www.sec.gov/ complaint.shtml.

Step 3: Consult Experts in the Real Estate Field

Before you start pouring your hard-earned money into the real estate market, you'll want to assemble a competent team of experts who can advise you on how to make the best possible financial decisions.

Here are some of the most important professionals you'll want to have on your team.

Tax Advisors

 Some 55 percent of Americans now rely on professionals to file their returns. That need becomes even greater when you establish a business or a sideline that requires tax advice. As you begin your research into various types of property you might buy, do not forget to ask professionals, property owners, and other knowledgeable people if there are good attorneys in the area. You can get referrals the following ways:

◆ Talk to friends, family members, and coworkers, or your state's bar association.
◆ Talk to local real estate agents or brokers.
◆ Call a local real estate association.

Identify a number of possible attorneys and call each one. Then:

◆ Prepare a list of questions pertaining to your situation. Most lawyers will answer simple questions over the phone at no charge.
◆ Ask how much each lawyer charges per hour and request an estimate of the time required to complete the tasks you require— looking over contracts, handling disclosures, and helping with the closing.

Real Estate Agents

A good real estate agent or broker can make a valuable addition to your investment team. Their commissions (typically paid by the property seller) average 5 to 6 percent of a property's selling price, and can get pretty hefty (depending on the property's price), but when you factor in the time and expertise required to search, negotiate, and ensure a smooth transaction closing, an agent might prove invaluable.

Many owners who try to sell on their own quickly discover the benefits of having a professional in the field to work with, as evidenced by the real estate signs that often appear in yards several weeks after the for-sale-by-owner signs. To find a good agent, ask for recommendations from friends, family, and other real estate professionals, including lenders. Then ask the agent the following questions:

- Do you specialize in selling properties like mine? What other properties similar to mine have you sold recently?
- What price do you think my properties should sell for and why?
- What are your marketing plans for my property?
- Do you provide à la carte services? That is, is there a way I can reduce my commission payment by removing some workload from you if my investment business becomes active? If not, explain what I will get for that full fee.
- Do you provide special services for investment clients? Explain them.

Experienced Investors

Not every real estate investor will want to share his or her best secrets with you. But if you meet a successful investor, it may be worthwhile to offer to buy him or her lunch. Keep the discussion respectful and not overly intrusive. Asking for information from others successful in the field is good practice for the real world of investing where you should always be asking questions.

Credit Scores

In the past decade, credit scores have become the most important determinant of whether an individual will be approved for a credit card, car loan, business loan, mortgage, and sometimes even a job. According to myFiCO.com, a division of Fair Isaac Corp., the company that helped develop modern credit scoring, a person's credit score is a number based on the information in their credit file that shows how likely they are to pay a loan back on time—the higher their score, the less risk they represent. The credit score that lenders use is called a FICO score. A FICO score helps a lender determine whether a borrower will qualify for a loan and what interest rate they will pay.

Credit scores range from 300 to 900. The best credit rates are given to people with scores above 770.

IMPORTANT TIP

Request a Copy of Your Credit Report

MyFiCO.com is a clearinghouse for credit reports from all three major credit reporting agencies—Equifax, Experian, and TransUnion. To make credit reports more accessible to consumers, these agencies have set up AnnualCreditReport.com, which allows you to get your hands on your own report without having to go through all three agencies. This central site allows you to request a free credit file disclosure once every 12 months from each of the nationwide consumer credit reporting companies. Check it out at www.annualcreditreport.com.

Chart

FICO scores are calculated from various different credit data in an individual's credit report and grouped into five categories, according to myFiCO.com:

Payment History

- On-time payment history for credit cards, store card accounts, installment loans, finance company accounts, mortgage, and so forth

(continued)

Payment History (*Continued*)

- Adverse public records (bankruptcy, judgments, suits, liens, wage attachments, etc.)
- Collection items and/or delinquency (past due items)
- Degree of delinquency for any of the above
- Past due time on delinquent accounts or accounts turned over to collection agencies
- How recently the individual went delinquent on accounts
- Number of accounts still past due
- Number of accounts paid on time

Amounts Owed

- Amount owed on all accounts
- Amount owed by specific class of accounts
- Accounts without specific balances
- Overall number of accounts with balances
- Proportion of credit lines used
- Proportion of installment loan balances still owed

Length of Credit History

- Age of accounts
- When specific categories of accounts were opened
- How long accounts were inactive

New Credit

- Proportion of accounts that were recently opened by account type
- Number of new accounts
- Number of recent credit inquiries
- Time since recent account openings by type of account
- Time since last credit inquiries
- Time it took to reestablish positive credit history after payment problems

Types of Credit Used

- Number of credit cards, retail accounts, installment loans, mortgage, and consumer finance accounts

Are Credit Scores Fair?

According to the PBS series *Frontline*'s 2004 broadcast "The Secret History of the Credit Card," a single number to define one's complete credit history may seem daunting, but credit lending is actually fairer now than it used to be. According to the report, despite the drawbacks, credit scoring has dramatically improved the efficiency of credit markets. "What credit reporting does, and does especially well in the United States, is that it improves risk assessment," says Michael Staten, director of the Credit Research Center at the McDonough School of Business, Georgetown University. "It gives the lender a better picture of whether the loan will be repaid, based entirely on how the consumer has handled loans in the past. You could say that it takes out a lot of the factors that you would consider discriminatory" (*Rental Property Investing*, Minotaur Media LLC, 2006).

Staten goes on to say that one major advantage of credit scores is that they allow investors who buy securities to get a more accurate assessment of the underlying risk in these loans. Investors who purchase the securities buy a share of the stream of revenue that flows as loans are repaid, allowing the lender to get the loans off their books and shift some of the risk to outside investors.

How does that help consumers who are seeking credit? According to the *Frontline* broadcast, these investments make available large quantities of additional funds to the lender that can then be awarded in consumer credit markets. This lowers the price of loans or the interest rates to the consumer and makes credit more widely available.

IMPORTANT TIP

While it may seem like an easy entry into the real estate investing market, tapping home equity and retirement accounts isn't always a good idea. See Chapter 14 for better financing, loans, and lending options that are available to you.

A Final Point

A decision as important as a real estate investment requires a careful overview of your own financial situation. Do this before you start your property search, and consider meeting with a financial planner to review your current savings, investment, and debt picture. From there, get the right guidance about taking on debt and risking personal funds in real estate. Only then can you be assured that you will be adequately braced for success in the field.

CHAPTER 3

Your Options: Self-Directed Real Estate IRAs, 1031 Property Exchanges, and Tenants-in-Common

As a real estate investor, you have various financing options available that go beyond the traditional mortgage that you've probably used in the past when purchasing a primary home. Cash is always king, of course, but there are other options that may be more applicable for your specific situation.

In this chapter, we look at three financing alternatives that you'll definitely want to consider: the self-directed real estate IRA, the 1031 property exchange, and the tenants-in-common arrangement. Each comes with its own set of pros and cons, so you'll want to consider them carefully before signing on the dotted line.

Self-Direction

Breaking out of the mold of the typical individual retirement account, the self-directed IRA allows individuals to invest both in traditional investments (stocks, bonds, mutual funds) and nontraditional options (real estate, mortgages, mobile homes, and limited partnerships). Designed for the investor who is savvier than the average person who is looking to stash money away for future retirement, the self-directed IRA can be a good financing vehicle for someone looking to invest in real estate.

The pros of self-directed IRAs include:

◆ The ability to apply your investment knowledge to an IRA and diversify out of stocks, bonds, and mutual funds.

◆ The opportunity to purchase raw land, houses, condos, and/or commercial properties.

◆ Investments grow in a tax-free or tax-deferred manner.

◆ Those investments help create a more diverse, broad retirement portfolio.

◆ The rate of return will be based on your knowledge of investing in real estate (not the fluctuations in the stock market).

◆ You have absolute decision-making power and don't have to ask permission of anyone else when making investment choices.

IMPORTANT NOTE

Self-directed IRAs are an excellent option for the hands-on real estate investor who isn't afraid to make key decisions about his or her retirement portfolio.

There are also some cons of using self-directed IRAs, including:

◆ Unlike traditional IRAs, they require knowledge of exactly *what* type of assets you want to purchase.

◆ They also require a reasonably sound knowledge of the subject matter (investing, real estate, retirement).

◆ These investments can be complex, particularly when it comes to structuring the IRA and real estate entities, evaluating investment opportunities, and complying with the self-directed IRA rules for setting up investments. (This is where a good IRA advisor will prove invaluable.)

◆ Your business cannot lease space from your IRA property.

◆ You (the IRA owner) cannot live in an investment owned by the IRA.

◆ You also can't directly (or indirectly) buy, sell, or lease property between the IRA and a disqualified party (such as your grandparents, children, grandchildren, stepchildren, daughter-in-law, or son-in-law).

Usually you will open a self-directed IRA through your bank, insurance company, or stock brokerage, but for real estate investors a better option may be an independent administrator (the actual company through which you will invest) to serve as the trustee or custodian for the account. This alternative is usually best because those options offered by banks, for example, may limit the investment options or products that are available to you as an investor (real estate, for example, may be excluded).

IMPORTANT NOTE

The self-directed IRA is often overlooked by real estate investors because many trustees incorrectly tell their clients that they cannot use the accounts to invest in real estate.

You cannot take real estate property you already own or occupy and stuff it into your IRA, even if you sell the properties to the IRA at fair market value (FMV). If you have to liquidate a portion of the IRA's ownership in the property at the time of required minimum distributions—70½ in order to remain IRS compliant—you can do so incrementally. In doing so, the portion that is sold off can be taken as an IRA distribution.

Section 408 of the Internal Revenue Code allows individuals to purchase land, commercial property, condominiums, residential property, trust deeds, or real estate contracts with funds held in many common forms of IRAs, including a traditional IRA, a Roth IRA, and a Simplified Employee Pension plan, or SEP-IRA.

To find an advisor who specializes in real estate, and who can help you set up a self-directed IRA, start by searching for keywords like "real estate IRA" on a search engine such as Google. Find an advisor who has worked with real estate investors in the past, and who is knowledgeable about the types of investment you're interested in. The fees you'll pay this person can vary, so pay close attention to how these additional costs affect your investment strategy and potential ROI.

When you find the right property to invest in, your IRA custodian will purchase it, with the title reflected in his or her name for "your benefit." All property expenses (taxes, insurance, and repairs, for example) must be covered by the funds that are in your IRA and all income generated will be deposited into your IRA account (and used to cover those costs).

Owners of self-directed IRAs can make annual contributions. At press time, the maximum you could contribute to such accounts annually was $3,000 for a traditional or Roth IRA ($3,500 for those 50 and older) or 15 percent of annual salary (up to $40,000) for a SEP-IRA.

Like any investment, be sure to educate yourself on the fine points of self-directed IRAs and/or work with a professional who has in-depth knowledge and hands-on expertise in the field. The process, rules, and requirements can be daunting, but when approached in a tactical manner can be quickly overcome to reveal a viable financing option for real estate investors.

Swapping It Out

It almost sounds too good to be true. Sell a piece of investment property and defer both capital gains and depreciation recapture taxes, as long as 100 percent of the equity is reinvested into a "like-kind" property of equal or greater value. Known as a 1031 exchange, the tax law applies to any property held for investment purposes, or for productive use in a trade or business, and is often referred to as a "tax-free" exchange.

In a typical transaction, the property owner is taxed on any gain realized from the sale. However, through a Section 1031 Exchange, the tax on the gain is deferred until some future date, which is usually triggered by another exchange, sale, or purchase. In other words, no gain or loss will be recognized on the exchange of property held for productive use in a trade or business, or for investment. In a tax-deferred exchange, a property owner trades one or more sold properties for one or more new of "like-kind," all the while deferring the payment of federal income taxes (and some state taxes) on the transaction.

IMPORTANT NOTE

Many 1031 exchanges involve vacation homes, second homes, and single-family rental properties.

To qualify for the tax relief, the investor must select up to three investment properties within 45 days of the close of escrow of the sold property, and must successfully complete the new purchase(s) within 180 days of closing. As determined by IRS Code Section 1031, a like-kind exchange simply means exchanging any property considered real property under state law with another such property.

For a Section 1031 exchange to be eligible for the tax relief, the value of the replacement property must be equal to or greater than the value (the purchase price adjusted for actual closing costs) of the sold property sold. A $150,000 property whose sale requires closing costs of $8,000, for example, would be valued at $142,000.

Real Estate Investor Insights

The criteria for 1031 exchanges is very explicit and sometimes complicated. You have to dot your i's and cross your t's and use a reputable exchange service (an IRS requirement). Use someone who doesn't know what they're doing and it can be fatal if the IRS audits you.

—Florida-based financial advisor

IMPORTANT NOTE

Sometimes, the six-month window just isn't long enough for an investor to pick out a good property and get it closed in time. As a result, people will buy something they shouldn't, thinking, "Well, I'm going to save all this tax, so I'll buy it." This can result in a poor investment decision and should be avoided at all costs.

Certain property types do not qualify for Section 1031 exchanges, including:

◆ Property held primarily for sale
◆ Inventories
◆ Stocks, bonds, or notes
◆ Securities or evidences of indebtedness
◆ Partnership interests
◆ Certificates of trusts or beneficial interest

What Is Like-Kind?

Replacement property acquired in an exchange must be "like-kind" to the property being sold. All qualifying real property located in the United States is considered like-kind. The relinquished property must be exchanged for other property, rather than sold for cash and then using the proceeds to buy the replacement property.

For the most part, deferred exchanges are facilitated by qualified intermediaries who assist the taxpayer in meeting the requirements of Section 1031. This person is an independent party who facilitates tax-deferred exchanges pursuant to Section 1031 of the Internal Revenue Code.

The qualified intermediary, who can't be the taxpayer or a disqualified person (anyone close to the investor who is presumed to be under the control of that buyer), will purchase the relinquished property and sell it to the buyer, then hold the sales proceeds until the taxpayer has selected his or her like-kind exchange property to buy (this must take place within the six-month window). The qualified intermediary then purchases the replacement property and transfers it to the investor to complete the exchange within the appropriate time limits.

IMPORTANT NOTE

When using a 1031 exchange, the properties you select must be identified in writing, signed by you (the taxpayer), and delivered to the qualified intermediary.

IMPORTANT NOTE

Once the closing occurs, it's too late to take advantage of the 1031 tax-deferred exchange. You must arrange this aspect of the real estate deal in advance, and with the help of a qualified intermediary, or you will not qualify for the tax savings associated with the 1031 exchange.

Follow the Rules

Here are the rules governing property selection when using 1031 exchanges:

- *The three-property rule:* You can select up to three potential replacement properties, without regard to their value.
- *The 200 percent rule:* Any number of properties may be identified, but their total value cannot exceed twice the value of the relinquished property.
- *The 95 percent rule:* Select as many properties as you want, but before the exchange period expires you have to buy replacement properties with an aggregate fair market value equal to at least 95 percent of the aggregate fair market value of all the identified properties.

A 1031 exchange is completed when the investor is given the proceeds from the sale of the relinquished property. The process may seem complicated, but it's one of the few "breaks" that Uncle Sam provides to real estate investors who follow all of the rules when selecting and purchasing real estate, and can be a great financing vehicle for the person who has an existing property to sell.

Tenants in Common

The last financing option that we'll discuss in this chapter is the tenants in common (TIC) 1031 exchange, which is a form of real estate ownership in which two or more persons have an undivided, fractional interest in the asset. In this setup, ownership shares are not required to be equal, and ownership interests can be inherited. Each co-owner receives an individual deed at closing for an undivided percentage interest in the entire property.

IMPORTANT NOTE

A TIC owner has the same rights and benefits as a single owner of property.

Through the TIC, investors can receive monthly income and are entitled to all tax advantages (for each of their pro-rata percentage shares). The TIC option can be particularly beneficial for the landlord who wants to free herself from having to handle property management. Ready to give up the hassle of tenant relations, facility maintenance, and bill paying, the TIC allows the owner to enjoy the income from the property while leaving the management to someone else.

It works like this: The owner exchanges a management-intensive property for an institutional-quality property with the potential to generate steady income, tax benefits, and appreciation. Via a management contract, a manager will be retained to manage the asset while the owner enjoys the financial benefits, including a replacement property income that could be higher than what was being netted from the original property.

Through the TIC exchange, no capital gains taxes are due until the replacement property is eventually sold.

IRS Rules

In 2002, the IRS issued guidelines (Revenue Procedure 2002-22) governing the unique structure of TIC property investments. According to these guidelines, a TIC, also known as co-ownership of real estate (CORE), should have no more than 35 investors. The typical structure for this includes from 12 to 20 TIC investors in one particular property.

The benefits of a TIC arrangement for real estate investors include:

◆ The ability to invest in larger, institutional grade properties (like warehouses, shopping centers, industrial property, and so forth) that cost a few million dollars or more and that are out of reach for the individual investor.

◆ The opportunity to diversify a real estate investment across different types and sizes of real estate investments, as well as in different geographic markets.

◆ The potential to increase your net cash flow.

◆ The chance to take advantage of tax write-offs and property appreciation benefits.

As with all real estate financing vehicles, you'll want to do your homework and work with a competent advisor before getting into the TIC arena. This investment vehicle isn't for everyone, but with the right partners and advisors—and with the help of the experienced CompleteLandlord team—you'll be well positioned to take advantage of this financing option.

CHAPTER 4

Legal, Financial, and Tax Considerations

Property owners often have been described as having a bundle of legal rights that are protected by state and federal laws. The bundle includes, for example, the right to:

- ◆ Control how the property is used—within the law's parameters.
- ◆ Benefit from the property—that is, to receive benefits such as rents or mining income.
- ◆ Transfer, sell, mortgage, will, or otherwise dispose of the property.
- ◆ Exclude others from entering and using the property.

Not every interest in real estate conveys the entire bundle of rights to a purchaser. For example, some individuals may have only the right to enjoy property at some point in the future or for a term of years, while others may have interests that terminate upon the occurrence of a specified event. Others simply may possess a leasehold interest in property, which means the title is not theirs to transfer.

Due to these parameters, it's critical that all real estate investors understand the different forms of ownership that exist today. Some types give the owners absolute ownership of the property for unlimited duration. These owners can sell, rent, mortgage, and transfer the property to heirs as they like. Other forms of property ownership, such as a life estate, are valid only during an individual's life and do not confer unlimited ownership rights.

In this chapter, we examine the different types of interests in real estate, including fee simple estates, life estates, and leasehold estates. We also discuss which ownership options are available when more than one owner is involved. Exactly who is named as owner on a deed becomes important when property is later re-conveyed, when a co-owner dies, or if property becomes subject to a creditor's lien. Finally, we look at the different ways in which real estate can be owned by trusts and other legal entities.

The Impact of English Law

As feudalism declined in England, a system of private land ownership slowly evolved. It recognized six basic types of estates, distinguished primarily by their duration:

- *Three freehold estates:* Fee simple, life estate, and fee tail, which last for an indeterminate length of time, such as for a person's lifetime or forever.
- *Three nonfreehold estates:* Tenancy for years, periodic tenancy, and tenancy at sufferance, also called leasehold estates, which last for a fixed period of time.

All of these estates, with the exception of the fee tail, are part of the American property system today.

Freehold Estates

Fee Simple

Today, the most common form of property ownership is called an estate in fee simple—sometimes called a fee simple absolute. Essentially, this is the highest interest in real estate that is recognized by law. It gives the owner the entire bundle of rights and title to property for an unlimited duration, unlike some older forms of ownership, such as a life estate, where title reverts to another beneficiary after a certain time.

In addition, the owner has absolute ownership rights in the property, which means that he or she can sell it, lease it, and eventually transfer it to heirs. The only limits placed on fee simple absolute interests are public and private restrictions, such as zoning laws and restrictive covenants.

Origin of the Word

The term *fee simple* has its origins in feudal England. A noble landowner would grant an estate called a fee to a third party in exchange for service or money. In the thirteenth century, a fee simple could be created by making a grant to person X and his heirs. It became a rigid common-law rule in England that a fee simple could be created only by using the words "and his heirs" in the grant.

Today, statutes in almost all U.S. jurisdictions provide that a grantor or testator may pass a fee simple interest by conveyance or will, unless the document affirmatively shows a contrary intent. As a result, a fee simple interest will be created simply by using the words "to X" rather than to X and his or her heirs if that is the grantor's or testator's intent.

Today, in residential real estate transactions, land is almost always granted in fee simple absolute. In commercial real estate transactions, the same also holds true; the only other significant estate in such transactions is the leasehold estate. Thus, when a contract requires the seller to convey title to land, the seller is obligated to convey property in fee simple absolute, unless a smaller estate is intended. If a property owner tries to place any total or absolute restraint on alienation of a fee simple estate, a court will find the restraint void.

> For example, a conveyance of land is given to Alison. However, if Alison ever attempts to sell the land to Bob, she would give Bob no interest whatsoever in the property. Alison would own the property in fee simple and could do with it what she pleased. However, partial restraints on alienation of a fee simple may be allowed if reasonable in nature, purpose, and duration.

Fee Simple Defeasible

While most fee simple estates are absolute, meaning that they provide the owner with full possessory rights, an owner of a defeasible fee simple estate has a limited use of the land. Essentially, a defeasible fee simple is created by language sufficient to create a fee simple followed by a special provision that may end the estate prematurely if a particular event occurs.

There are two types of defeasible fees: a fee simple subject to a condition subsequent and a fee simple subject to a special limitation, also known as a fee simple determinable. If a fee simple estate is qualified by a condition subsequent, the new owner is not allowed to perform a certain action or activity. If the condition is broken, the former owner retains a power of termination or right of reentry that allows him or her to retake possession of the property through legal means. Note that upon the occurrence of a designated terminating event, the fee simple does not terminate automatically; the person who created the estate has the power to terminate the estate but need not do so.

> For example, a fee simple subject to a condition subsequent is created by a grant of land to Adam on the condition that there be no consumption of alcoholic beverages on the property. If alcohol is served, the grantor and his or her heirs shall have a right of reentry and repossession.

 To create a fee simple subject to a condition subsequent, words of limitation such as "subject to the following", "on the condition that", or "but if" typically are used. In contrast, with a fee simple determinable, the estate ends when the new owner fails to comply with the limitation that has been imposed. If the designated terminating event occurs, the estate automatically ends, and the former owner or his or her heirs obtains full ownership once again. Unlike the fee simple subject to a condition subsequent, there is no need to reenter the land or go to court to regain possession of the land.

> For example, a fee simple determinable is created by a grant of land to the ABC Church so long as the land shall be used for church purposes. In this case, if the church ever decides to use the land for another purpose, the original owner or his or her heirs or successors reacquires ownership to the land.

The operative words needed to create a fee simple determinable are "so long as", "while", or "during".

IMPORTANT NOTE

Today, estates in fee simple determinable and estates subject to a condition subsequent are rarely created in commercial transactions. However, they are often used when property is given to religious, educational, or other charitable organizations.

Life Estate

Another type of freehold estate is the life estate, which is limited in duration to the life of the owner or another designated person. Unlike fee simple estates, the owner of a life estate cannot transfer the property by will or intestacy.

> For example, John Smith has a fee simple interest in his house and would like to give his wife a life estate in the property at his death. To do this, John could provide in his will that "I hereby bequeath the property at 123 Elm St. to my wife, Pamela, for her life and then to Charles, our son". In this case, Pamela is considered the life tenant, and Charles is the person to whom the property will pass when Pamela's life estate ends. In legal terms, Charles is known as the remainderman and merely has a future interest in the property. When Pamela dies, Charles automatically becomes the fee simple owner.

> A life estate can also be based on the life of someone other than the life tenant. In the above scenario, for example, John could convey a life estate to Pamela for the duration of the life of Henry, John's elderly uncle. While Pamela is still considered the life tenant, the measuring life is Henry's, and the life tenancy ends at Henry's death. This form of a life estate is known as a life estate *pur autre vie*.

Rights and Duties of Life Tenants

The life tenant has the exclusive right to use the property and to receive income from it as long as he or she is living. If the tenant tries to sell, lease, or mortgage his or her interest, the purchaser would receive only the tenant's interest—that is, an interest for a lifetime.

In practical terms, a life tenant's ability to transfer his or her interest is limited since a life estate is much less desirable than a fee simple estate.

The holder of a life estate also has certain duties with respect to the property. For example, a life tenant cannot injure the property—by allowing it to fall into disrepair, for example. Legally, this type of injury is known as *waste*. Affirmative waste occurs when the present owner's voluntary acts significantly reduce the property's value—destroying a valuable house, for instance.

Permissive waste stems from the present owner's inaction causing damage to the estate (such as failure to repair a leaky roof or replace broken windows). With either type of waste, the eventual property owners can sue the life tenant for damages or seek an injunction to stop the harmful conduct.

IMPORTANT NOTE

While it is still possible to transfer property to others as a life estate, it is no longer common to do so. Instead, trusts often are used to accomplish the same purpose. The trustee holds title to the land for the life of the beneficiary, and the beneficiary is entitled to all proceeds from the land during his or her lifetime. At the beneficiary's death, the land is distributed as directed by the creator of the trust.

Estate in Fee Tail

The last type of freehold estate is the estate in fee tail, whose duration is measured by the lives of the lineal descendants of a designated person.

For example, an estate in fee tail is created by granting land to Adam and the heirs of his body. The estate would last as long as Adam's bloodline continued, and the land could not be alienated out of the prescribed line of succession.

This type of estate is largely obsolete today; most states have enacted legislation that precludes its creation.

Nonfreehold Estates

In contrast to a freehold estate, a nonfreehold estate does not involve property ownership. Instead, it simply gives a tenant the right to possess—that is, lease—property for a specified term. Nonfreehold estates include tenancies for years, periodic tenancies, and tenancies at sufferance.

A tenancy for years is a leasehold estate that begins on a specific date and expires on a fixed date, such as after a specific number of years, months, or weeks. When the ending date arrives, the tenancy terminates without either party having to give notice. A periodic tenancy exists for a set term, such as from month to month or year to year, and automatically continues if neither party takes steps to terminate the tenancy. Today, leases for real property and buildings typically use periodic tenancies.

Finally, a tenancy at sufferance arises when a tenant continues to occupy property after the right of occupancy has expired. In this case, the landlord either can object to the holdover and evict the tenant or accept rent offered by the tenant. If rent is accepted, a periodic tenancy is created.

Forms of Ownership

Just as there are many different types of interests in land, owners have numerous options regarding how property can be titled. Who is named as owner on a deed and how ownership is shared, if there is more than one owner, becomes important when property is later re-conveyed, when a co-owner dies, or if property becomes subject to a creditor's lien. Marital status also impacts which title options are available to joint owners.

The three main ways in which a fee simple estate may be owned include:

1. *In severalty:* Only one person holds title.
2. *In co-ownership:* Two or more individuals hold title jointly.
3. *In trust:* A trustee holds title for the benefit of another person called the beneficiary.

Let's look at each of these options in depth.

Ownership in Severalty

When only one person owns property, the person is said to own property in severalty. This term comes from the idea that as sole owner, a person is severed or cut off from all other owners. Only one name appears on the property's deed. Because there is no one else with ownership rights, the owner has sole discretion with respect to how to use or transfer the property.

 An important concern when deciding whether to place property in one spouse's name only is the risk of liability for court judgments. For example, if a doctor does not have malpractice insurance, his or her assets could be attached by creditors if an adverse judgment is rendered against him or her. He or she can avoid this risk by putting title to the family's house in his or her spouse's name. Note that if a married man or woman is titling real estate in his or her name only, the title insurance company will require the other spouse to specifically disclaim his or her right, title, and interest in the property.

Joint Ownership or Co-Ownership

In many cases, real estate may be held jointly by two or more individuals called co-owners. There are four basic forms of joint ownership:

1. Tenancy in common
2. Joint tenancy
3. Tenancy by the entirety
4. Community property

> **Joint Estates and the English Common Law**
>
> Joint ownership was first recognized in the English common law, which held that joint estates in land exist whenever two or more persons have a concurrent and equal right to the possession and use of the same piece of land. Early common law recognized several forms of concurrent estates: joint tenancy, tenancy by the entirety, tenancy in common, tenancy in coparcenary, and tenancy in partnership. Today, only the first three types still exist in the United States.

Co-owners who are not married have more limited options when choosing a form of co-ownership: They can either be tenants in common or joint tenants with right of survivorship. Married co-owners, on the other hand, can choose either of these options or can hold property as tenants by the entirety or as community property, depending on the state.

Tenants in Common

The most common way that real estate is owned today by joint owners is as tenants in common. With this type of ownership, each person owns an undivided fractional interest in the property, although the ownership interests need not be equal. For example, a tenant in common may hold a one-half or one-fourth interest in an apartment complex, with the other tenant holding the remaining interest.

For example, in a deed, words such as "to Harry, Jane, and Sally as tenants in common" are sufficient to create a tenancy in common. A deed may or may not state the fractional interest that each owner holds. If the fractional interest is not stated, the tenants are presumed to hold equally. If three people are tenants in common, they would each own a one-third interest in the real estate.

As tenants in common, each tenant owns half—or whatever fractional share is specified—of the value of the real estate. Each tenant also is entitled to a pro rata portion of the income from the property and must pay an equivalent share of expenses.

Each tenant also can sell, mortgage, or transfer his or her interest to a third party without having to obtain the consent of the other co-owners. However, a tenant does not have the right to transfer or sell the entire property. When a co-owner dies, a tenant's interest passes to his or her heirs named in the will, who then become new tenants in common with the surviving tenants.

Generally, if two or more individuals purchase real estate but do not specify the form of ownership in the deed, it is presumed that they have acquired title as tenants in common. Every state has created by statute a presumption in favor of tenancies in common over joint tenancies. This means that a transfer to two or more persons other than husband and wife will create a tenancy in common, unless the grantor clearly has expressed his or her intent to create a joint tenancy.

However, this presumption may not apply if the owners are husband and wife. In some states, they will be presumed to own the property as tenants by the entirety, while in others they will own it as community property.

Joint Tenancy

Two or more people also may own real estate as joint tenants. The distinguishing characteristic of this form of ownership is the right of survivorship, which means when a joint tenant dies, his or her interest automatically passes to the surviving joint tenant by operation of law. Unlike tenants in common, a joint tenant's interest does not pass to heirs through a will but instead passes to the surviving tenant without going through probate. The last surviving joint tenant takes title alone and possesses all the rights of ownership, including the right to transfer the property by will.

To create a joint tenancy, property owners must state specifically their intention to do so in the deed, and the owners must be identified explicitly as joint tenants. Unlike tenants in common, joint tenancy cannot be implied or created by operation of law. Some states, however, have abolished joint tenancies and created a presumption in favor of tenancies in common instead.

For example, to create a joint tenancy, words such as "to Harry, Jane, and Sally as joint tenants with rights of survivorship and not as tenants in common" may be used.

To create a joint tenancy, the law requires that the following four unities must exist:

1. *Unity of time:* All joint owners must acquire their interests at the same time—that is, all joint owners must sign and execute the deed at the same time.
2. *Unity of title:* All joint owners must acquire their interests by the same document—only one deed is executed to convey the property.
3. *Unity of interest:* All joint tenants must own the same fractional share.
4. *Unity of possession:* All joint tenants have an undivided right to possession of the property.

Because these four unities must be satisfied, the common law did not allow a person who owned property alone to create a joint tenancy between himself or herself and another person. To avoid this problem, owners sometimes would convey the entire interest to a third party called a *straw man,* who then conveyed it back to the entire group of intended joint tenants. In some states, however, the need to use a straw man has been eliminated by statute. In effect, these statutes have eliminated the requirement that there be unity of time and title to create a joint tenancy.

Many married couples own property as joint tenants because the property automatically passes to the other at the first spouse's death, thereby avoiding probate. As a result, the surviving spouse gains title to the entire property quickly and without the expense and time required to probate most estates.

A joint tenant is legally free to transfer his or her interest to a third party at any time. However, doing so destroys the joint tenancy. The new owner becomes a tenant in common with the remaining original owners rather than a joint tenant. The other owners remain joint tenants and their rights are unaffected.

> For example, Harry, Jane, and Sally own an apartment complex as joint tenants. Ten years after starting their real estate venture, Sally decides that she no longer wants to own part of the complex. If Sally sells her interest to Ben, Harry and Jane will continue to be joint tenants with respect to two-thirds of the property but tenants in common with respect to Ben's one-third interest. Ben now has a one-third interest that he can convey or leave to his heirs.

A joint tenancy also may be severed if the joint tenants expressly agree to terminate the joint tenancy and to hold as tenants in common. In addition, a joint tenancy may be terminated as a result of an involuntary transfer of a tenant's interest—for example, if a trustee in bankruptcy sells the joint tenant's interest or a judgment against the tenant is rendered requiring the sale of the property.

Tenancy by the Entirety

Married couples can own real estate through a form of co-ownership called *tenancy by the entirety* in about half of the states. Each spouse has an equal, undivided interest in the property. As with joint tenancy, the surviving spouse receives the entire estate upon the other spouse's death and automatically becomes the sole owner.

In states where tenancies by the entirety can be created, they often are used because property can be transferred to the surviving spouse without having to make a will or go through probate proceedings. In some states, property held as a tenancy by the entirety cannot be seized and sold to satisfy the claims of creditors of either spouse.

However, this form of ownership differs from joint tenancy because neither spouse can sell the property without the other's consent. Title to property can be conveyed only by a deed signed by both parties. In addition, neither spouse generally has the right to partition or otherwise divide the property unilaterally.

IMPORTANT NOTE

To create a tenancy by the entirety, words such as "Harry and Sally, husband and wife, as tenants by the entirety" may be used.

A tenancy by the entirety may be terminated in several ways:

- *By the death of one of the spouses:* The surviving spouse becomes the sole owner.
- *By the parties' agreement:* A new deed can be executed showing a different form of ownership.
- *By divorce or annulment:* Property is then held by the parties as tenants in common.
- *By a court-ordered sale of the property to satisfy a judgment against the husband and wife as joint debtors:* The court dissolves the tenancy so that the property can be sold.

IMPORTANT NOTE

Married couples who own real estate either as tenants by the entirety or as joint tenants with right of survivorship are presumed to own the property equally even though one spouse may have contributed most or all of the money to buy the property.

Partition

What happens if a person no longer wants to own property with his or her co-owners? In such cases, a co-tenant can file an action in court to partition the property. Partition is a legal way of dissolving the co-tenant relationship. It results in the property being sold or divided into distinct portions that can be owned individually.

An action for partition may be voluntary or compulsory. To voluntarily partition property, all of the co-tenants must consent and agree to the specific division of the property. Typically, a deed is executed in which each co-owner is allocated part of the property by the other co-tenants. In contrast, compulsory partition occurs when one or more of the co-tenants wants to end the relationship but the owners cannot agree on how the property should be divided. In this case, judicial action is necessary.

Partition can be carried out in several ways. First, a court may order the property divided and allocate a share to each co-tenant. However, if a property cannot be divided into equally valuable portions, a court may require those tenants receiving more valuable portions to make monetary payments to the other co-tenants. In cases where equal division of the land is not possible or physical partition would destroy the land's value, a court will require the real estate to be sold and the proceeds from the sale distributed among the joint tenants according to their fractional interests. Most partition actions today result in a court order for sale and division of the proceeds.

Community Property

In community property states, all property held by a spouse is classified as either the separate property of one or the community property of both. Community property laws are based on the idea that a man and woman become equal partners when they get married. As a result, all property acquired during the marriage is considered to be obtained by mutual effort and is deemed community property. This remains true even if title to property is in one spouse's name only.

Community property also includes:

◆ Property that both spouses agree to convert from separate to community and
◆ Property that cannot be identified as separate property.

A typical state statute describing community property is the Texas Family Code, which states: "Community property consists of the property, other than separate property, acquired by either spouse during marriage."

In most states, community property is nearly always described by exclusion. In contrast, separate property is property that either spouse owned separately before marriage. It also includes:

- Property that either spouse inherited or was given separately while married
- Property purchased with separate funds while married
- Property bought with separate funds or exchanged for separate property during the marriage
- Property that both spouses agreed to convert from community to separate property in an agreement valid under state law
- Income earned while living in a noncommunity property state

In addition, if a spouse's separate property generates income—such as rent from a rental property—the income typically belongs to that spouse only, although a few states hold that such income is community income. Each spouse also has the power to mortgage or transfer his or her separate property without the consent or signature of the other spouse.

A married couple cannot transfer community property unless both spouses agree and sign the conveyance. At a spouse's death, the survivor automatically owns his or her half of the community property. Unlike joint tenancy, there is no automatic right of survivorship. Instead, the deceased spouse's one-half interest in the community property passes according to his or her will. If there is no will, the surviving spouse typically inherits the property, or the decedent's other heirs may inherit, depending on state law. Each spouse also has the right to dispose by will of all of his or her separate property.

The following states have a community property system:

- Arizona
- New Mexico
- California
- Texas
- Idaho
- Washington
- Louisiana
- Wisconsin
- Nevada

The marital community is dissolved either when a spouse dies or when the spouses divorce or annul the marriage. In a divorce proceeding, a court typically will award separate property to the spouse who owns it. With respect to the community property, most states require substantially equal division of such assets between former spouses.

The marital community also may be ended if a decree of legal separation or of separate maintenance has been issued. Depending on the state, the court issuing the decree may terminate the marital community and divide the property between the spouses.

Ownership of Real Estate

Real estate can be owned by individuals. However, real estate often is owned by trusts and other legal entities when multiple owners are involved. It is critical to understand the different forms of ownership. Some types give owners absolute ownership of the property for unlimited duration, while others only give ownership during an individual's life. There are also many ownership options to consider when there is more than one owner. Real estate can also be owned by trusts and other legal entities. Be sure to review your options before making a decision, factoring in all of the legal, financial, and tax considerations before coming up with the best possible action to take.

Next we briefly review some of the options you need to consider.

Trusts

A trust is an arrangement in which a grantor transfers legal title to property to another person to hold or manage the property for the benefit of a third party. Essentially, there are four components to a trust: a trust agreement, a grantor, a trustee, and a beneficiary.

The trust agreement sets forth the trust's terms, such as what rights the beneficiaries have to the property. The three main parties to a trust are:

1. *The grantor:* The person creating the trust
2. *The beneficiary:* The person who benefits from the trust
3. *The trustee:* The person who is considered the legal owner and is charged with carrying out the grantor's instructions regarding the purpose of the trust

In all states, the trustee is considered a fiduciary, which means that he or she has a special relationship with the beneficiary that requires the utmost trust and confidence. A trustee possesses a fiduciary duty to the beneficiaries to follow the terms of the trust as well as the requirements of applicable state law. Most trusts grant trustees extensive powers that usually include the ability to make new investments, manage real estate, sell property, collect and distribute income, and mortgage property.

All states allow real estate to be held in trust. The trustee, grantor, and beneficiary can be individuals or legal entities, such as corporations. In many cases, the grantor and the beneficiary are the same individual.

Trusts also can be characterized as living or testamentary. A living trust is one that the grantor creates during his or her lifetime. It may continue after his or her death, if so desired. A living trust may be used to minimize estate, inheritance, and income taxes and to transfer real estate privately rather than have it go through the probate process. In contrast, a testamentary trust becomes effective only at the grantor's death.

IMPORTANT NOTE

In many cases, a trust may give real estate owners great flexibility in managing and transferring their property. However, because the legal and tax implications of setting up a trust are complex and vary from state to state, it is advisable to seek legal expertise.

Land Trusts

In some states, real estate can be owned by a land trust. As with other trusts, a land trust is an arrangement where title to property is held by a trustee and all the rights of ownership belong to the beneficiary. Typically, the beneficiary is also the grantor, and land is the only trust asset.

Note that the beneficiary does not have a legal interest in real property, only an interest in personal property—that is, the beneficiary has a beneficial interest in the trust rather than title to the property. The beneficiary has the right to sell, pledge, or assign his or her beneficial interest in the property.

Land trusts are used for many reasons, including:

◆ *Privacy of ownership:* When a person buys real estate, his or her name is listed in public records as the legal owner. Anyone who is interested in the details of another person's property ownership can check property records that are available through the county assessor's office to see the purchase price and the amount of real estate taxes paid each year. However, if a land trust is created to own property, the trust is named as the legal owner in the property records; the beneficiary's name is not listed, which allows homeowners to buy and hold property anonymously. Many celebrities and public figures hold property in this manner in order to keep their addresses and assets private.

◆ *Ease of conveyance:* Property owned by a land trust can be mortgaged and sold easily without having to get deeds from all the beneficiaries and their spouses, as would be the case if the property were held jointly. Also, since a beneficiary's interest is considered personal property, the beneficiary can pledge such interest as security for a loan without having to comply with the restrictions and formalities of mortgages and title reports.

◆ *Ease of succession:* With a land trust, the grantor retains control over the property during his or her lifetime and can provide for succession in the property's ownership upon his or her death without having to go through probate. This can be especially beneficial to individuals who own property in several states since additional probate costs and inheritance taxes can be avoided.

◆ *Legal protection for owners:* If property is held in a land trust and a judgment is rendered against one of the beneficiaries, the judgment does not constitute a lien on the real estate. Title to the property also is not adversely affected by other legal proceedings against any of the beneficiaries.

Real Estate Syndicates

Another means of investing in real estate is through a real estate syndicate. Generally speaking, a real estate syndicate involves two or more people or entities that join together to finance the purchase and sale of real estate properties, typically those requiring significant capital.

However, a syndicate is not an actual form of ownership. Instead, the investors involved must decide what legal form to use to hold the real estate. For example, the syndicate might be organized as a corporation, general or limited partnership, joint venture, or limited liability company. The corresponding responsibilities, obligations, and relationship between the investors are determined mainly by the form in which the syndicate is organized.

Corporations

A corporation is a legal entity that is created under state law. A corporation's charter—sometimes called its articles of incorporation—sets forth the powers of the corporation, including its ability to buy real estate. While some corporate charters permit the purchase of real estate for any reason, others limit it to buying land necessary to fulfill the entity's corporate purposes.

One of the main advantages of the corporate form of ownership is that its shareholders enjoy limited liability. This means that if the business were to incur significant debts, only the business itself would be liable. The shareholders' investment in the corporation is limited to their investment in company stock, and they are not responsible for any company losses.

The biggest disadvantage, on the other hand, is that corporations are subject to double taxation. A corporation must file an income tax return and pay tax on its profits. Then, when a corporation distributes dividends to shareholders, it must pay tax on the dividends at its own personal income tax rate.

As a result, many real estate investors use a modified corporate form known as the S corporation. This alternate form of ownership allows limited shareholder liability but eliminates double taxation. Essentially, an S corporation allows the syndicate to pass income through without taxation at the corporate level. Shareholders only pay tax on distributions at their personal income tax rate. S corporations are limited, however, to smaller businesses; a maximum of 75 shareholders are permitted.

In addition, the corporation must elect to be treated as an S corporation. Failure to do so or to comply with other requirements governing their structure and operation will result in the loss of the favored tax status. In general, S corporations typically are used for somewhat smaller real estate transactions.

Real Estate Partnerships

Real estate partnerships have long been used to acquire, operate, and hold real estate. Essentially, a partnership is an association composed of two or more individuals to operate a business for profit as co-owners. By pooling their resources, partners have greater leverage in buying property and can combine their skills in managing the property.

In today's real estate investing environment, there are many kinds of partnerships. For example, a person can invest in a:

- *General partnership:* All of the partners actively participate in the management and day-to-day business operations. Any business losses are shared among the partners, who are fully liable for all partnership debts. To mitigate this risk, a partnership typically will purchase insurance. However, if one partner dies, withdraws from the partnership, or files for bankruptcy, the partnership automatically terminates. To continue operations, the remaining partners must enter into a new partnership agreement.
- *Limited partnership:* Consists of one or more limited and general partners. The limited partners typically provide capital and arrange the financing but do not take an active role in running the business. The limited partners receive a share of the profits for their role as limited partners but are not liable for the business's debts. Instead, their liability is limited to their capital contribution. However, if limited partners begin actively taking part in the control of the business, they will lose their limited liability.

A majority of states have adopted the Revised Uniform Limited Partnership Act (RULPA), which expressly authorizes limited partnerships to own real estate and recognizes the limited liability of limited partners. It also provides that profits and losses are to be passed through the partnership to the partners, who are taxed on any profits at their own personal income tax rate.

RULPA also lists certain actions that limited partners can take without losing their limited liability status. For example, a limited partner may vote on whether:

- A general partner should be admitted or removed.
- The nature of the business should be changed.

- The business should be dissolved.
- Assets of the limited partnership should be sold, leased, mortgaged, or otherwise transferred.
- The limited partnership should incur debt other than in the ordinary course of business.

When creating a general or limited partnership to own real estate, the following issues, among others, should be addressed in the partnership agreement:

- Allocation of partnership interests
- Capital investment of each partner
- Legal structure—limited partnership, general partnership
- Management strategy
- Tax issues—allocation of tax benefits, sharing of accounting costs
- Failure to pay contributions
- Timing of meetings and voting requirements
- Liquidating distributions when partnership is dissolved
- Effect of the death of a partner
- Dispute resolution

Joint Ventures

A joint venture is a type of partnership in which two or more individuals join together to conduct a specific business enterprise. While a joint venture must be created by agreement between the parties to share in the venture's losses and profits, it is created for one specific project only rather than to carry on a continuing business relationship.

Most partnerships, in contrast, carry out a general business purpose over a period of years. Moreover, the death of a joint venture member does not automatically dissolve the joint venture. Another difference is that a participant in a joint venture does not have the power to bind the others, whereas partners may agree that each has full power to bind the partnership.

Limited Liability Companies

The limited liability company (LLC) is a relatively new legal entity created by statute and recognized in all of the states today. An LLC is a hybrid entity, combining the most attractive features of limited partnerships and corporations. Like a corporation, LLC members are protected from individual liability for the LLC's debts and losses. However, an LLC need not comply with the formalities of corporate minutes, bylaws, directors, and shareholders, but has a more flexible management structure.

For tax purposes, the LLC itself pays no income tax. Like a partnership, all of the income and losses flow through directly to the members, who must report such items on their individual income tax returns. Because each state has enacted its own legislation on LLCs, laws vary widely regarding how such entities may be created and organized. LLCs have become one of the most popular and versatile means of owning real estate.

Winning Residential
Investment Strategies

CHAPTER 5

Which Is the Right Strategy and Property for You?

Buying a primary residence is one thing, but investing in real estate that you plan to own and manage for whatever length of time you plan to hold onto the property is a much different scenario. It takes different skill sets, considerably more research, and a time investment that not everyone is willing to put forth to succeed. The good news is that those who do go the extra mile to create a successful real estate investment strategy typically end up with significant financial rewards. In this chapter, we look at how you can create the best possible real estate investment strategy and select properties that will deliver those rewards on a consistent basis.

Nuts and Bolts of It

Investing in real estate is significantly different from putting money in a vehicle like the stock market. If a fire starts at IBM's headquarters, for example, your stock price may temporarily drop a fraction of a penny. But if a fire starts at a home, condo, or apartment building you own, your entire investment may be wiped out. Insurance often pays considerably less than necessary to recover fully from a disaster, particularly if you are highly leveraged.

There are also maintenance and repair costs, financing issues (since most investors tend to borrow money to buy), and closing costs to consider. These fees may run into the thousands of dollars, particularly if there are unexpected delays or problems with titles or other legal issues. There are property taxes and utilities to pay, and there are also lifestyle adjustments that come along with owning real estate (like dealing with tenants, contractors, and potential buyers, to name a few).

Despite options like "no-money-down" financing, you're going to need cash flow to support investments in real estate, even if you plan to live in the investment property and tackle renovation tasks yourself. Unexpected expenses usually arise, and you need to be able to handle contingencies with a healthy financial picture already in place.

Landlord Insights

More often than not, I hear about a client's real estate investment after they have made it. They have found something great and they have not really considered what may happen if they pour a bunch of money into it and then it sits with a for sale sign for months. Or what may happen if they decide to rent it and it is not snapped up in a weekend. Real estate is all about staying power and not using up all your assets to make it happen.
—Phillip Cook, Certified Financial Planner (CFP), Cook and Associates

Determine Your Risk Tolerance

Getting involved in real estate may test your personal definition of risk tolerance. Before you get into it, ask yourself the following questions:

- Am I more concerned about maintaining the value of my initial investment or about making a profit from that investment?
- Am I willing to give up that stability for the chance at long-term growth?
- How would I feel if the value of my investment dropped for several months?
- How would I feel if the value of my investment dropped for several years?
- Am I in a financial position to handle setbacks?

Your answers should reveal a picture of your risk tolerance and help you make investment decisions that you will be comfortable with.

Find a Healthy Starting Point

No one starts a new job expecting every day to go perfectly, but many people do expect their investment ideas to be foolproof. So what is a healthy investment picture? To answer that, we'll start with the definition of *asset allocation* and what it really means for your financial life.

Asset allocation involves dividing an investment portfolio among different asset categories, such as stocks, bonds, real estate, and cash. It's based on very personal decisions about your age, your risk tolerance, and your plans for the future. The asset allocation that works best for you at any given point in your life will depend largely on your investment time frame and your ability to deal with problems along the way.

Any investments you make should consider the following important issues:

◆ *Time horizon:* How many months, years, or decades will you be spending with this investment to reach a targeted financial goal? An investor with a longer time horizon may feel more comfortable taking on a riskier or more volatile investment because he or she can wait out slow economic cycles, the inevitable ups and downs of various markets, and the effect they have on each other. However, older investors or investors with substantial financial pressures—college tuition, young children, and substantial debts—might need to take on less risky investments.

◆ *Risk tolerance:* How willing or able are you to lose your original investment in exchange for the potential of maximum returns? An aggressive investor, or one with a high risk tolerance, is more likely to risk losing money in order to get better results. A conservative investor, or one with a low risk tolerance, tends to favor investments that will preserve his or her original investment. That may or may not be the case with real estate.

◆ *Portfolio options:* Historically, real estate has been thought of as a minor investment category that's included only with other options (such as precious metals and private equity), although anyone looking at where investment money has gone in the past 13 years may argue otherwise.

Next we describe the asset categories that make up a diversified portfolio.

Stocks

A stock is a share of ownership in a corporation. Stocks have historically had the greatest risk and highest returns among the three leading asset categories that make up most investors' retirement plans and investments. As an asset category, stocks generally offer the greatest potential for growth, and for those who remember 2008, the greatest potential for loss. Stocks hit home runs, but they also strike out. The volatility of stocks makes them a risky investment in the short term. Large company stocks as a group, for example, have lost money on average about one out of every three years. And the losses have sometimes been dramatic. But investors who have been willing to ride out the volatile returns of stocks over long periods of time have generally been rewarded with strong positive returns.

Bonds

Bonds are debt instruments—meaning that each bond entitles the holder to a portion of the company's borrowings that are typically paid back with interest. Bonds are issued by corporations, nonprofit entities, and governments that issue bonds to fund programs and expansions. Bonds are generally less volatile than stocks but offer more modest returns. As a result, an investor approaching a financial goal might increase bond holdings relative to stock holdings because the reduced risk of holding more bonds would be attractive to the investor despite their lower potential for growth. You should keep in mind that certain categories of bonds offer high returns similar to stocks. But these bonds, known as high-yield or junk bonds, also carry higher risk.

Cash

Cash and cash equivalents—such as savings deposits, certificates of deposit, treasury bills, money market deposit accounts, and money market funds—are the safest investments but offer the lowest return of the three major asset categories. The chances of losing money on an investment in this asset category are extremely low. The federal government guarantees many investments in cash equivalents. Investment losses in nonguaranteed cash equivalents do occur, but infrequently. The principal concern for investors investing in cash equivalents is inflation risk. This is the risk that inflation will outpace and erode investment returns over time.

Real Estate

Whether individually owned houses, office buildings, apartment buildings, condos, or assortments of these properties owned in a real estate investment trust (REIT), real estate is generally thought to be a better earner during tough stock markets. Though we discuss REITs later in the book, these trusts that can be bought like mutual fund shares have been around since President Eisenhower signed a law creating them in 1960. Indeed, while the 500 Index lost nearly 40 percent over a recent two-year period, REIT investments measured during the same time period were up 50 percent, as measured by the Wilshire REIT index.

Precious Metals

Be it gold, platinum, or precious coins, people view precious metals as tangible or material wealth—it can be carried and held in their hands. Depression-era babies have a particular love for it and have been known to put it in safe deposit boxes. Unless there is a national emergency—such as the events of September 11, 2001, or a war, which sent gold prices from about $260 an ounce in 2001 up to their fall 2005 levels of $475—metals are often the most stagnant investment out there. It literally takes a crisis to budge metals. But as your grandmother or great-grandmother might say: When you really need it, it is there.

Energy

Rising gasoline, heating oil, and natural gas prices have skyrocketed in recent years, making energy a close contender to real estate. It is impossible to stockpile gasoline or heating oil on our property, so the least complicated way to buy energy as an investment is in energy stocks or mutual funds that invest in various companies that discover, refine, or support the sale of energy products. Many people who started buying energy stocks at the start of the Iraq war have not been disappointed. In 2001, crude oil prices hovered between $20 and $30 a barrel. By 2008, the price of oil had eclipsed $100 a barrel, with no end in sight to the escalation.

Investing by the Numbers

There are some common financial calculations that are used to determine property value and income-generating potential for buyers. Real estate investors would be wise to consult with tax and financial experts before making any purchase, but it's also important to familiarize yourself with these key calculations to help determine the cost and future profitability of the property.

Play around with the calculations and ask questions, but don't use the formula as a final determinant on whether to close a deal. Realize that these figures can be skewed on a comparative basis because all buildings—including those that are similar in layout—may have different income streams and features.

Net Operating Income

The net operating income (NOI) is a property's yearly gross income minus its operating expenses:

$$NOI = Gross\ income - Operating\ expenses$$

Gross income includes rental income and other income, such as parking fees, billboard advertising (some property owners allow billboards mounted on their property if they are zoned for it), and laundry machine and other vending revenue. Operating expenses are what you pay to maintain and operate a property, including maintenance, property taxes, insurance, management fees, supplies, and utilities. It is also important to know what does not count as an operating expense, such as principal and interest on your mortgage, major capital expenditures, depreciation, and income taxes.

Capitalization Rate

A capitalization rate (cap rate) is an indicator of the current value of an income-producing property in the marketplace. The cap rate is a property's net operating income as a percentage of its asking price:

$$\text{Cap rate} = \text{NOI} \times 100$$

WRONG!

$$CAP = \frac{NOI}{\text{price of prop.}}$$

Generally, a lower cap rate occurs when you are valuing highly attractive properties in good neighborhoods. Sellers are trying to get the highest price for their property, so they want to have a low cap rate. Buyers, meanwhile, want to get a low price, so they are looking for higher cap rates because the lower the selling prices in a neighborhood, the higher the cap rate.

Cash-on-Cash Return

This calculation is used to evaluate the profitability of income-producing properties before you buy. It measures, in percentage terms, your cash income on the cash you plan to invest:

$$\text{Cash-on-cash return} = \text{Before-tax cash flow} \times 100$$

wrong!

$$CoC\ \text{return} = \frac{\text{income}}{\text{money invested}}$$

For instance, if you want to purchase a two-flat and put only 10 percent down, cash-on-cash return would tell you the annual return you would make on that property relative to the down payment.

Gross Rent Multiplier

This is a common calculation and an easy one to make—all you need is a sale price and the annual income of a property:

$$GRM = \frac{\text{Sale price}}{\text{Annual gross rent}}$$

Low gross rent multipliers (GRMs) may indicate either run-down or mistakenly undervalued properties. Again, this calculation is not a final answer, but rather a starting point.

Price per Unit

This is a good equation to use when comparing various rental properties:

$$\text{Price per unit} = \frac{\text{Asking price}}{\text{Number of units}}$$

If you find that other properties in the neighborhood have sold for a much higher per unit figure, you may have a bargain. By researching why the price per unit is so low—you might find problems, or a real gem.

Price per Square Foot

Like price per unit, this is an easily calculated figure you can use to compare similar buildings:

$$\text{Price per square foot} = \frac{\text{Asking price}}{\text{Total square footage}}$$

Why Cash Is King in Real Estate

In future chapters, we explore the various ways to borrow money as you start your real estate investment plan. Though borrowing has its merits, we often suggest that the ability to purchase property with cash (not always big properties, but definitely smaller ones) is the most desirable position to be in.

Paying cash means you avoid paying interest fees and whatever you buy is completely yours. You control all the equity. Controlling all the equity, despite whatever tax benefits you get from borrowing to buy property, should be your eventual goal in investing in real estate. True ownership without any encumbrances sets true investors ahead of dabblers and those who put themselves at substantial risk.

Borrow if you must and if you have a solid strategy to get into real estate investing, but make it a goal to pay off those loans. If the economy goes south, equity will save you.

IMPORTANT NOTE

Consult a financial advisor before you buy investment real estate. There are many financial issues to consider before you buy property—your cash flow situation, your preparedness for the lean times, your desire to be a multiproperty owner—and you need to consider where real estate investing fits into your tax and retirement picture. Are you prepared to make this choice without an informed review of your financial situation? A solution may be a Certified Financial Planner. These professionals are trained to advise individuals on the major financial choices in their lives. Likewise, potential investors should also consult a tax advisor if they do not already work with one—an individual's tax picture changes substantially when making a real estate investment. To find a qualified financial planner in your area, visit the Financial Planning Association's web site at www.fpanet.org.

The Big Picture

In real estate, diversification and planning are important. By including asset categories with investment returns that move up and down under different market conditions within a portfolio, an investor can protect against significant losses. Historically, the returns of the major asset categories have not moved up and down at the same time. Market conditions that cause one asset category to do well often cause another asset category to have average or poor returns.

By investing in more than one asset category, investors reduce their risk of losing significant assets because losses in one category may be counterbalanced with impressive gains in another.

It is all about finding the right balance, and combining your overall financial picture with your investment goals. A financial evaluation—and possibly a tune-up—may be in order before you put down your first dollar on a piece of property. For more information on getting your financial house in order, turn back to Chapter 2.

Do Your Homework

Once you have the financial aspect of your investment strategy in order, you'll want to turn your attention to successful property selection. That starts with gathering critical information and data about communities where you want to invest. To get there, the most prolific investors stay apprised of local and regional news, talk to local real estate professionals and government officials, and most importantly, keep their eyes and ears open for new information.

National and international events can also have far-reaching effects on local real estate markets. Changes in the prime rate set by the Federal Reserve Board affect interest rates, which impacts the entire economy, especially real estate markets. Changes in oil and other energy markets are also important because higher cost-of-living expenses may slow some segments of the housing market, such as vacation home buying.

Following local and national changes in economies will help investors make informed decisions. Here are some specific ways to stay on top of the information.

Read the Local Papers

If you are investing in a large regional market with many community newspapers, you may want to subscribe to several, or check the news online. Look for the following information as you scan the local news:

- *City council news:* Review the council meeting summaries for decisions that affect the community's tax base or zoning laws.
- *Real estate classifieds:* Follow current property listings on a daily basis. Though Sunday may be the large-volume day for ad listings, you may get an early lead on a new property by checking the classifieds daily.
- *Police blotter:* Crime is an issue anywhere you invest. Even if an area is on the brink of gentrification, it is difficult to interest people in property if it is located in a crime-ridden area. Smaller communities typically list summaries of police reports of disturbances and arrests. Where and when they happen can tell you a lot about a neighborhood.
- *Legal notices:* These are the pages of listings in small type that most people thumb past on a normal day. Investors, however, may find bankruptcies, foreclosures, unclaimed property, or other real estate events from which they may benefit.

◆ *Sales transactions:* Many local and county governments put a great deal of data online. See if your local paper reports recent property sales in your area (some allow you to search by street name or specific address) so you can follow property sales and prices in specific areas.

◆ *The business section:* Most newspapers provide a short summary of current interest and mortgage rates, but equally important is any news that will affect local employment. Companies often cut jobs when the economy or their business slows, but they can also make cuts for other reasons—legal disputes or mergers, for example. Fewer jobs and fewer buyers with cash equal lower housing prices.

Follow Demographic Changes

Many smaller communities struggle with the loss of local white- and blue-collar employers. Seemingly overnight, a community with citizens of all ages can turn gray. Chapter 1 covered several major demographic and population trends expected to change the real estate forecast over the next 40 years. Could a sleepy small town become part of a megapolitan area in the next 5 to 10 years?

Here are some Internet sites that can help you identify trends in a particular area:

Bureau of Economic Analysis (www.bea.gov)
Overview of national economic statistics.

Federal Financial Institutions Examination Council (FFIEC)
Geocoding System (www.ffiec.gov/geocode/default.htm)
Population, housing, and income data based on U.S. addresses.

Bureau of Transportation Statistics (www.bts.gov)
All statistics related to U.S. transportation trends.

U.S. Census Bureau (www.census.gov)
State and national population statistics and other demographic data.

Current population and migration statistics are available from many sources and provide investors with critical information concerning past migration patterns of specific areas. Use this information to determine whether construction and property resale will continue to be strong.

Local newspapers often report on community growth and decline. The arrival of a major corporation or several major retail outlets, for example, could indicate increased growth in the community. Likewise, the departure of a major corporation or the closing of any established retailers may signal a downturn in the local economy, which will be reflected in local real estate prices.

Watch What Boomers Do

A key indicator of real estate investment performance will be what the baby-boomer generation does with its overall investment wealth. A recent Congressional Budget Office report predicted that many people from this generation will delay retirement because of recent investment market downturns and cutbacks in retirement benefits at their companies.

Boomers are also beginning to downsize. Once their children leave the nest, their parents are moving into smaller residences in big cities or selecting vacation homes in places that will become a permanent home upon retirement. This trend has left many experts wondering when the boomers move away, where will it leave the overall residential market of larger, more recently built homes? Will these large properties continue to sell at a premium?

The best communities have a mixture of housing to accommodate differing space needs. It is important to watch where the real estate dollars are being spent as you make future investment decisions in real estate. By keeping track of economic and demographic trends, you'll gain an edge in the investor pool and you will be well equipped to purchase properties that yield the best results.

CHAPTER 6

Your Choices: Single-Family, Condo, Co-Op, Vacation Home, and Multiplexes

As a real estate investor, the world is literally your oyster. There are many choices out there on the market. And while single-family homes, condominiums, and apartments top the list of most real estate investment portfolios for rental, rehab, and vacation property, townhomes and even mobile homes might be a worthwhile investment in certain geographic areas.

Before you make your selection, first consider location—the key tenet of any real estate investing strategy. Property tends to conform to what makes sense economically and aesthetically in a specific area. That is why, before you invest your money, you need to review what types of property are located in a particular neighborhood (as opposed to a city or state, which are both too broad to use in this situation).

As you can see, getting involved with real estate requires more than just a "quick read" of a property listing. You have to get out there in person to gauge its condition and determine whether it is in a desirable part of the neighborhood, right down to the block level. In this chapter, we look at the basic steps you'll want to take when selecting among the various options.

Useful Definitions

When someone says "single-family home" or "condo," most people understand what they are referring to. But making an investment in any of these properties requires a more in-depth knowledge of exactly what these terms refer to. Here's a primer for you to use.

Single-Family Homes

The single-family detached house is the most common type of residential property. Though they are available in all shapes, sizes, and prices, what distinguishes a single-family home from other kinds of housing is that the structure resides on its own piece of property.

Maintenance

You, the homeowner, are generally responsible for all of the expenses associated with ownership and maintenance of a single-family house, including real estate taxes, garbage removal, water, and sewage. Though some developments charge assessments for shared services, most homeowners pay all maintenance and care costs.

Financing

Single-family homes are easier to finance, refinance, manage, and liquidate when compared with larger, multifamily property investments. But residential property investments require up-front cash, financial feeding, management, and maintenance—especially during the early years.

Best Bets for Investments

For the best returns, consider fixer-uppers that do not need major upgrades. Buy the least expensive home in the most desirable block, or buy into the most affordable neighborhood in a sought-after community. Buy in areas where demand for housing will eventually exceed supply. If possible, buy in a down market to enjoy the equity-building benefits of an upturn. Many homes are part of a homeowners' association. Sellers should provide a Homeowner's Association Disclosure similar to the one shown in Figure 6.1.

IMPORTANT NOTE

Leave out-of-town investing to experienced professionals. When you start buying real estate as an investment, consider property that you can get to within an hour—and preferably much less, especially if you plan to rent it out. It will save you the time and trouble of traveling to and from the property to handle problems as they arise. Landlords close by can also keep an eye on tenants and changing circumstances in a neighborhood.

Homeowner's Association Disclosure

Purchaser(s) should not execute a real estate sale or purchase contract until receiving and reading this disclosure summary.

1. This is a disclosure summary for _____ (name of community).

2. As Purchaser of property in this community, you will be obligated to be a member of a homeowner's association.

3. There have been, or will be recorded, restrictive covenants governing the use and occupancy of properties in this community.

4. You [check only one] ❏ will ❏ will not be obligated to pay assessments to the association, which assessments are subject to periodic change. If applicable, the current amount is _____ Dollars ($_____) per _____.

5. Your failure to pay these assessments could result in a lien on your property.

6. There [check only one] ❏ is ❏ is not an obligation to pay rent or land use fees for recreational or other commonly used facilities as an obligation of membership in the homeowner's association. (If such obligation exists, then the amount of the current obligation is _____ _____ Dollars ($_____).

7. The restrictive covenants [check only one] ❏ can ❏ cannot be amended without the approval of the association membership.

8. The statements contained in this disclosure form are only summary in nature, and, as a prospective Purchaser, you should refer to the covenants and the association governing documents.

_____   _____
Date   Purchaser

_____   _____
Date   Purchaser

This disclosure must be supplied by the developer, or by the parcel owner if the sale is by an owner who is not the developer.

Figure 6.1 Homeowner's Association Disclosure

Condominiums

Once the province of cities and high-rises, condominiums—also known as condos—now exist in virtually every community of any size. Condos became popular in the 1970s when state legislatures passed laws allowing their existence. Apartment buildings are commonly converted to condos by means of a condominium declaration that divvies up the percentage of ownership, defines which areas are commonly held by all owners, and states the building rules.

When you purchase a condo, you are purchasing an actual unit—meaning the person owns the walls, ceiling, and floor of the unit, and may also own the plumbing and perhaps a parking space if one is allotted to that unit. In some condos, the buyer owns what are known as common elements, which may include the roof, plumbing, lobby, laundry room, garden area, or the garage.

Owning a condominium requires shared decision making, which works well for people who are comfortable allowing others some control over property management decisions. A joint governing body called a condominium association oversees maintenance and care of all external structures and common areas of the property. The association gathers facts, bids, and decides how money for repairs and other projects will be collected and paid out. Condominium owners—particularly investors who do not live on-site—need to stay on top of all condominium association activities and decisions.

Maintenance

A condominium association raises money for maintenance through monthly assessments, which increase over the life of ownership. The building's expenses are tallied, divided by the percentages of ownership and then by 12 to ascertain the monthly fee. If your annual share of building maintenance cost is $1,200, you will pay $100 per month in assessments in addition to the costs of your mortgage and real estate taxes. The good news is that the maintenance work on the property, from grass clipping to roofing, will be hired out. The bad news is that you will be making the hiring and spending decisions on these projects as a team, which may not appeal to you.

Financing

Financing a condo purchase is similar to obtaining a mortgage on a single-family home, except that your lender may have restrictions on the types of condos approved for Federal Housing Administration (FHA) financing. Some lenders may question you if you are not planning to live in the property. Typically lenders like to see owners on-site because tenants are sometimes late or skip on the rent, putting owners in a cash squeeze that may delay repayment of their loans. Some tenants may damage the property, which decreases the value of the lender's investment in you. Ask potential lenders if they have particular requirements or higher fees and rates connected with financing investment loans for condominiums.

Cooperative Apartments

A housing co-op (short for cooperative) might look like an apartment or a condo, but the ownership structure is very different. Co-ops are apartment buildings owned by a corporation, typically formed by developers or by the original residents of the building. Individual tenants do not own their apartments in the same way they would own a condominium or home. They own shares of stock in a corporation. These shares are apportioned based on the size and floor level of the apartment, and ownership is established by a stock certificate and occupancy is governed by a proprietary lease. The corporation pays all real estate taxes, maintenance expenses, and the underlying mortgage on the building. The co-op owner's portion of the payment depends on the number of shares owned in the corporation.

Cooperative ownership is the most common form of apartment ownership in New York City. There are three times as many co-ops as there are condominiums in Manhattan. As a result, there are more cooperative apartments on the market that are likely to be more affordable than similarly sized condominiums. But co-ops do have complex requirements. Co-op owners have the same tax benefits as other homeowners, including taking their share of the mortgage interest and real estate taxes as an itemized deduction on their 1040 federal income tax return. Tax laws also treat co-op owners the same as other homeowners when they sell.

According to the Washington, DC–based National Association of Housing Cooperatives, there are three types of housing cooperatives. Each deals with an owner's equity in a different way:

◆ *Market-rate housing cooperative shareholders:* These shareholders are allowed to buy or sell a membership or shares at whatever price the market will bear. Purchase prices and equity accumulation are similar to condominium or single-family ownership.

◆ *Limited-equity housing cooperative members:* These owners are restricted in what proceeds they can receive from the sale of their unit. Typically located in economically challenged neighborhoods, these types of co-ops benefit from below-market interest rate mortgage loans, grants, real estate tax abatement, or other features that make the housing more affordable.

◆ *Leasing cooperative (or zero-equity cooperative) members:* These members do not have any equity in the property because the co-op leases the property directly from an outside investor (usually a nonprofit set up specifically for this purpose). If set up as a corporation, however, the co-op can elect to buy the property later and convert it to a market-rate or limited-equity corporation. When considering a co-op purchase, a potential buyer needs to ask: What is my equity?

Questions You Should Ask about Co-Op Ownership

Because you are buying a share of a corporation that owns real estate, you will want to find out about the financial health of the corporation. You will also want to understand what your financial obligations to the cooperative will be and learn about all the rules and regulations of the community. Here are some sample questions to ask before making your investment:

◆ What is the equity participation of each of the members?
◆ What is the current share price for buying in?
◆ Where can I get financing?
◆ What is the underlying mortgage on the whole property, if any?
◆ Do I have to live in the building or can I sublet my unit?
◆ What are your policies on pets or children?
◆ Can I renovate or alter my unit in some way?

Maintenance

Though condominium owners are allowed to do largely whatever they please with the interior of their unit (as long as they do not weaken support structures or otherwise interfere with the structural integrity of the building), co-op boards may tell potential buyers that they have the right of approval on all renovation activity within individual units, depending on their bylaws. Co-op members pay a monthly assessment(maintenance) that also includes their portion of taxes paid by the corporation on the building.

Financing

Co-op boards often require a large cash down payment of at least 25 percent. This may be primarily to ensure the financial stability of the co-op, but high down payments—or an all-cash purchase price—are also a good way to keep out buyers with limited means. Investors may want to bypass co-ops that require an owner to occupy the unit because they will not be allowed to rent their unit. Selling may also be troublesome because co-op sellers typically must have the new buyer approved by the board, and sometimes there are special fees—called a *flip tax*—charged to new residents moving in.

Multi-unit Apartments

Apartment buildings come in all shapes, sizes, and numbers of units. Whether a two-flat or a structure holding six units or more, owners are landlords—they maintain the building; pay the taxes, utilities, and maintenance; select the tenants; and collect the rents. They are also responsible for all legal challenges brought their way by tenants. For anyone who rents or sublets property and who does not hire resident or offsite building management companies to handle their affairs, multi-unit apartment ownership is extremely hands-on.

Maintenance

Maintenance is the sole responsibility of the owner, not the tenants. Owners must adhere to landlord/tenant laws in their own community that make specific provisions for maintenance, utilities, sanitation, and other provisions. Unlike a single homeowner who can elect to do upkeep whenever he or she has the time, money, and inclination, landlords are subject to risk and oversight if they do not do minimum upkeep on their property.

Financing

Multi-unit purchasers have two options when borrowing to buy property—residential loans and commercial loans. The tipping point for either option is generally the number of units in the building. Typically, for four units or less, you can qualify for residential financing. Any units above that, you are in commercial loan territory. Commercial loans are an entirely new ballgame; lenders are more concerned about the income-producing potential of the property, the down payment demands are larger (at least 20 percent), and fees at all stages tend to be higher. Experts generally agree that new investors—who may be highly leveraged—should stick with smaller properties that can be financed with residential loans, preferably of the owner-occupied variety.

Townhouses

Like condominium and co-op dwellers, townhome owners typically share a wall in common with their neighbors. But townhome property may be held in a variety of ways. Most townhouses built in the twentieth century—called row houses—were held fee simple, meaning that owners hold legal title to their structure and the land it sits on, and are personally responsible for all taxes assessed to that property. Today, townhouses may be held as condos, but most are a hybrid, falling somewhere between condos and single-family homes.

Maintenance
Like condos, townhouse developments often have a homeowner's association that manages the common elements of the property. Owners pay a monthly assessment covering the maintenance of the common elements, which may include the roof; common outdoor, recreation, or parking areas; and any laundry facilities.

Financing
Townhome financing is similar to financing for single-family homes or condominiums.

Mobile Homes

Mobile homes are usually less expensive than traditional brick and mortar homes, but can be surprisingly complex to own. Sometimes called manufactured homes, the main identifying characteristic of a mobile home is that it is prefabricated and can be moved to any location. If a mobile home is placed in a specially zoned mobile home park, the mobile home turns into a house. When buying or investing in a mobile home, it is important to decide where you will be placing the home because management structures vary widely.

Mobile homes may or may not be treated as a single-family home—it depends on the land ownership structure underneath. In some parks, you must buy the lot for your home; in others you can lease or purchase a lot as a share in a corporation, much like buying a co-op. Property taxes are handled in various ways based on these distinctions. Like condo communities, co-op buildings, and townhomes, mobile home parks have rules that must be followed by the residents.

Maintenance

Mobile home maintenance costs vary depending on the park and its management policies. According to Consumers Union, zoning or restrictive covenants may limit an owner or an investor's ability to place mobile homes on some private lots. Investigate your land rights, and find out what types of mobile homes are allowed in a particular park or development and for how long. Consumers Union also advises that some parks do not allow homes of a certain age to be resold, which means you may be forced to tow away an older home in order to sell it. That involves extra cost and possibly a substantial loss of your original investment. Mobile homes are less expensive compared with traditional homes, but there are risks worth exploring before you buy. Visit www.consumersunion.org for more information about mobile home maintenance.

Financing

Consumers Union advises potential buyers and investors to research their financing options well before making a purchase. Banks and credit unions will often provide loans for mobile homes, though most manufacturers do so as well. Traditionally, dealers finance mobile homes using personal property loans rather than mortgage loans, at rates two to four percentage points higher. Dealers often get a commission for obtaining credit for buyers, so buyers may be better off talking directly with the lenders. It also makes sense to talk to your tax advisor before borrowing to purchase this type of home.

Vacation Homes

Owning a second home is a great way for a first-time real estate investor to test the market without wandering into the tougher arena of multiple-unit apartments or other rental property. Investors can pour their money into a vacation area with growth prospects and possibly rent out the property a fraction of the time, working gradually into full-time landlord status.

 People buy second homes for more reasons than to have a getaway place. Investors can pay off the property by renting it out, and if the timing and location are right, they can realize a significant profit that can be used for other rental properties, either locally or out of town.

Things You Should Know When Shopping for a Vacation Home

- ◆ Start with good tax advice. Depending on your individual tax situation and your plan for the property—year-round use, part-time use, or full-time rental—there are tax ramifications that need to be considered. Find a good tax advisor as a first step.
- ◆ Even if you are planning to spend only minimal time there, make sure the property is in an area where you want to spend a lot of time. If the house becomes a chore, it is not a good investment.
- ◆ Research renting options for the property, and double-check local restrictions on rentals. Make sure you also know how much rental income the average property owner gets. If your rental income does not make the overall investment work, there is no point in buying it.
- ◆ If you cannot pay cash, start shopping for a mortgage before you find a place, and find a lender in the place where the property is located. Lenders are generally not eager to loan money for a second home to people still carrying a balance on their primary residence. You may be forced to tap home equity or other investment sources.
- ◆ The best vacation home investments tend to be two to three hours in driving time from major metro areas. Also, you want to make sure there are plenty of recreational opportunities near the property you are buying. You also want to see upscale commercial investment going into your vacation community. Chains always attract a more upscale clientele that will increase property values over time.

(continued)

Things You Should Know When Shopping for a Vacation Home (*Continued*)

- If you are buying waterfront property—which will cost more than inland residences—check on access to flood insurance or other disaster coverage.
- Interview several real estate agents in the vacation area before selecting one. Ask how many vacation homes they have listed and whether there might be lending resources in the vacation area.
- Consider all maintenance costs, including renovation if necessary. Check into hiring someone local to cut the grass and check up on the property when you are not there. This is particularly important if you are renting out property—it needs to be a consistently good experience for renters if you are going to build repeat business.
- Try out sweat equity on a vacation home. A fix-up property that you plan to spend time in will teach you a lot about your skills and limitations in getting a more elaborate investment property strategy off the ground.

Financing

Any time you consider buying real estate, it is important to find the least expensive way to purchase that property, but it is particularly important with vacation homes. Why? Because if you are already carrying a mortgage on your primary residence, lenders may be leery of lending you money for a second home. Here are two options you should consider:

- *Pay cash if possible.* If you have access to liquid investments that may be tapped intelligently from a tax perspective, do it. It is best not to take out a mortgage.
- *Tap home equity.* If your tax and financial advisors clear it, you might want to consider tapping a significant store of home equity to make a cash payment for that vacation home. A home equity loan is almost always cheaper than a vacation property loan. Vacation property loan rates are higher than conventional residential loans because owners are not living in the property full time, and that subjects the property to particular risks.

Tax Issues

The good news if you borrow is that mortgage interest on a second home is fully deductible. You may be able to rent out that second property for part of the year and still take an interest deduction. IRS rules allow it as long as you spend at least 14 days at the property (or 10 percent of the number of days that you rent it out, whichever is longer). To avoid dealing with IRS regulations, it is generally best to pay cash if you plan to treat the vacation property as full-time rental property.

For more details, look at IRS publication 527, "Residential Rental Property" (including Rental of Vacation Homes).

What Areas Are Hot?

San Francisco-based EscapeHomes.com, an online real estate marketplace focusing exclusively on the second homebuyer and seller, does a regular ranking of top vacation home destinations. Here are the most recent results:

Top 10 Vacation Home Destinations

1. Orlando, FL
2. Destin, FL
3. Naples, FL
4. Myrtle Beach, SC
5. Ocean City, MD
6. Phoenix, AZ
7. Venice, FL
8. Galveston, TX
9. Bend, OR
10. Las Vegas, NV

As a real estate investor, it's important to understand that every type of property comes with its own pros and cons in terms of ownership, maintenance, and financing. Some of the obstacles may be specific to a locality (due to zoning rules, for example), so be sure to investigate all factors before you sign on the dotted line.

7

Understanding Zoning and Building Codes

You may not have much interest in government or politics, but as a new investor you should consider attending a zoning board meeting in your community to understand how decisions are made. You will learn valuable information such as what might trigger a challenge from the local zoning board and whether local inspectors are easy to work with. You might also receive another type of payoff such as firsthand news that a particular parcel is being cleared to make way for property that you're interested in.

In this chapter, we walk you through some of the most important aspects of zoning and building codes, and help you understand how they affect you as an investor.

Use Restrictions

In general, use restrictions refer to the ways in which buildings and land are used. A particular property may be restricted for residential, commercial, office, professional, or industrial use. By reading the use restrictions, you might discover that one parcel in a commercially zoned area allows residential loft development on a certain block. As more municipalities take a step back to try and understand how to best distribute their populations and keep property in use, use restrictions are in a constant state of change. It is always worth a look at the use restrictions in your area of interest.

Environmental Restrictions

 Though federal and state laws provide important guidelines to protect the environment, municipalities may define the term *environment* differently. Cities might be more particular about ozone, trees, or hazardous materials stored on your property than rural areas. It is critical that you and your contractor understand these restrictions to avoid any conflict with the authorities. A good place to start is your state or local environmental protection agency.

Occupancy Rules

Occupancy regulations are established by local zoning commissions and dictate the number of people who can live in a rental unit. This is a particular concern for landlords in neighborhoods where certain populations have large, extended families living in a small space to save money. Regardless of how you feel, the local government also has a say about the number of people living in your apartment.

Heights and Setbacks

Though many zoning issues may surface in the process of a condo conversion or some other major exterior change to a property, guidelines on building heights and setbacks are another issue. Local officials are often concerned that buildings in a particular area maintain a cohesive appearance—that is, no towering rooflines or homes built two feet from the sidewalk. Before you buy a property with plans for improvement that might extend its footprint or height, you need to check the building guidelines for that area.

Architectural/Landmark/Design Restrictions

No public arguments are as heated as those over historic buildings or architectural gems in a community. If you own such a property, you are likely aware of how difficult it can be to make changes to the structure. Even for investors who don't own an "architectural gem," many communities place limits on everything from exterior paint colors to what type of siding and windows are allowed. Others will reject new construction that does not conform to existing building styles or height restrictions. If you like a community for its look and feel, be assured it did not get that way by peaceful cooperation. There are usually detailed laws behind building appearance in a community. If not, you may find yourself free to do anything you want, but the property values will probably be lower.

Keeping a Low Profile

As you learn the zoning codes in a community, refrain from broadcasting your plans for the property. Individuals with little knowledge and big plans often draw attention, and that may create problems when it comes time to get your plans approved. Take it from the team at CompleteLandlord and its many constituents: be nice, courteous, and quiet as you investigate this important area of the real estate investment process. Obviously, if you have a chance to make friends on the zoning board, do so in a decidedly low-key manner. Being vocal about your plans can sometimes have negative consequences.

Arm Yourself

When it comes to complying with zoning and building codes, you can count on your contractor—who deals consistently with these restrictions during the course of business—for advice in this area. Even with that assistance, long-term real estate investors should commit themselves to having at least a working knowledge of their local zoning requirements.

Being armed with that knowledge can give you an advantage in the marketplace, especially if you find out about new proposed uses of land and property.

CHAPTER 8

The Flipping Phenomenon, Preforeclosures, Foreclosures, and Short Sales

Flipping, by definition, is the practice of buying existing or preconstruction property with a buyer waiting closely in the wings. Investors who flip properties often complete minor repairs or renovation work to increase the value of the property. The practice of flipping is profitable mainly in markets where prices are increasing rapidly.

Though flipping has gained a reputation as a quick and easy way to make money in real estate, there are pitfalls, too. A less-than-thorough inspection before purchase can result in expensive repairs. A buyer's financing can fall through. The market may cool and you, the investor, may be left with holding costs that far outstrip your cash flow until the property finally sells. In addition to these problems, you may find the U.S. government is after you.

IMPORTANT TIP

Here's a note worth repeating about the content in this entire book. We describe general situations about the way lending and tax practices work, but you are strongly advised to get individual tax and legal assistance before making any real estate investments. Because each person's financial situation is unique, tax and investment issues should be reviewed individually.

The Nothing-Down Movement

In the 1970s, credit investor Robert G. Allen created the nothing-down movement, which, depending on who you talk to, was either a legitimate milestone in real estate investment or one more multilevel marketing program that made some rich and others poor. One might wonder what Allen wrought, considering that during the real estate boom of the late 1990s and early 2000s conventional lenders made it progressively easier for homeowners to borrow 100 percent of their equity or more to get into real estate investing.

Regardless, Allen's initial ideas about finding distressed properties and creative financing are put into practice by individuals all over the country today. The stock investment clubs of the 1990s are the real estate investment clubs of today.

By nature, flippers practice the speedy purchase and resale of homes. They also:

◆ Buy, hold, and resell fixer-uppers without repairing them.
◆ Buy and repair fixer-uppers to sell at a profit.
◆ Sign lease-option-to-buy deals in which investors rent out a property at above-market rent to a tenant who wants the right to buy the place at the end of the lease.

While the word *flipper* can bring with it a negative connotation, there are some ways to safety get involved with this practice and reap the financial rewards that come from making excellent investment choices and quickly reselling at a profit. They include:

◆ *Know your neighborhood forward and backward.* Find a neighborhood that you know really well and stay there. Learn everything about that neighborhood.
◆ *Get to know bankers personally.* If you plan to take advantage of the foreclosure market, steer clear—at least initially—of the dozens of web sites out there purporting to have every foreclosure listing in your neighborhood. Go directly to the source to gather information. Knowing the local banker will possibly help you find out when they will be filing preforeclosure actions. Why

aim at preforeclosure? The answer in two words—motivated sellers.

◆ *Hang out at the courthouse.* Depending on the size of the community you live in, the clerk's office might let you know when up-to-date foreclosure records are filed and when the next public foreclosure auction will be held. This is valuable information if you have it before everyone else, and it gives you extra time to look at the properties coming up for bid.

◆ *Develop a dream team of advisors.* Find a lawyer, an accountant, and a favorite real estate agent or broker you can work an exclusive deal with for lower commissions or some other break for your repeat business. Most importantly, find a lending officer who will run numbers on any property you plan to buy before you buy it. Every member of your team should be delivering reality checks on a continuous basis.

◆ *Start as an owner-occupier.* Learn to paint, spackle, refinish, and love the smell of paint and sawdust in the morning. Avoid supporting two households and start your investment career with sweat equity. You may get more favorable loan terms as well.

◆ *Insure properly.* Your experts should tell you this, but make sure you are properly insured for your renovation work. A fire or injury could wipe out your reserves and disrupt your timetable.

◆ *Have some cash in the bank.* Problems and contingencies are common and may lengthen your time frame for fixing up and selling. Do not let the loss of one month's cash flow sink you; it may lead to financial disaster.

Learning Tough Lessons about Financing

Loans and lending strategies are discussed in more detail in Chapter 3, but there are a few basic issues to understand about financing real estate investments. The first is that mortgage rules for buying second and third properties are different from those for buying your first home. The money you can borrow for a rental or investment property is sometimes restricted, with the limitations of borrowing described for vacation homes.

This is the main reason why so many investors are highly leveraged and exposed to cash flow trouble if they cannot sell the house right away or if unexpected problems with renovation end up delaying the sale. Before you jump into flipping, consider whether you have enough cash to service your debt—and all your other living expenses—while you renovate. You have to be able to carry the mortgage until you are in a position to sell the home, which will likely take at least a few months, at the same time you carry your usual debts.

Locating Properties You Can Flip

Flippable properties are everywhere. Part of the aggressive housing boom in warm areas of the United States, like Las Vegas and Phoenix, in the early part of the twenty-first century came from speculation in existing and preconstruction condos. Investors would buy units right off a developer's blueprints and sell them the moment the last nail went in for healthy double-digit profits. It is a perfect example of tap-the-market-while-it-is-hot investing, though markets may not always be that hot.

With so many Americans in trouble right now due to the overuse of alternative financing methods and a faltering economy, distressed housing is another natural area for flippers looking for deals. To succeed in this area, investors educate themselves on the neighborhoods and those areas' chances for gentrification and appreciation.

 The "We buy ugly houses" movement you see advertised on billboards is perfectly legal, based on the oldest principle in investing— buy low, sell high. In this case, individual investors and national companies that have sprung up to meet this need act largely as pawnbrokers to people who need cash immediately and do not have the time or wherewithal to get a conventional real estate agent or broker to sell the property. Dangling cash, ugly house investors do deals quickly, fix up the property at lightning speed, sell for a profit, and move on.

Distressed properties can be profitable and certainly fill a need, but inexperienced investors need to study hard to identify value in appreciating neighborhoods. Investors must also consider their personal safety as much as the potential profit in this game. Foreclosure and preforeclosure homes are also ripe areas for flipping and provide an opportunity for investors who aren't afraid to roll up their sleeves and dig around at the courthouse to find out what's coming up for sale.

The Owner-Occupancy Route

On-site owners maintain property better than renters. This is why owner-occupants are far more attractive to lenders, and why becoming an owner-occupant is typically the easiest way for investors to start making money in real estate. Lenders are willing to make high loan-to-value (LTV) loans to legitimate owner-occupants who want to fix up property. They are available from most common lenders—banks, savings and loans, mortgage bankers, mortgage brokers, and credit unions.

In most cases, you have to tell your lender that you intend to live in the home for one year—a convention in that type of financing—but many experts say it is possible for owner-occupants to change their mind on this point before the year is up.

As long as you have paid the loan in good standing and have lived in the house during its renovation, it will be hard for a lender to prove you did not originally intend to live in the home for a year at the start. Besides, lenders would rather chase down bad customers than good ones, and chances are that if you want to continue investing and fixing up, they will want your business on the next loan.

Target Numbers—What to Shoot For

Every real estate deal is different in some way. There are always unexpected surprises—good and bad—in the buying, renovation, lending, and sale process. But when it comes to profits, some experts zero in on target numbers you should keep in mind.

Buy properties at least 30 to 50 percent below the market value. That way, after you fix them up and subtract the rehab expenses, commissions, financing, and miscellaneous costs, your target is a minimum 20 percent profit margin. Some might say that is a breakeven percentage as most interest-only loans cover only 80 percent of a home's expected market value.

Consider Tax Consequences

Over the past decade, there has been good and bad tax news for people who buy homes. Before May 7, 1997, the only way a seller could avoid paying taxes on a home-sale profit was to use the money to buy another, costlier house within two years. Sellers age 55 or older had one other option. They could take a once-in-a-lifetime tax exemption of up to $125,000 in profits. Everyone faced heavy tax paperwork to show the IRS that they followed the rules.

But when the Taxpayer Relief Act of 1997 became law, the home-sale tax burden got easier for most ordinary residential taxpayers. The rollover or once-in-a-lifetime options were replaced with the current per-sale exclusion amounts. (Visit www.irs.gov for more information.)

This is all good news for anyone selling a primary residence after years of living in it, but what about the investor who has never lived in a property? In this case, we are talking about investment property, and the tax considerations are completely different and definitely more costly.

 Be forewarned that the IRS keeps a careful watch on flippers, as they do all business owners. If you are buying and then quickly selling properties you do not live in, you need to talk to your tax advisor about organizing that activity as a business. When you complete several real estate transactions in a short time, do not be surprised to learn that the IRS considers your property transactions a business or trade rather than an investment strategy. That means you might pay ordinary income tax rates as high as 35 percent, which will put a significant dent in your profit margin.

For the vast majority of investors who hold the property for a year or more before selling, sale proceeds are considered long-term capital gains and are taxed at a 15 percent rate. One way to defer any tax obligation on the sale of investment property that is not owner-occupied is to funnel the proceeds into property equivalent in value under Section 1031 of the tax code, known as a like-kind exchange (see Chapter 3). Owners have up to 45 days to identify a comparable property and 180 days to conclude the transfer. A real estate professional can help you find the property and make the sale, but an exchange intermediary must handle the exchange end of the deal.

That is why it is critically important to consult a tax professional and a real estate attorney before investing. Learn more about selecting these key advisors in Chapters 10 and 11.

IMPORTANT NOTE

Ways Flipping Can Kill Your Cash Flow

- Failing to set aside three to six months of holding costs before buying.
- Vastly underestimating the time and cost of renovation. Get several bids from contractors with good recommendations, and build in incentives for finishing jobs early as long as they meet precise specifications.

One Flipper's Story

Wells Fargo lending executive Henry Apfelbach does an exercise with prospective customers who want to become real estate investors. He also does it with his experienced customers who have invested in real estate in the past, and it goes like this:

An individual wants to buy and flip a condominium with a market price of $250,000. She is able to put 20 percent down ($50,000), so she is holding a mortgage of $200,000 at 5.25 percent interest (assume a three-year adjustable rate mortgage at 5.25 percent).

Her dream: to put $40,000 into the $250,000 property and sell it for $360,000 in 10 months—a $70,000 profit.

Here's a more detailed look at the numbers: First, figure the cost of that loan. The loan origination fee is probably going to be one point, or $2,000, so when adding title costs, attorney fees, and other local fees that crop up, closing the sale alone will cost roughly $4,500. Next, consider her monthly expenses on the purchase, known as holding costs. The moment she gets the keys, she will be paying $890 a month on the mortgage, $250 a month for property taxes, and an extra $250 a month in condo assessments. This represents basic monthly holding costs of $1,390.

Now to renovation expenses. This condo needs a new kitchen and bathroom, and the budget should not exceed $40,000. She will now need a construction loan, which will run an additional $125 in payments a month, not counting the $3,000 for closing costs she will pay going into that loan.

Here's a quick rundown of what she will have on the line for this investment when she wants to sell at the end of 10 months:

One Flipper's Story (*Continued*)

Mortgage	$200,000
Down payment	50,000
Lending costs	10,140
Holding costs	22,790
Total investment	$282,930

Now she places the home on the market for $360,000, and she gets 94 percent of the asking price, which would be $338,400—not bad.

However, because she used a real estate agent to sell the property, she owed closing costs on the sale. A safe estimate of those costs would probably be around 6.5 percent of the sale price, or $21,996.

So what are her actual proceeds on the property in 10 months?

$$\$338,400 - \$21,996 = \$316,404$$

And how much profit did she make?

$$\$316,404 - \$282,930 = \$33,474$$

This is less than half of what she expected.

It is always possible to cut costs in some way—doing all the renovation work yourself (unless you have the skills, this can be tough to handle) or choosing to list the property yourself (for sale by owner) to save on commission expenses—but these tasks can be time-consuming if you do not know what you are doing.

The bottom line is that the costs associated with owning property can be high, and overruns in any area can have a serious impact on your expected earnings. It is also important to consider the possible tax consequences involved in every purchase.

The lesson to learn here is to proceed cautiously and seek the advice of seasoned professionals before you make your move.

Beware of Fraud

Mortgage fraud has grown rapidly during the housing boom and is now a multibillion-dollar problem for the industry. Mortgage-related suspicious activity reports more than double annually, with most cases involving a number of misrepresentations—the most common of which is falsification of applications by individual borrowers (56 percent of all cases), fake or incorrect tax and financial documents (33 percent), bogus employment verifications (12 percent), and fabricated or intentionally inflated appraisals (10 percent).

Investigators have noted that fraud often involves stated income and no-income or no-verification mortgages, property-flipping scams, or unscrupulous loan officers who help borrowers falsify their income.

The Foreclosure Option

A foreclosure occurs when a buyer defaults on his or her loan payments, often as a result of bankruptcy or other hard times. As the real estate market heated up in the 2000s, so did the market for web sites and other clearinghouses offering to help people find quality foreclosed properties. But beware of the hype; foreclosures are out there, but to get the pick of the litter, you need to build relationships first.

Another myth about foreclosures is that they are offered at 40, 50, or 60 percent below market rates. This is simply not true. Lenders—who own and oversee the sale of the property—know that foreclosed properties are a hot commodity on the real estate market and will not sell them for less than they are worth. In reality, 5 percent to 10 percent below market price is the norm.

One piece of good news, however: Foreclosures can be found in all types of neighborhoods. When times get tough, foreclosures happen everywhere. You may be surprised at the number of foreclosed homes found in affluent neighborhoods.

Buying a Foreclosure

There are three primary ways to buy a foreclosure property:

1. Attend a public or private foreclosure auction. You will usually get a chance to inspect the property first this way.
2. Buy a preforeclosure, which allows limited review time and requires a buyer to take on the mortgage and any other outstanding debts on the property.
3. Buy a real-estate-owned (REO) property that the bank has purchased at auction.

Do Your Homework

As discussed in previous chapters, it is important to invest in your own neighborhood. That is why it is best to learn how the foreclosure process works among lenders in your neighborhood.

Lenders have different methods by which they pursue foreclosures, but when the decision is made, they will file a notice of default (also called a *lis pendens*) with the clerk of the appropriate local court that handles foreclosure issues. This document is a public record available for anyone to see, and it gives notice to the borrower that there is a claim on the property. Your local newspaper may publish new filings.

Keep an eye out for these filings on a regular basis—they are your first step in identifying foreclosure property to buy. Assuming the borrower does not rescue himself by bringing his payments up to date, his property will be retained by the lender for sale, or possibly auctioned by city, county, or state officials designated to do so.

This is where experienced local real estate attorneys come in handy. For the cost of one to two hours of their time, you can learn the steps you will need to follow to enter into the foreclosure business. You may also learn about the difficulties of the process so you can correctly judge whether you have the skill, and the temperament, to be successful. All states have their own particular rules related to foreclosure and property sales. These rules may affect the way you learn about these opportunities. Again, do your research beforehand.

It is also important to understand that public officials can be swamped with new investors excited about the possibility of buying foreclosures. Therefore, limit your questions and be organized. It is fair to ask if most local lenders keep the properties to market—meaning they end up as real estate owned properties (REOs), or those that have been returned to the lender who must then resell them—or whether they cash out immediately and turn the property over to public agencies. Such agencies include the U.S. Department of Housing and Urban Development (HUD), the U.S. Department of Veterans Affairs, the Federal National Mortgage Association (Fannie Mae), and the Federal Home Loan Mortgage Corporation (Freddie Mac).

Information You Will See in a Foreclosure Notice

Most foreclosure notices contain the following:

- The type of property being sold
- The address of the property
- A description of trust including the balance, interest rate, and date
- The deed book and page that describe the trust, obtained from land records
- The location and date of the sale
- A legal description of the property, and the book and page that contain the street address
- The terms and conditions of the sale—foreclosure properties are sold as is
- The names of the trustees
- The primary contact information for the foreclosing attorney

Your Bank Is Your Ally

If you have worked to build a relationship with a bank's REO officer—the best way is to start doing business with the bank, not by walking in cold and demanding their REO list—buying directly from the lender is usually the safest way to go. Most foreclosures are taken back by the bank during auction, and though well-located homes in good shape generally do not sell for deep discounts, run-down properties can often be found at bargain prices.

Again, you need to know the neighborhoods—that is part of the research you will want to do in advance for any type of real estate investment, and particularly for foreclosures. In busy times, banks sometimes hire real estate agents to handle the sales to keep investors from hanging around the bank and pestering officers. Do not be afraid to ask the bank which agents they use and their contact information.

If you have an inside track, do not hesitate to use it. Try to contact the REO officer to see if they might want to start dealing directly. Agents cost a lender commissions, after all, and bulk-marketing foreclosures during tough times gets expensive, too. Show up well informed with a pleasant disposition, your financing prepared, and ready to go (again, cash is best in these situations) and, most importantly, enough knowledge to get you through the process.

Another benefit of buying directly from a bank is that the complicated issues (such as unpaid liens and taxes or owners who refuse to move) have been resolved. Banks typically settle up the liens and taxes before they remarket, and tenants and owners should have vacated the property when the foreclosure order was issued. Although other grassroots strategies may net you a better deal, the complications may prove much greater.

Preforeclosure

Buying a preforeclosure involves negotiating a sale directly with the owner shortly after notice of pending foreclosure has been issued (but before the lender has repossessed the property).

To find out what properties have been listed as pending foreclosures, find the person in your county clerk's office who records all mortgage or deed of trust foreclosure actions. That official might be the clerk, registrar, recorder, or prothonotary, and may work in the circuit court, county court, or bureau of conveyances. Each community, county, and parish has its own name for this position.

These officials will be the first ones to place into public record a notice of default—the first step in a foreclosure action. Some of these preliminary filings may be provided online with your county government, or they might be listed in the local newspaper's legal notices section.

With this information, a buyer can contact the owner directly; many experts agree it is best to do this by mail first just to break the ice. But first-time investors should be forewarned. People this close to foreclosure are often living in homes without phone service, heat, and are possibly far behind on maintenance. Given their circumstances, it is best not to expect an enthusiastic response. When you write or phone, simply introduce yourself politely and request an inspection of the property.

An investor who decides to pursue preforeclosures must be ready for the unexpected, such as quick payment for an agreed-upon transaction or immediate filing of legal documents to satisfy the banks, the county, or anyone who demands proof that the transaction is legal (here again is a strong argument for working with a knowledgeable attorney). Investors must also be ready for the human side of what they are trying to do. Owners may have nowhere else to go, so getting them out of the property may be problematic. Some owners are bitter enough about the loss of their property that they damage it before vacating.

Foreclosure investors need to be a bit fearless. They also need to be prepared to work with different groups of people in a variety of neighborhoods. The ability to read people quickly and resolve problems fairly are other important skills. Most important, foreclosure investors need to keep a healthy distance from the tough circumstances faced by the person they are buying from. This type of investing can be a cold, hard business.

Short Sales

When a homeowner hasn't paid for his or her mortgage for a certain period of time, but isn't yet in the foreclosure process, a short sale can take place. In such situations, a homeowner and a lender work out an arrangement that permits the homeowner to pay less than what is owed on the total loan balance. As an investor, your role would be to purchase the property, thus allowing the owner to "pay off" the negotiated amount and walk away from the home without having to deal with a foreclosure on his or her credit report.

There's a plethora of buyer-investors out there looking for foreclosed properties and short sales, and a growing number of homeowners who are finding themselves burdened by these types of properties (and lenders that are grappling with the overflow of such loans). These lenders would rather work out a short sale than pay out the average $80,000 that it costs them to manage, reclaim, and sell these foreclosed-upon properties. The scenario is also beneficial for buyers, who get competitively priced properties. It's truly a win-win situation for everyone involved, including the homeowner, who gets to sell his or her property with dignity, rather than losing it to a foreclosure sale.

Landlord Insights

When I first started in this short sale and foreclosure area of the market five years ago, I was skeptical when someone told me that people would be grateful that I came knocking on their doors, ready to help. "They're losing their homes, how could they possibly be grateful?" I said, but have since learned that a real estate professional's services are sorely needed in this arena, where an increasing number of homeowners are grappling with foreclosure. It all pays off when sellers tell me that they've had their best night's sleep in months, and that I'm the answer to their prayers. I hear both these comments in 90 percent of the deals that I work in this market, and it's very gratifying.

—Florida real estate agent

Public Auction Approach

Property retained by county governments is sometimes sold on county property with public notice posted in public buildings and local newspapers. Depending on how your county or municipality runs these auctions, you may not be able to fully inspect these properties before they are sold (which is not a problem for investors planning to knock them down and build something new), and you may have to be ready with a certified check to cover the bid you are willing to make. Attend an auction first before you attempt to buy anything, but first find out the answers to the following questions:

◆ What is the typical inspection process for these auctions?
◆ If my bid is accepted and for some reason there is a problem obtaining the property, do I lose my money?
◆ When do I get the deed and title to the property, or do I have to go through a separate process for that?
◆ If there are liens on the property, how will they be paid?
◆ Is there any way I can get out of this transaction if for some reason I am unsatisfied? (The answer to this is usually no, but it is best to ask an attorney or a clerk before the process starts than to suffer later.)

In many cities, you will find private auction houses that are either contracted out by banks to sell property or by other entities, including the property owners themselves, to unload property near or at foreclosure. They will also sell property that is not in financial peril—the owners, for whatever reason, have decided that an auction is the most efficient and low-cost way for them to sell. Do not let your search for foreclosures in process keep you from investigating these options. Private auctioneers tend to work in multi-unit residential and commercial properties or large estates with plenty of land; smaller properties do not always interest them.

Learn the Lingo

If you're going to take the public or private auction route, it helps to learn the lingo. Here are some terms you will likely encounter:

- *Open outcry:* This is the type of auction we know most about, where bids are shouted or verbally communicated with the auctioneer. Bidders sometimes compete by telephone with on-site bidders until the bids slow at the highest level and the auctioneer declares a winner.
- *Sealed bids:* Bidders submit their bids on a contract form submitted by a particular date and time. This way, the seller gets to review all the bids for a variety of conditions other than price—zoning issues on various parcels, for example.
- *With reserve:* In this kind of auction, a suggested opening bid for a property is set by the auctioneer to discourage frivolous bids. The auctioneer also reserves the right to accept or reject the high bid for any reason.
- *Multipar bidding:* This is an auction held in several stages, typically for undeveloped land, where bidders first bid on individual tracts of land within a development, then on the tract in its entirety. Based on what they know at that point, the auctioneer packages various tracts of lands in various configurations to get the best price for the seller.

IMPORTANT NOTE

A public records search ensures that no liens exist on the property because these can drive the purchase price above market value. You should also look for assessed values and sale prices of neighboring properties to make sure your bid is reasonable.

Paying for Auctioned Property

There are very few options in this area aside from having cash or acceptable lines of credit ready to go. In cases where a bank has only a few chances to sell the property, it may loan the full price of a foreclosure to acquire a good borrower. That gives the bank the opportunity to clear the property off their inventory and to maintain a good relationship with you—the client. Also, that lender may allow the foreclosure investor to convert the expensive short-term financing used for the original deal into conventional financing later. Again, remember that success in real estate investing—foreclosure and otherwise—is built on the relationships you form along the way. Lenders want to deal with informed investors who make the process easy for them.

Federal Agencies Sell Homes, Too

Many federal agencies and quasi-federal agencies have a process for selling homes to homeowners. In most cases, they give priority to owner-occupants looking to buy, not offsite investors or developers. Following the priority period for homeowners, the agencies will accept bids from off-site investors. In HUD's case, homeowners can start by finding a participating real estate agent. Your real estate agent must submit your bid for you.

Normally, HUD homes are sold in an offer period scheduled by the agency—your agent will know the schedule. At the end of the offer period, all offers are opened and, normally, the highest reasonable bid is accepted. If the home is not sold in the initial offer period, you can submit a bid until the home is sold. Bids can be submitted any day of the week, including weekends and holidays. They will be opened the next business day. If your bid is acceptable to HUD, your real estate agent will be notified, usually within 48 hours.

Visit www.hud.gov/homes/index.cfm for more information on available HUD properties.

Contacts for Other Federal Foreclosure Programs

Federal Home Loan Mortgage Corporation/Homestep Program
(www.freddiemac.com/corporate/buyown/english/properties)

U.S. Department of Veterans Affairs
(www.va.gov)

Federal National Mortgage Association
(www.mortgagecontent.net/reoSearchApplication/fanniemae/
  reoSearch.jsp)

U.S. Department of Agriculture
(www.resales.usda.gov)

Hidden Foreclosures

Some foreclosed homes and properties come from contractors and developers who could not make a sale in time, fell behind on their payments, and had the bank call in their loan. These are referred to as hidden foreclosures because they rarely appear on national lists and nobody refers to them as foreclosed homes. Sometimes it helps to have contacts in the contractor community to help you locate individuals in lending trouble, but this is also where your efforts to make contacts at the bank and with informed brokers will make the most sense.

Other Public Agencies

Foreclosed and seized property, including buildings and vacant land, turn up at auctions offered by the IRS (www.treas.gov/auctions/irs/), the U.S. General Services Administration (http://propertydisposal.gsa.gov), and the Small Business Administration (http://app1.sba.gov/pfsales/dsp_search .html). There is also a clearinghouse site for the federal government's housing properties (www.homesales.gov/homesales/mainAction.do/).

It is interesting to look at the various types of properties the government has listed on these web sites. If you have the time, get to know someone in local law enforcement who might know of local foreclosure/seizure resources related to criminal activity.

Probate

If a property owner dies with no written, legal will to dispense of his possessions—and there are no heirs—it is up to the court to dispose of the property. Depending on how your city or county government works, you might be able to buy a house below-market in probate court. Be prepared for significant fix-up work, however. People who are sick or very old typically have not put much work into property maintenance.

Develop a System for Inspecting Properties

Foreclosure properties can be problematic. In situations where you have little time to inspect, you need a system. Plan to bring a contractor or licensed inspector with you to the inspection and make sure you have a review plan to make the best use of time. Remember, owners in the midst of foreclosure actions have more problems than you being there, so lingering about the property and asking a lot of questions may not be greeted in the friendliest of ways. Use a form similar to Figure 8.1 when inspecting properties.

Good Reasons to Take a Pass on Foreclosure Property

- *Lack of equity:* If the current owner has no equity left in the home, there are probably more problems there than you want to deal with.
- *Holding costs:* Getting the home in your name is just a start. If you do not have six months' worth of cash in the bank to cover the mortgage, attorney, title, brokerage fees, renovations, and other contingencies, you might run out of cash before you can sell at a profit.
- *Not knowing precisely what you want to buy:* Any successful real estate strategy involves focus and niches. You need to pick categories of property that are predictable from a purchase and renovation standpoint so the financial structure of each deal is predictable. Unless you know the particular neighborhoods, structures, and transaction issues inherent in the properties you want to invest in, take a pass at buying just any foreclosure.
- *Auctions may be confusing, or possibly fixed:* Public entities have an obligation to make sure auctions are publicly disclosed and run legally. But certainly you have read about communities where certain people seem to get the sweetest deals first. Such situations are the result of everything from favoritism to outright corruption, and that is why you need to learn the system. Everyone is looking for an advantage. If you can find one that is legal, use it.

Residential Inspections:
Buyer's Walk-Through Inspection Form

This systematic review of the building's components prior to settlement, or as soon thereafter as possible, will assist you in acquiring a baseline of the building's condition and will provide a report on any agreed-on repairs or modifications.

General	Yes	No	Comments
Any major changes to the property?			
Agreed-on modifications or repairs completed?			
Receipts/warranties/guarantees provided by repair contractors?			
Pest control clearance provided?			
Roofing			
Age of covering in good condition?			
Good drainage flow around foundation walls?			
Indications of roof leakage?			
Good condition of flashing between chimney damper and exterior wall?			
Gutters and downspouts secure?			
Attic			
Needs ventilation such as windows			
Need insulation?			
Needs vents or vented soffits?			
Is insulation blocking air circulation?			
Is there an attic fan?			
Exterior			
Exterior door condition and testing of locks?			
Good insulated glass seal quality?			
Storm door condition?			
Do windows open and close easily?			
Cellar door condition?			
Concrete: condition of steps, sidewalks, and driveway?			
Window and storm window condition?			
Evidence of new cracks, paint peeling, or other visible defects?			
Plants/vegetation growing on the building exterior?			
New cracks or indications of retaining wall failure?			

Figure 8.1 Residential Inspections: Buyer's Walk-Through Inspection Form

Figure 8.1 *(Continued)*

Signs of inadequate surface drainage		
Openings into the building at trim, flashings, chimneys, etc.		
Stairway, deck, porch, and other railings secure and properly installed		

(continued)

Figure 8.1 (*Continued*)

Heating/Cooling/Air Filters

- ☐ System functional?
- ☐ Forced-air furnace noisy
- ☐ Serviced recently?
- ☐ Flame not centered in heat exchanger
- ☐ Draft is poor in heat exchanger
- ☐ Type of air filter on furnace?
- ☐ Condition of hot water heater
- ☐ Pressure safety valve in place
- ☐ Burn marks at lighting panel

Fireplace

- ☐ Safety check on older fireplaces and chimneys?   ☐ Dampers operational?
- ☐ Fire boxes need repair?   ☐ Spark arrestor and rain cap installed?

Flipping, foreclosures, and preforeclosures, perhaps more than any other type of real estate investment, highlight the importance of doing your research before jumping in and purchasing a property. Not only do potential buyers need to understand how the process works, but they need to know the relevant players at each stage of the process to give them an advantage. They also need the kind of people skills specific to these kinds of deals. It is certainly possible to hire an agent or broker and buy foreclosures, but any part of the process you outsource cuts your potential profit.

CHAPTER 9

Creative Real Estate Investing

So far you've learned about the more traditional methods and strategies for investing in real estate. In this chapter, we show you some of the more "creative" financing options that are available to today's investors, with the intention of giving you a brief picture of the full scope of available opportunities. These go far beyond cash and bank deals to include such options as tax liens, tax deeds, mortgages, and wholesaling. Here's a look at your options.

Tax Liens

Using tax lien certificates, investors can acquire real estate at a budget price. Such liens attach to a property when an owner fails to pay the real estate taxes due. When this happens, the government auctions the responsibility for payment of the tax to the highest bidder, who in turn becomes owner of the property.

Investors looking for a creative investing option will definitely find it in tax liens. TaxLiens.com reports that $7.6 billion in delinquent property taxes are created each year with total size of the market at any given time being in the $20 billion range.

The tax lien process is highly localized, so be sure to find out how it works in your area before proceeding. The county may announce tax liens online, in the paper, or on a list at the courthouse. Delinquent nontax-paying individuals (or companies) are subject to tax liens. Those liens typically sell for more than the outstanding debt due on the home, and require some liquidity to acquire.

IMPORTANT NOTE

Don't bid on a tax lien certificate without visiting the houses or land first. Municipalities release lists of properties before the auctions so you can visit them. Do your research before undertaking any tax lien certificate investing.

Tax Deeds

With a tax deed sale, you will bid on the actual deed to a property that's come up for sale due to nonpayment of taxes by the owner. Not all states offer this option, but those that do have created a viable avenue for real estate investors. Through the process, you will acquire the property and then be able to sell it, rent it, or live in it.

Tax deeds are cash-intensive in that they require more money up-front to purchase. The upside is that properties can be acquired for a very low price through this process. In exchange, the deeds are issued at the tax sale auction.

IMPORTANT NOTE

In some states, after the tax deed has been issued, the successful bidder must comply with the state's statute of redemption, which is a law that allows the delinquent owner to reclaim the property by paying all back taxes, expenses, and accrued interest within a specified period of time. In most states, all lien holders of record must be served notice, and they are also given the opportunity to redeem the property prior to the expiration of the redemption period.

Wholesaling

Wholesalers buy properties at below-market prices and then turn around and sell at below-market rates, thus earning a $500, $1,000, $2,000, or higher spread on their investment. The deals are usually closed within a short period of time, and could be considered a "quick flip" in real estate terms.

For the wholesale deal to make sense, the property and/or owner must be in distress. Maybe he can no longer afford the mortgage, or maybe she has had a death in the family and must move immediately to a new state.

IMPORTANT NOTE

Wholesale real estate is essentially buying cheap to sell for a profit to another investor. It is the other investor who will then retail the property.

Speed counts when it comes to wholesaling real estate. Your offer probably allows for only a few days or a week to find an investor, and that investor needs a property that sells fast to avoid holding costs and market risk. The best approach is to come up with a list of investors before you start looking for properties, and focus only on those houses that are selling fastest (usually those that are near the median price for properties in the area).

Buying Mortgages

Mortgages are often sold by lenders to other lending institutions. Once that happens, investors can broker transactions by arranging meetings between buyers and sellers, or by buying them and immediately selling them for a profit.

It works like this: An investor buys a mortgage, or "note," often from a seller of a property, at a discounted price and receives the monthly principal with interest until the mortgage is paid off. If an investor pays $22,000 for a $36,000 mortgage, for example, the borrower makes payments on a $36,000 mortgage, with the investor pocketing the difference.

Once you've agreed to purchase a mortgage, you'll send the check to the title company, where the money is held in escrow until the transaction is closed. The seller of the property (and mortgage) sends the original documentation of the transaction and the mortgage to the title company along with the signed assignment of the mortgage. The title company records the transaction, then the money is given to the seller and the documentation is given to the investor. You then officially own the mortgage.

Navigating the investment options covered in this chapter can be a complex task, so be sure to confer with an experienced attorney, accountant, and/or financial professional before taking advantage of any of these opportunities. For the right investor, however, these creative strategies can be a great way to break into the market without having to take out a mortgage or take too much cash out of the bank.

Creating Your Action Plan

Your Winning Business Strategy, Action Plan, and Team Building

If there's one piece of advice that the CompleteLandlord team would like to share with any new real estate investor, it's this: Don't go it alone. Even if you're the hands-on type who believes that a job doesn't get done right if you don't do it yourself, there are still myriad resources that you can take advantage of. Doing so means that you won't have to reinvent the wheel, do everything yourself, or spend 24/7 worrying about whether important tasks get done.

In this chapter, we look at the role that a good real estate agent can play on your team. Then, in Chapter 11, we walk you through the intricacies of finding and working with lawyers and accountants. Combined with a number of other service providers (such as home inspectors, repair personnel, and lenders), these professionals will serve as your "right arm" as you embark on the real estate investment process.

The Real Estate Agent

Imagine that you have a $600,000 investment home to sell and the agent you have hired to handle the entire transaction is charging you a 6 percent commission for the work. That's $36,000 off the top, not counting fees, taxes, and other items you need to pay at closing. The agent did a great job, selling the property in a week. But 6 percent? That is a pretty big slice off the top, and many people who have seen their real estate assets skyrocket during the past 10 years are asking that question a lot more often.

The more they make, the more they have to pay out to professionals. But before you decide to sell your property yourself, it is worth looking at what it takes to sell property through an agent or broker and on your own. The reason for selecting one alternative or the other should be based on:

♦ The time you have to learn the intricacies of the sale process
♦ Your skills as a negotiator
♦ The types, frequency, and complexity of the deals you want to do
♦ The time you have to show your property and answer questions about it

Time and complexity drive the process of hiring an agent or broker in most cases. If you have ever attempted to sell a home or other real estate property, you know that the paperwork piles up fast. It is easy to lose track of the various deadlines and players who are part of the process—inspectors, mortgage loan agents, real estate agents, and title officers.

An agent will not only negotiate the deal for you, but also make sure everything you have agreed to actually happens. Perhaps most important is that you are hiring a professional who knows far more about the marketplace than you do. If you find that you know more about what and where you plan to buy or sell than the agent, then find another agent.

IMPORTANT NOTE

Dual agency occurs when a real estate agent or broker represents both the buyer and the seller in the same transaction. Both parties must consent to this situation in writing because the agent is promising a duty of confidentiality, loyalty, and full disclosure to both parties. Because of this, these situations should be limited.

Real estate agents normally work on commission, not salary, and most commissions start at 5 percent, to be split when two agents are working the deal. Agents receive their share of the commission after the transaction is complete.

Commissions Are Negotiable

As you search for an agent, ask friends, family, and other contacts about qualified agents who not only would meet your service needs but are willing to negotiate the commission based on the price of the property or the possibility of sharing some of the duties. There are rare situations when brokers work on a discount basis or for an hourly fee—sometimes for commissions as low as 1 percent—but these situations work best only when duties are spelled out clearly and both agent and customer are experienced at real estate transactions.

To save a few dollars you might consider doing most of the work yourself, such as showing the house, and hiring an agent to handle:

- Setting the price of your house
- Advertising your home in the local multiple listing service (MLS) of homes for sale in the area (a database managed by local boards of real estate agents)
- Handling some of the more complicated paperwork when the house closes

For real estate investors, there is one more incentive for hiring a real estate agent: most of them specialize in a specific niche. In the foreclosure arena, for example, there are agents who act as intermediaries between banks and buyers. If your goal is to transact business in distressed or reclaimed properties, working with a good agent may be an excellent way to train for the process.

How to Hire a Real Estate Agent

You wouldn't pick the first doctor that you meet to handle an important surgery, so don't rush into working with the first real estate agent who hands you a glossy brochure and flashes a toothy smile. Always talk to two or three agents before you settle on your choice. If you have access to the Internet, conduct a short search for background information before interviewing possible candidates.

Here are some of the key questions to ask in a face-to-face conversation:

◆ *How long have you been working in this area?* Though every professional has to start somewhere, newer agents who want to make it will generally work harder to please. However, try to hire agents with at least five years' experience in the neighborhood where you are listing. Also, make sure you have checked their web site for biographical and professional information so you know a little about their committee work and local activities. Agents need to network because the more contacts they have, the more they can help you.

◆ *Is your primary specialty residential, or do you handle other types of property work?* Most good agents are not all things to all people. Residential, investment, commercial, industrial, and vacation properties all require different skill sets in the brokerage process, so make sure you are talking to the specialist you need.

◆ *How do you allot your time when working for a client?* This is an important question because it gives you an opportunity to see whether the agent is hands-on or hands-off. Do they staff their own open houses? Are they only available by phone during certain hours? Do they routinely attend closings to make sure everything wraps up properly? These are all important issues. Some agents have been known to assign various parts of their workload to junior staff, which is fine if you are aware of this before you hire the agent. However, if you feel uncomfortable with what the agent describes, then you might want to interview other candidates.

◆ *How much do you think you could get for my property?* Experienced agents provide thorough market assessments for their clients. What goes into a market assessment? Many things, but key items include a complete list of comparable sales in your area (and access to gossip about what really happened in those deals), a report on how quickly properties are selling on the market right now, and a frank assessment of what you need to do to your property to make it more salable. Watch carefully to see if an agent or broker is factoring in another important variable—the convenience factor. Some agents who would rather be working with higher-end properties may suggest a bargain price for a lower-end property so they can keep their work to a bare minimum. This is why it is especially important to know comparables on similar properties going into the interview process with any agent. An agent may indeed be wiser about the market than you are, but make them prove it to you.

◆ *What kind of marketing will you do for my property?* If the agent's firm has a standing advertisement in the community paper, ask whether your property will appear in it and for how long. See if your property will be featured on the real estate agent's Internet site and related mailing lists. Ask how the master property listing in your community works and how the broker works with other agents. Word-of-mouth from an influential agent is often the best sales tool.

◆ *Do you have good financing contacts?* If you are selling, you might need financing on your next property. Always ask whom an agent or broker likes to work with. He or she might give you a better deal for the bulk business the agent sends to them. It is another way to find out how good the agent's connections are.

◆ *How do you keep your clients' homes secure during open houses?* It is particularly important that the agent or broker you hire staff your open house for security reasons. See how he or she considers the question; a signup sheet is not the only protection. The agent should tell you at that time what he or she believes should be hidden safely from view (such as jewelry, medications, valuable artworks, other valuables) and what the agent does to protect his or her own security during the open house process.

◆ *Under what conditions would you offer a lower commission?* Do not ask the agent or broker to lower his or her standard commission unless you are prepared to take a reduction in services. If an agent raises the possibility of a lower commission first, ask what traditional services you will have to give up as a result. Newer brokers may offer commission breaks in order to build their business, but a lower fee almost always means a tradeoff in service. In a hot market, why should an agent accept only half of his or her normal commission to do the same amount of work? However, if the market is hot and you are seeing homes move in just a few days, propose to the agent a discounted commission if the property sells quickly—say within 24 to 48 hours. Before signing any agreement, be clear on what the agent's average fee buys you before you start looking for a break. Maybe that full 6 percent will buy you an immediate sale while other agents' homes languish on the market. Consider carefully what the full commission may be worth to you.

◆ *Can you provide references?* If you have done your homework, you will have already received a recommendation on this agent or broker and researched his or her professional background through various sources on the Internet. Asking an agent for references from past property sales similar to yours may yield the most important information. You will learn whether he or she is hesitant to share performance information, and you may learn valuable information from those past clients about their experience working with him or her. Good real estate agents should be eager to provide these references.

◆ *How often will we be in contact?* Problem clients are ones who call several times a day to find out if there are any nibbles; problem agents and brokers are ones who dodge your calls. When interviewing an agent, find out what he or she thinks is a reasonable way to stay in touch. If there are specific times during the day when you cannot vacate your property for a showing, tell the agent. Likewise, if there are nonnegotiable scheduling issues for the agent, you should know what they are. Set up a specific time during the week to chat, even if nothing is going on; it is a way for you both to briefly catch up. Most agents work odd hours, but there needs to be a mutual respect for time and boundaries.

◆ *How busy are you right now?* This is a way to know how much time the agent has for you, and most important, how hot the market is right now.

◆ *Will you ever represent anyone other than me in a transaction?* Make sure the agent verbally guarantees—followed by a written statement in the service contract—to represent only you. You cannot have an agent or broker negotiating for you and the seller, though most ethical brokers would never do this.

The answers to these detailed questions should give you a good idea of whether an agent is a good candidate to work with . . . or not. Use your best judgment when finding the right partner and you're sure to benefit from the association.

Going It Alone

While some states require that purchasers or sellers of real estate have legal representation, no states dictate whether the consumer must use a real estate agent. While the process can be time-consuming and complex, many property owners successfully manage the transaction on their own. Those who choose to go the for sale by owner (FSBO) route may or may not have their homes included in the local multiple listing service (MLS)—an aggregation of all listings for a particular area. Once the domain of the real estate agent, MLSs are now used by FSBO service companies, which will handle the listing for a small fee.

Be aware that real estate agents have historically pointed their clients to properties that are listed by commissioned agents. This approach has changed in recent years as FSBO service firms have sprung up around the country. Agents know that it may behoove them to at least stop by your property, if only to try and snag your business when the FSBO route doesn't work out.

Real Estate Investor Insights

You see a lot of FSBO homes go off the market after a month or two because the owners are tired of the work, and an agent who is willing to treat them nicely during FSBO might get their business later.

—Henry Apfelbach, Wells Fargo mortgage executive

If you want to go it alone, check out a few of the web sites that are dedicated to helping the FSBO owner including www.forsalebyowner.com, www.buyowner.com, and www.homekeys.com. These sites offer everything from market data to help you competitively price your FSBO to yard signs, sample contracts, and even access discount real estate agents that will provide services to you at a fraction of full-service agent fees.

Those real estate investors who want to list and buy properties on their own should know that—according to Henry Apfelbach of Wells Fargo—anywhere from 60 to 80 percent of FSBOs fail to sell. So while you may save tens of thousands of dollars by *not* paying a commission to a real estate agent, you should know that handling an FSBO is not something you learn in a weekend. You need to know how to accurately research the market to come up with a fair price for your home, and you need to know whether buyers in your neighborhood are FSBO friendly. In fact, some people see an FSBO sign and ask themselves whether you are up to the task of making a problem-free sale.

If you're going to take the FSBO route, you would also be wise to secure a good real estate lawyer who will be available whenever you need him or her to read documents. You must also know the legal rules that govern real estate transfers in your state, such as who must sign the papers, who can conduct the actual transaction, and what to do if and when situations arise that slow down the transfer of ownership.

You also need to be aware of any state-mandated disclosures on the physical condition of your house—if you fail to tell a buyer the house has a cracked foundation or leaky roof, you might find yourself in court later.

Most important, you will need to know exactly what to do with earnest money—an informed buyer will be hesitant to hand you a check unless you have specific information on escrow. Then there is the complexity of title insurance. In some states, the buyer pays for the title insurance policy. In other states, it is up to the seller. Details such as these require a good deal of homework.

Disclosure Dangers

State and local laws vary, but if you are selling your own property, you also have to know about environmental risks common to your community. For instance, if you are selling a house built before 1978, you have to comply with a law known as the Residential Lead-Based Paint Hazard Reduction Act of 1992, also known as Title X. You will have to:

- Disclose all known lead-based paint and hazards in the house.
- Provide buyers with a pamphlet prepared by the U.S. Environmental Protection Agency (EPA) titled "Protect Your Family from Lead in Your Home."
- Include certain warning language in the contract as well as signed statements from all parties verifying that all requirements were completed.
- Keep signed acknowledgments for three years as proof of compliance and give buyers a 10-day opportunity to test the house for lead.

Disclosure Dangers (*Continued*)

FSBO sellers must be aware of any issues that might occur surrounding their property. You would have to know, for instance, if a major development is being considered near your property because any possible buyers are going to have to deal with the racket for the next year or two. You have to be ready for any question a potential buyer might have and be as good as the best agent in your neighborhood at answering them.

In the current real estate market, you'll need strong negotiating skills to justify your asking price. Many buyers—particularly those represented by experienced agents—will argue that because you are not paying a commission, you should be willing to take less for your house. Use a form like the one in Figure 10.1 to ensure full disclosure to the buyer.

IMPORTANT NOTE

Some owners opt to get their licenses in order to handle their own deals. This may not be a bad idea, as long as you are prepared to make the time and cost commitment. Keep in mind, however, that real estate agents must disclose that they are licensed agents, so you must provide this information up front before beginning any negotiations. Also, agents are governed by a state licensing board and are held to high ethical and business standards.

The decision of whether to buy or sell properties on your own or with assistance is a critical one. Though there is a large FSBO movement, and successful transactions will save thousands in an inflated price environment, individuals need to educate themselves for weeks and possibly months to compete with established agents. Know exactly what you want to do with your real estate activities, and then decide whether you can best accomplish your goals with a professional or by yourself.

Real Estate Sales Disclosure
Also called Seller's Disclosure or Transfer Disclosure

The prospective buyer and the owner may wish to obtain professional advice or inspections of the property and provide for appropriate provisions in a contract between them concerning any advice, inspections, defects, or warranties obtained on the property. The representations in this form are representations of the owner and are not representations of the agent, if any. This information is for disclosure only and is not intended to be a part of the contract between the buyer and owner.

Seller states that the information contained in this Disclosure is correct as of the date below, to the best of the Seller's current actual knowledge.

Date _____ Property Address _____

The Condition of the Following Property Is:	N/A	Defective	Not Defective	Unknown
1. Electrical System				
a) Air filtration system				
b) Burglar alarm				
c) Cable TV wiring and connections				
d) Ceiling fans				
e) Garage door opener				
f) Inside telephone wiring and jacks				
g) Intercom				
h) Kitchen range hood				
i) Light fixtures				
j) Sauna				
k) Smoke/fire alarm				
l) Switches and outlets				
m) Amp services				
n) Plumbing				
o) Other				
2. Heating and Cooling				
a) Attic fan				
b) Central air conditioning				
c) Hot water heater				
d) Furnace heater: gas, electric, oil, solar				
e) Fireplace				
f) Humidifier				
g) Ventilation				
h) Propane tank				

Figure 10.1 Real Estate Sales Disclosure

Figure 10.1 (*Continued*)

The Condition of the Following Property Is:	Yes	No	Unknown
3. **Foundation and Structure**			
a) Are there any problems with the foundation?			
b) Are there any structural problems with the building?			
c) Have any substantial additions or alterations been made without a required building permit?			
d) Are there any violations of zoning, building codes or restrictive covenants?			
e) Are there moisture or water problems?			
f) Is there termite, rodent, or insect damage?			
g) Is there damage due to wind or flood?			
h) Is the property in a flood plain?			
i) Is the property located within 1 (one) nautical mile of an airport?			
j) Is there any threat of or pending litigation regarding the property?			
k) Are the furnace, wood stove, chimney/flue in working order?			
4. **Roof**			
a) Age in years_____			
b) Are there any current leaks?			
c) Is roof currently damaged?			
d) Is there more than one roof on the structure? If yes, how many_____?			

Additional Comments (attach additional pages if neccessary):

_____

_____

5. **Hazardous Conditions:** Are there any existing hazards on the property (e.g., methane gas, radioactive material, radon, or lead paint in house or well, or expansive soil, toxic materials, asbestos insulation, landfill, mineshaft, or PCBs)? If yes, explain: _____

_____

_____

6. **Major Damage:** Do you have any actual knowledge if there has ever been any material damage to the property or structures such as movement, shifting, cracks in the floors, foundation, walls, or ceilings? If yes, give details: ____

_____

_____

_____

(*continued*)

Figure 10.1 (*Continued*)

7. **Termites/Insects:** Are you aware of any existence of any wood boring insects/termites currently in or on the property or any existing, unrepaired damage caused by same? _____

_____

_____

_____

8. **Water Service:** Is there a well on the property? If yes, is it in working order? If it is not in working order, has it been sealed? If so, when _____

_____

_____

9. **Sewer Service:** Is the property serviced by a municipal sewer? If not, what is the date of installation of the private septic system? Date last pumped? List dates and describe any repairs to the system: _____

_____

_____

_____

10. **Lot:** Is there an oil/fuel tank on the property? If yes, where is it located? Is the oil/fuel tank in use? Is the oil/fuel tank underground? _____

_____

_____

_____

11. **Structural:** Are you aware of any code violations on the property? If yes, attach explanation. Is the exterior siding synthetic stucco, Exterior Insulating Finish System (EIFS), or hardboard siding? If yes, which type? _____

_____

_____

_____

12. **UFFT/Asbestos:** Is there any urea-formaldehyde (UFFT) or asbestos material present? _____

_____

_____

_____

13. **Mold/Mildew:** In the course of preparing your property for sale, did you clean up any mold or mildew? If yes, name where and the method of remediation: _____

_____

_____

Figure 10.1 (*Continued*)

14. **Radon Gas:** Has the property been tested for radon gas? If the property was tested for radon gas, the results of all tests known to seller(s) are attached. Tests disclose level of radon on test day(s) only and no representations are made as to the level of radon at any time prior to or after the test(s). _____

_____

15. **Roof:** Have there ever been any material repairs or replacement made to the roof as the result of any water problems in the past five years? What is the roofing material? _____

_____

_____

_____

16. **Additional comments or explanations:** _____

_____

_____

_____

_____

Seller and Buyer hereby acknowledge receipt of this Disclosure Form by signing below.

_____   _____
Seller's Signature   Date   Buyer's Signature   Date

_____   _____
Seller's Name   Buyer's Name

CHAPTER 11

Accountants and Lawyers

Some investors are capable of drafting a contract without the aid of an attorney or filing their taxes without the help of an accountant. But for the rest of us, hiring a professional to guide us through the process is a necessity. When you are buying and selling or owning and managing investment property, you are running a business and you need to handle business matters professionally. With the complexity of ever-changing regulations, and tenant and tax laws affecting real estate today, you may need an attorney *and* an accountant to keep you from landing in court. In the end, their guidance may save you far more than their fees.

According to Gary Wendland, a Chicago attorney who specializes in real estate, experienced attorneys do more than simply review contracts; they are necessary guides to the specific ins and outs of property management in every community.

When is the best time to consult an attorney or a tax professional? Before you leap into any investment. Buying investment property is a huge undertaking, and it is a good idea to secure an hour or two of a professional's time to discuss planning all aspects of the transaction. You may have an idea of a specific property in mind or only a general idea of what you want to do. But an initial, exploratory conversation with an attorney, a tax advisor, or both may radically shape your view of what you are buying, when and where you buy it, or if you should be buying it at all.

Choosing a Professional

Friends and trusted advisors are always the first and best source for finding a real estate professional. After that, real estate agents or other experts in your circle are good choices. You might also contact your local bar association or certified public accountant (CPA) society for names of those who specialize in your particular financial interests and investment strategy.

Landlord Insights

The biggest mistakes I see new real estate investors making are usually due to their lack of awareness of local requirements for converting a property or, when purchasing a property, bringing it up to code. Real estate attorneys who know and work in your neighborhood are paid to see these obstacles before you hit them. The unexpected costs of buying and renovating real estate are a big surprise to many people.

—Gary Wendland, attorney.

Big or Small Firm?

If you are planning to invest narrowly, it may be wise to consolidate your personal and business tax duties at a small to midsize firm. There is no need to pay big-firm fees unless they have a particular type of practice that serves you well and charges you fairly. As for choosing an attorney, there is little reason to go with a large firm if you know of competent neighborhood attorneys who handle real estate. Like good agents, they should be knowledgeable about the area and local properties for sale and may help you locate the best properties for your needs.

Some states require a licensed attorney to prepare home purchase documents and close the deal. Everywhere else, involving an attorney is strictly optional. But paying for expertise up front can be a wise decision. Though a real estate agent—if you are using one—will be handling the negotiations on the property, your attorney can be an important backstop on what the agent has delivered to you.

If you are planning to rent property and are inheriting tenants that may become problematic for you later, an attorney can help you think through a battle plan before problems occur. Think of the best attorneys as you would the best contractors or agents. You are buying their knowledge and expertise, so prepare a list of questions before each meeting. If you are paying $150 an hour, make it worth your while. The attorney you hire should:

- Have integrity and a plain-spoken manner.
- Work in real estate most of the time and with clients who own the type of property you want to own (do not hire a lawyer who works with commercial real estate developers if you only plan to own a couple of two-flats).
- Respond to your tastes and individual needs.
- Be licensed in the states where you want to buy and be a member of a major trade organization in the real estate field that helps him or her stay abreast of issues in the marketplace or at least a local association that helps him or her network in real estate.
- Carry certifications from the local real estate agent's trade association that show training in agent activities and residential and commercial property issues.

Before you select an attorney, ask him or her the following questions:

- *How long have you been working in real estate?* There is no specific time frame that connotes expertise, but you do want someone with a strong knowledge of the real estate market.
- *Do you own property yourself?* Attorneys with personal experience as an investor often provide better advice.
- *Are you a member of any local or national real estate trade groups?* Attorneys can be members of NAR or other major real estate groups. Ask them what that membership brings to them and their clients.
- *What are the three biggest problems you see facing investors today?* Pay attention to how he or she answers this question. If he or she responds with general issues, such as interest rates and high property prices, probe further. The attorney should be telling you detailed information about the local market you plan to buy into; if not, it is better to know before signing on for services.

(continued)

> *(Continued)*
> ◆ *What is your fee structure?* Ask how fees are generally paid and if there are any opportunities to get fixed-priced services for certain tasks.
> ◆ *If there is criminal activity involving a tenant or the property, what can you do for me?* This, or any other worst-case-scenario question, should be asked in the interview before you buy. The worst time to hire an attorney is during legal disputes related to your property. The attorney's answer will reflect his or her expertise with crisis situations.

Accounting 101

The complexity of the U.S. tax code has convinced many Americans of the importance of professional guidance; fewer and fewer Americans are able to complete their own tax returns without the help of an accountant. Tax issues related to real estate investments are highly involved because laws, rules, and regulations change nearly every year at the national, state, and local level.

The most important assistance tax professionals can provide for your real estate activities involves helping you plan the life cycle of that investment. This will allow you to focus your goals, avoid overpaying taxes when you renovate, buy more property, or close out your holdings. Your accountant, in conjunction with your attorney, can also help you decide whether you need to make the transition to a formal business structure to accomplish these goals.

Consider the following issues:

◆ The type of business entity—an S corporation, C corporation, or limited liability company (LLC)—and ownership structure needed to facilitate your ownership of one or more properties.
◆ The design and setup of your accounting system so that year-end tax reporting will be easier.
◆ The proper payment of tax and in the correct amounts.

◆ The proper delivery of W2 and 1099 forms to the appropriate people—if you work with employees or contract employees.

◆ Advice on deductions and how to separate your personal and business expenses.

◆ Guidance on how to get through an audit if you ever face one.

◆ Specific transactions related to property ownership, such as whether it is better to lease or buy certain equipment.

◆ Compilation of financial records for the past period.

◆ A general understanding of your financial statements. If you neglect to do this, you will not know as much as you should about how your investments are really doing.

Before you select an accountant, ask him or her the following interview questions:

◆ *Do you work regularly with clients who own property like mine or the property I want to buy?* It is important to find an accountant with some experience in the type of real estate investing you plan to do—residential, commercial, or rental property.

◆ *What is your training?* Choose someone with at least several years' experience in the field.

◆ *How much do you charge and how do you itemize those fees?* Make sure you have a clear sense of how you will be billed and what the hourly rate is. Ask to see a sample billing statement.

◆ *Are there any particular kinds of real estate transactions you would steer me away from, given my personal tax issues?*

◆ *In planning my real estate investments, are there any estate or inheritance issues I should be thinking about right now?*

◆ *If I buy a certain property, when do you think I should sell or divest it in some way?* A good accountant with experience in real estate should be able to answer this question easily. If not, look elsewhere for an accountant.

◆ *What do you know about 1031 exchanges?*

◆ *Do you deal with certified intermediaries?*

◆ *Are there any personal financial issues we should discuss before I start investing in real estate?* Your accountant should provide a complete review of your present financial situation, offering advice on future planning and goals.

A Note on Job Descriptions

Tax professionals may handle various roles and have a variety of training. An enrolled agent, for example, may or may not be an accountant who is federally licensed to represent taxpayers in audits, collection proceedings, or appeals before the IRS.

A CPA has the highest certification in the tax field and may be a specialist in a particular area of law. Tax lawyers tend to be necessary for complicated tax planning or defense against audits. Some trained accountants and CPAs may also train to become financial planners, though there are stringent rules regarding financial products they can sell and the types of advice they can give.

Lawyers and accountants are an important part of any real estate investor's advisory team and should be hired and consulted before any investment. They can help a new investor plan a strategy for buying and selling property and improving profitability in the long run. By adding these professionals to your team, you will be gaining an edge in the field and protecting yourself from future financial and legal issues.

CHAPTER 12

Networking Your Way to Success

It's a known fact that people do business with those whom they know, love, and trust. It only stands to reason that networking—the process through which people get to "know" one another in both business and social settings—would be one of the best ways for real estate investors to find properties, locate buyers for their properties, secure tenants, and tap other business opportunities.

By getting out into the limelight to press flesh, exchange business cards, and then follow up with phone calls, e-mails, and/or snail mail, investors can build client and vendor pipelines that would be otherwise unattainable.

IMPORTANT NOTE

Thanks to the Internet and the communication opportunities that it has opened up, networking has grown in popularity. Using sites like Facebook and LinkedIn, online boards run by professional associations and other venues, businesspeople are interacting with one another on the Web, sharing information and making valuable connections that very often carry into the offline world.

As a real estate investor, you'll quickly find out that having a network of other investors, buyers, tenants, and professionals can be a vital asset for your business. These connections not only help you find properties, but they also can help you find investors who want to buy your properties, locate tenants, and find reputable service personnel.

Where to Start

Networking is an essential part of the real estate investment business. But you don't have to feel intimidated by the fact that you're getting going with a very small—or no—networking contacts. As you close deals and view local properties, you will gradually develop your own network.

  Some of the best starting points for investors are the Chamber of Commerce, trade associations, and local business group meetings that are designed to open networking opportunities for local businesspeople. Get involved with major organizations and go the extra mile to participate in local mixers, annual functions, and other events designed to create networking opportunities.

While at these events, don't expect business opportunities to simply fall into your lap. Do your homework beforehand, however, and your chances of having a successful interaction will be enhanced. Chambers of Commerce, for example, typically have member profiles that other members can review as a way to narrow down their networking approach before any interaction starts. And remember that the same "80/20 rule" used in business holds true in networking (with 80 percent of a firm's business coming from 20 percent of its clients).

In other words, 80 percent of all business in Chambers, nonprofit organizations, and business groups is done by 20 percent of the members. That 20 percent comprises the people who use networking day in and day out, and who are in it for the long haul. The rest pay an annual membership fee, go to two or three events without generating any business, and cancel the following year.

Maximize the Interaction

Leave a networking event with a feeling of accomplishment and there's a good chance that you'll walk away without experiencing the true benefits of your efforts. That's because many of the rewards come after the initial interactions—once you get back to your office and start following up on the connections that you've made. So while handing out business cards is a good first move, taking the next step by sending out those e-mails and making phone calls is the sure path to the Holy Grail of networking: new clients and new business opportunities.

"Networking does not happen overnight," says one accounting professional who uses the strategy to find new clients and form new partnerships. "One of the biggest mistakes people make is going to the event and then waiting for the phone to ring. Then, when no leads come their way they say networking doesn't work." The reality is that networking is a long-term play that rarely yields results when used one or twice a year at cocktail parties thrown by local business groups.

To make the most impact, real estate investors should conduct some type of follow-up with his or her new contacts within 24 hours of the event, preferably via phone. Let the potential client or business partner know of your intention to make contact (a simple "I will call you within the next 24 hours to discuss opportunities with you," will suffice), and follow through on your promise.

Finally, investors looking to maximize their networking efforts should understand the difference between networking and socializing. Roughly 95 percent of attendees at networking events are there to socialize, while the remaining 5 percent are there to build their businesses and make money. To make sure they fall into the second group, real estate investors should turn light conversations about the weather and sports teams into real business opportunities (by doing your homework in advance, putting yourself out there to meet people, and doing the necessary follow-up). This is the critical part of networking that, when mastered, can yield impressive results.

CHAPTER 13

Legal and Asset Protection Strategies

So far in this book we've covered the many different aspects of getting started in real estate investing. In this chapter, we go a step further by taking a look at a much longer-term plan that centers on using your investment drive to build a business. Within this plan, you will incorporate a number of legal and asset protection strategies that will legitimize your real estate investing business, essentially bulletproofing it from potential harm, lawsuits, and failures in the future.

The need for business planning may seem obvious, but many new investors skip this very important step and just start pouring their money into the real estate market. For some people, this spontaneous approach works well. Others pay the price for their unorganized approach to business. Why take a chance?

Business Planning 101

Despite the critical importance of a business plan, many entrepreneurs drag their feet when it comes to preparing a written document. They argue that their marketplace changes too fast for a business plan to be useful or that they just don't have enough time. But just as a builder won't begin construction without a blueprint, eager business owners shouldn't rush into new ventures without a business plan.

Before you begin writing your business plan, ask yourself these four questions:

1. What service or product does your business provide and what needs does it fill?

(continued)

133

> **Business Planning 101 (*Continued*)**
>
> 2. Who are the potential customers for your product or service and why will they purchase it from you?
> 3. How will you reach your potential customers?
> 4. Where will you get the financial resources to start your business?
>
> As fundamental as they may seem, the answers to these four core questions are critical to your business success—whether that venture is a hair salon, bookstore, or an individual real estate agent who sells homes. Know your service, your customers, how to reach them, and what resources you'll need to get there, and you'll soon find yourself on the path to success.

The Business Plan

For real estate investors, putting together a business plan is a crucial step that not only helps them organize their day-to-day business operations, but that also helps them focus on their growth expectations and create steps to meet those goals.

Growth expectations are directly connected to your need for capital. The bottom line is that most lenders will not give you their best rates until they see a business plan that makes sense.

Even if you do not need to borrow money, the business plan is critically important for other reasons. Putting your goals on paper can be a wake-up call—it forces you to define what it is you want to do and how you want to do it. It is also useful for attracting talent. When a prospect wants an overview of your business, you can hand them a copy of your business plan.

IMPORTANT NOTE

If you made a business plan years ago when you launched your business and you are now ready to change its structure, rewrite it. It is a great way to review your current goals.

> **Why Write a Business Plan?**
>
> ◆ To create supporting documents for a loan application
> ◆ To create supporting documents for a merger

> ## Why Write a Business Plan? (*Continued*)
>
> - ◆ To raise equity funding
> - ◆ To better define your objectives
> - ◆ To lay out a plan to achieve those objectives
> - ◆ To set out a specific timetable for the life of the business
> - ◆ To outline the types of products and services you will create and sell
> - ◆ To articulate your business logic and attract talent

Visit www.ebizstartups.com/businessplan.html for more information on writing a business plan.

The Process

Preparing a business plan can seem like an overwhelming task for some people, but the process will allow you to think through why you are going into business and how you want your business to run.

The components of a business plan include:

- ◆ *Executive summary:* Writing the executive summary is best left for last, after you have worked through the rest of the plan. An executive summary encapsulates in one page the description of the franchise, products and services, risks, opportunities, target market and strategies to reach it, competition, finances, and, above all, projected return on investment.
- ◆ *Mission statement:* This is a one- or two-sentence statement that describes the culture of your business and its goals. Some states require you to write a statement of corporate purpose as part of your application for a certificate of incorporation, so you might as well think in those terms while doing this.
- ◆ *Business concept:* Explain the type of business you plan to run, how it will be financed, and the concept or strategy on which it is based.
- ◆ *The team:* List the CEO and key management by name, experience, and past successes.
- ◆ *Industry analysis:* Reviews changes in market share, leadership, players, market shifts, costs, pricing, or competition that

provide the opportunity for your company's success. This is another section that needs updated every few years.

◆ *Competition:* Discuss the competitive challenges that exist in this business and how you plan to overcome them.

◆ *Goals and objectives:* This is your five-year plan. State measurable objectives for market share, revenues, and profitability. It may be useful to have your accountant or financial advisor help you with this.

◆ *Description of day-to-day operations:* Describe staffing options and training. Also discuss your resource needs, such as supplies, advertising, and marketing.

◆ *Financing:* Provide a statement of your current assets and funding needs. If you are seeking money from lenders, outline how your business will help you repay this debt efficiently.

◆ *Appendix:* Lenders want to see tax returns, current articles about the industry, and any other third-party information that will help them learn about the business.

Projecting Income and Cash Flow

If you are incorporating with the help of an attorney or an accountant, creating financial projections is an important thing to add to their to-do lists. It is useful to create a five-year projection by adding up all the possible costs of your business. This will help you calculate how much capital you are going to need to stay afloat. If your business outpaces your costs significantly, you can always pay off the loan early.

Using these elements, you'll be able to put together a viable business plan that you'll want to review and revise on a regular basis (such as quarterly, biannually, or yearly) and/or to share with those entities that request it. The business plan will be the foundation for your real estate investment venture and will help guide you through the ups and downs of entrepreneurship.

Your Business Entity

One good way to protect your real estate investment business is by starting it up under the right business entity. You have four basic options to chose from: sole proprietorship, partnership, limited liability company (LLC), and corporation. As you move from single ownership to incorporation, the complexities increase, as do organizational and tax issues.

Here is a brief overview of each business type.

Sole Proprietorship

If you are looking for the simplest form of start-up, this is it. A sole proprietorship is a single-owner business in which the owner is wholly responsible for all aspects of the operation. Many home-based businesses start out as sole proprietorships.

Advantages

- *Hook up a computer and go.* Your city or state may require business name registration, and you must adhere to tax and other registration guidelines, but most sole proprietorships simply buy stationery and apply for a DBA (doing business as) account at the bank and they are in business.
- *You have a simple tax treatment.* All business profits and losses are reported on the owner's personal income tax return each year. You will need to file a Schedule C: Profit or Loss from Business form with your 1040.
- *It is an easy transition.* If you decide to incorporate or form a partnership or an LLC in the future, there are no administrative costs other than the fees required to file for the new business structure.

Disadvantages

- *All debts and legal liabilities are your own.* More complex business structures, such as incorporation, protect business owners against lawsuit damages and excessive business debts. With a sole proprietorship, you stand to lose everything, including personal assets.
- *Beware of huge success.* If your business starts to make significant money, your income will be taxed at your personal rate, which is typically higher than the standard corporate rates.

Many corporations with substantial earnings do income splitting, which allows them to keep some earnings in the business that will continue to be taxed at the lower rate.

Partnership

A partnership is a legal entity jointly owned by two or more individuals (although in some cases partners may also be corporations or other entities). Partners agree to be in business and to share the profits equally based on the kind of partnership they have structured.

There are two basic types of partnerships:

1. *General partnerships:* This is a partnership in which two or more people go into business together and share all profits, losses, and liabilities equally. The act or signature of any partner can bind the partnership, and partners file a U.S. Partnership Return of Income that shows how profits, losses, and other tax issues are allocated. The partnership also issues individual Schedule K-1s to each partner at the end of the year, which reflects their share of profits or losses. All income and losses are then reported on each partner's personal income taxes.
2. *Limited partnerships:* One or more general partners manage the business while limited partners contribute capital and share in the profits but take no part in running the business. General partners are the parties responsible for debts, whereas limited partners do not have an obligation beyond their initial financial contribution.

Advantages

- ◆ *Less expensive to start than a corporation:* Partnerships tend to have less expensive filing fees than corporations.
- ◆ *Management flexibility:* Partnerships benefit from a broader management base than a sole proprietorship, and a more flexible management structure than a corporation.
- ◆ *Option to be taxed as a corporation:* Partnerships have the option of splitting earnings as a corporation, so part of those earnings can be taxed at a lower corporate rate. But based on

your situation, you should check with an accountant to see if simply converting to corporate status would make more sense.

Disadvantages

- *Unlimited liability:* At least one partner, and possibly all partners, might lose everything in a business failure or lawsuit except in limited partnership situations. The personal assets of the general partners are available to satisfy partnership debts.
- *Politics:* The life of a partnership is unstable and if partners die or leave, it can bring about a funding crunch that could cause a partnership to terminate.
- *Raising capital:* Partnerships cannot raise funds through stock offerings or bonds as S corporations do, so they either have to bring in more revenue or demand more funding from partners.
- *Unilateral decision making:* The acts of just one partner, even unauthorized acts in many cases, bind all partners.
- *Difficult to sell:* An individual partnership interest cannot be sold or transferred easily.
- *Limitations on benefits:* Most tax-supported fringe benefits, such as pension and profit-sharing arrangements available to corporations, are unavailable to partnerships.

Partnership Agreements

There is no law requiring a partnership agreement, but it would be wise to have one. If you do not have a partnership agreement, then state statutes determine many aspects of your ownership, decision-making, dissolution, and winding-down rights. Consider the problems and disputes that could potentially develop—disputes between partners, a partner who leaves, dies or becomes incapacitated, a partner who takes a partnership opportunity for himself or herself, or a partner who causes harm to the partnership.

At a minimum, your partnership agreement should state:

- Each partner's specific interest in the partnership
- How profits and losses will be split
- How former partners can keep the partnership going if they want to

The Limited Liability Company (LLC)

An LLC is not a corporation, and it may be a better fit for certain businesses than a corporation. The LLC got its start in Europe and Latin America and appeared for the first time in the United States in 1977, enacted by the Wyoming legislature. Since then, it has expanded to all 50 states and become popular with small business owners for its partnership-like pass-through taxation and liability protection similar to a corporation. That pass-through taxation feature was approved by the Internal Revenue Service (IRS) in 1988. A sole-owner LLC is treated like a sole proprietorship for tax purposes.

Different states have different rules about LLCs, so it is best to check with your secretary of state's office first to see what specific provisions might apply to your business. Some states impose an annual fee or tax on LLCs, so make sure you check all the costs.

Advantages

- *Debt and liability protection:* Similar to a corporate structure, LLCs protect personal assets from business debt and other liabilities.
- *No double taxation:* Like a partnership, LLCs pass through earnings to the personal income tax returns of owners, but owners must choose a form of business taxation and file accordingly.
- *Flexibility in management:* LLCs can be managed by sole owners, but the law provides for member management, which is co-management by all owners of the company. Additionally, LLCs allow the appointment of one or more specially appointed managers as well.
- *No foreign ownership restrictions:* S corporations tend to have foreign ownership restrictions; LLCs do not.

Disadvantages

- *Limited life:* Most LLCs are ordered to terminate after 30 years. Corporations do not have any expiration requirement.

- *Raising capital:* LLCs cannot issue stocks or bonds, so raising capital may be a problem.
- *Higher taxes:* Because LLCs are not corporations, they are taxed at a higher personal rate.
- *Higher fees:* Even if you do not hire a lawyer or an accountant to help you with the process, LLC fees range from $250 and higher as an average.

Like all other business structures, you can file for an LLC yourself. Establishing an LLC can get complicated, though, so it makes sense to have an attorney or qualified tax accountant review your decision and look over your paperwork before you file.

The C Corporation

The most common form of corporation—known as a general corporation or C corporation—is a standalone legal entity owned by an unlimited number of stockholders who are protected from the creditors of the business.

What makes C corporations unique is that they are a legal and tax entity apart from any of the people who own, control, manage, or otherwise operate the business. A stockholder's personal liability is usually limited to the amount of investment in the corporation and no more.

Advantages

- *Liability protection:* Owners' personal assets are protected from business debt and liability.
- *Longevity:* Corporations have unlimited life extending beyond the illness or death of the original owners who incorporated it.
- *Employee benefits:* Corporations have the unique ability to offer tax-free benefits such as insurance, travel, and retirement plan deductions.
- *Capital availability:* Capital can be raised through the sale of stock and bonds that the corporation may issue.

◆ *Easy sale of assets:* Transfer of ownership may be done through sale of all the stock in the corporation to a new owner.

◆ *Consistency of management structure:* A change in ownership does not require a change in management.

Disadvantages

◆ *Expense:* A C corporation is more expensive to form than a proprietorship or partnerships.

◆ *Paperwork:* Continuing C corporations have a significant amount of paperwork to file on an annual basis.

◆ *Stricter legal requirements:* C corporations are more complicated to establish and maintain because of the many legal requirements.

◆ *Greater regulations:* C corporations are subject to a greater number of state and federal rules and regulations.

◆ *Double taxes:* Double taxation requires that the C corporation and the owners file tax returns. C corporations are required to pay tax on its earnings, and its shareholders pay a second tax when corporate earnings are distributed to them in the form of dividends.

The S Corporation

Like partnerships and LLCs, S corporations—named for subchapter S of the tax code—can elect to take corporate tax treatment (dual taxation) or pass-through taxation at the individual level.

With the Tax Reform Act of 1986, the S corporation became a highly desirable entity for corporate tax purposes. An S corporation is simply a special tax designation applied for and granted by the IRS to corporations that have already been formed.

Chart

Here's a closer look at the details of each business entity:

Business Type	Control	Liability	Taxes	Administration
Sole Proprietorship	Total control of business operations and complete share of profits	All personal and business assets are at risk	All taxes reported on personal return	Local requirements may include registering trade name and obtaining a business license
General Partnership	Management and profits are shared between partners as established by the partnership agreement	General partners are generally liable for obligations and tort damages incurred by other general partners	General partners are taxed directly on their share of the profits	No formal administrative requirements other than obtaining proper licenses and permits
Limited Partnership	General and limited partners share in the control and profits of the partnership according to the partnership agreement	Limited partners are not personally obligated for the liabilities of the partnership	Partners are taxed directly on their share of the profits	Registration requirements are similar to corporations without the boardroom record-keeping and tax-filing requirements
Limited Liability Company	Members share profits based on operating agreement	Generally, members risk only their investment in the LLC	Either partnership-style pass-through to personal returns or corporate income if elected	Similar to corporate requirements for formation and operation
Corporation	Shareholders hold ownership rights and elect directors; directors govern general affairs and appoint officers; officers manage operations	Neither officers, shareholders, nor directors are liable for debts or judgments incurred by the firm	Double taxation unless it is an S-corporation, in which earnings are passed directly through	Formal incorporation process and annual registration with the secretary of state. Comprehensive record-keeping and tax filing requirements

Like the LLC, many entrepreneurs and small business owners like the S corporation because it blends the advantages of a sole proprietorship, partnership, and corporation. S corporations avoid double taxation (once at the corporate level and again at the personal level) because all income or loss is reported only once on the personal tax returns of the shareholders. However, like standard corporations (and unlike some partnerships), the S corporation shareholders are exempt from personal liability for business debt.

Advantages

- *Only one level of taxation:* Income generally is taxed only to the corporation's shareholders.
- *Deductibility of losses:* Shareholders are generally allowed to deduct their share of the corporation's net operating loss on their individual tax returns in the year the loss occurs. This works well for new companies expected to generate losses at the start.

Disadvantages

- *Difficulty in selling stock:* Stock can be transferred only to eligible shareholders (individuals, estates, and certain trusts; certain pension plans and charitable organizations are also eligible for tax years beginning in 1998), and an S corporation cannot have more than 35 (75 for tax years beginning in 1997) shareholders.
- *Limited fringe benefits:* S corporations cannot offer the same types of fringe benefits that C corporations can.

Keep in mind that this list does not affect every company considering S status. Choosing to file as an S corporation is particularly good justification for bringing an attorney or tax accountant on board to help you consider your options.

Factors in the Decision to Incorporate

- *Legal liability:* To what extent do you need to be insulated from legal liability? If you cannot personally afford the risk of a lawsuit, incorporation and the possibility of business liability coverage may be a consideration.

◆ *Tax implications:* Based on your goals and those of the business, are there opportunities here to minimize taxation? Which type of corporate structure would best fit those goals?

◆ *The cost of incorporation:* Starting and keeping a corporation going is expensive. It is important to total up all fees, not just filing fees. Usually there are fees that need to be filed with annual reports, and many states charge franchise taxes. Make sure there are enough benefits to outweigh the time and costs associated with being a corporation.

◆ *Estate and flexibility issues:* Do you know where you are planning to be in five years? Consider the anticipated time line of your business and your planned tenure because that might affect the type of business structure you eventually choose.

If you are working with a good lawyer or tax accountant in the early stages of defining your real estate investment strategy, the question of how you will operate that activity will undoubtedly come into play. Developing a business plan is appropriate in any situation—even if you do not choose to define your investments as a business—because it will force you to look ahead toward further investment or a possible exit strategy down the road. But if you do decide to form a business to pursue these investments full time, it makes sense to understand various business structures and how they work before selecting one that best fits you.

The Legalities of It All

While owning a property carries with it significant privileges of use and enjoyment, an owner's rights are not absolute; the right to use and control property is subject to certain public and private restrictions. These restrictions are designed to ensure that one owner's use of his or her property does not infringe on or otherwise harm another individual's use or enjoyment of property or the welfare of the general public.

Specifically, state and local zoning laws as well as environmental regulations are key tools in regulating the use of land. An owner's property rights also can be impacted by interests held by third parties that affect title to real estate. For example, liens, mortgages, and assessments constitute charges against property as a result of the debts or obligations of the owner. Encumbrances, which include restrictions, easements, and encroachments, also affect the condition or use of property and may decrease its value.

In all of these cases, however, the party holding the lien or encumbrance does not have a possessory interest in the property but merely the right to use or take something from the land. In the section that follows, we cover some of the key legal issues that you should be aware of as a real estate investor.

Eminent Domain

Eminent domain is a legal principle that allows the government to take private property for public use, such as for a school or new roads. This right is enshrined within the laws of all 50 states as well as in the U.S. Constitution. According to the Fifth Amendment: No person shall be deprived of life, liberty, or property, without due process of law; nor shall private property be taken for public use, without just compensation.

This clause empowers the government to take property as long as:

- The proposed use is for the public good.
- Just compensation is paid.
- The property owner's rights are protected by due process of law, which means that the government must give the owner notice and the right to a hearing.

Federal, state, and local governments can exercise the power of eminent domain and also may delegate this power to certain quasi-public agencies, including, for example, airport authorities, highway commissions, and community development agencies. Some nongovernmental organizations, such as railroads and utility companies, also are authorized to use eminent domain to take private property.

Public Use

According to state and federal law, the government can exercise its eminent domain powers only if property is taken for a public use. The most common example is land being taken to build roads or highways.

Other acceptable public uses include taking property to build schools or municipal buildings. In fact, when the United States was founded, the right of eminent domain arose because of the new government's need for land to build courthouses, town halls, and other government buildings.

Over the years, however, the government's right to take property has been expanded by the courts. For example, the term *public use* has been defined very broadly to include not simply the taking of private property to build bridges and libraries but also for commercial uses such as shopping malls or independent retail stores. The courts also have upheld the taking of property when the government itself does not intend to possess or use the land but instead plans to transfer it to individuals.

The Supreme Court articulated this principle in the landmark 1954 decision, *Berman v. Parker,* when it allowed a local government to condemn land for urban renewal and then transfer title to private parties.

Just Compensation

A taking by eminent domain also requires that the property owner receive just compensation for his or her property. The amount paid should be equal to the owner's loss, which is measured by the property's fair market value at the time of the taking. Fair market value is equal to what a willing buyer would pay to a willing seller in an arm's length transaction.

If the government and owner do not agree, appraisers are hired to determine the fair market value of the property. If the dispute goes to court, each side will present expert witnesses—real estate sales personnel and appraisers—who are familiar with the market prices of similar properties.

The Fight over Eminent Domain

Critics of the eminent domain process argue that local governments are often too quick to use it on behalf of big retailers because of the potential for generating tax revenues and jobs. Moreover, if developers cannot purchase the property on the open market, it is unlikely that a landowner will actually receive the fair value of his or her property through condemnation proceedings. Still others simply believe that it is an abuse of power to force private owners to sell their most important possessions—their homes.

Supporters, on the other hand, believe that eminent domain is often critical to the revitalization of cities. Because few projects in urban areas occur on small, isolated lots, larger parcels of land often are needed. When property owners refuse to sell or set an unreasonable price, they risk derailing projects that may ultimately benefit the community.

Steps in an Eminent Domain Proceeding
While eminent domain law and the actual legal procedures required to exercise this power vary among jurisdictions, the following steps typically are followed in an eminent domain proceeding:

1. First, the government must make a good faith effort to negotiate the purchase of the property.
2. If a property owner does not consent to the taking and refuses to negotiate with the government authority in question, the government will file a court action to exercise its eminent domain right and also must serve or publish notice of the hearing.
3. At the hearing, the government must prove that it has attempted in good faith to purchase the property but an agreement could not be reached. It also must show that the proposed taking is for a public use. The property owner has the right to rebut the government's claims.
4. If a decision is made in favor of the government, proceedings are then held to assess the property's fair market value. Payments first are applied to satisfy any existing mortgages, liens, or encumbrances, and the balance is paid to the owner. The government then holds title to the property. The process of exercising the power of eminent domain is commonly referred to as *condemnation*.
5. If the government's petition is declined or if the property owner objects to the decision, either party may appeal.

If a government's petition is granted, all or part of the property may be taken either permanently or for a limited period of time. For example, the taking may involve:

◆ *A complete taking:* The government takes title to all of the property at issue.

◆ *A partial taking:* Only part of a property is taken, such as a strip of land needed to expand a road.

◆ *A temporary taking:* Part or all of the property is taken for a specified time period only. In this case, the owner still retains title but is compensated for any losses associated with the taking. At the end of the specified period, the owner regains complete possession of the property. For example, a highway authority may need to temporarily use part of a person's property to finish building a new road.

◆ *An easement or right of way:* These may be needed to install power or water lines on private property. The property owner retains title to the property and can use it however he or she likes, provided the use does not interfere with the right of way or easement.

Kelo v. City of New London

In one of the most important cases addressing eminent domain issues in years, the U.S. Supreme Court issued a ruling allowing a government to take private land for business development purposes. In *Kelo v. City of New London,* property owners resisted plans by the city of New London's redevelopment authority to revitalize a neighborhood by buying properties—many of which were historic—razing them and then selling the land at discounted prices to private developers. The developers then planned to build new stores and offices to support a nearby research facility.

The city condemned the properties even though its plans or projects for redevelopment were not settled at the time. Several residents and business owners objected, stating that the government's right only extends to public projects like schools and highways, thereby setting the case in motion. In siding with the city, the U.S. Supreme Court continued to grant wide latitude to cities, counties, and state legislatures over when and how eminent domain can be used for redevelopment purposes. Writing for the majority in the decision, Justice John Paul Stevens stated that the court was embracing "the broader and more natural interpretation of public use as 'public purpose."

(continued)

Kelo v. City of New London (*Continued*)

Controversy over the decision has been widespread. As Justice Sandra Day O'Connor stated in a dissenting opinion, "The specter of condemnation hangs over all property. Nothing is to prevent the State from replacing any Motel 6 with a Ritz-Carlton, any home with a shopping mall, or any farm with a factory. . . . The beneficiaries are likely to be those citizens with disproportionate influence and power in the political process."

Restrictive Covenants

Less drastic than taking by eminent domain, property rights also can be limited severely by restrictive covenants. A restrictive covenant is an agreement, contract, or promise, usually included in the deed to a property, that restricts or prohibits certain uses of real estate. An owner may include them in a deed when selling property. They often are used when a person is selling part of his or her property and wants to prevent undesirable uses of such property.

Example

A deed for residential property may contain a covenant stating that the property owner agrees not to use his property for anything other than residential purposes. If the first owner breaks the covenant by opening a café on the property, the second owner can sue the other owner or seek injunctive relief to prevent the violation.

To be enforceable, restrictive covenants must be in writing and signed. To ensure that they will be effective against subsequent purchasers, restrictive covenants must be recorded with the land title office on the title of all of the pieces of land affected by covenant.

Generally, restrictive covenants are said to run with the land, which means that they will continue to apply to the real estate even after the original owner transfers the property to another person. However, most states have some limits regarding how long restrictive covenants may run, while others allow them to last forever.

Restrictive covenants typically are imposed by developers of subdivisions and condominium communities to maintain certain standards in a housing development. When property is under construction, developers may record a document called covenants, conditions, and restrictions (CC&Rs) that sets forth limits on how the property can be developed in the future. For example, a CC&R may place limits on matters such as:

◆ The color of paint on a house
◆ Whether fences are allowed
◆ The types of swing sets or other children's play equipment that are permitted
◆ The types of materials that can be used to build a chimney, addition, outbuilding, or roof
◆ The square footage requirements—minimums and maximums—that homes must meet
◆ Whether property owners can store motor vehicles on their property
◆ Whether satellite dishes are allowed

Even if a municipal zoning law permits a property owner to use the property in a certain manner, the owner may not be able to do so if the covenants affecting the property prohibit such use. Restrictive covenants typically will be upheld by the courts if the restraints are reasonable and benefit all property owners. In all cases, however, private restrictions may not violate local, state, or federal laws. For example, covenants written years ago that prohibited people from selling their homes to people of certain races or religions are not enforceable today.

If a person breaches a restrictive covenant, the person entitled to enforce it may recover money damages for the breach. However, the preferred remedy is usually injunctive relief, which directs the violator to stop the violation. If the owner refuses to heed a court order, the court may hold him or her in contempt of court. When a covenant is being breached, an action seeking injunctive relief must be brought quickly. In some cases, a court may hold that the right to seek enforcement of the covenant was lost through unreasonable delay or failure to assert a claim, termed *laches*.

Easements

Another right that affects a person's use of land is an easement. Generally speaking, an easement is the right to use some part of another person's property for a specific purpose. An easement may exist in any part of the real estate, including the airspace above a parcel of land so that a utility company can erect power lines. An easement also may be given to use the area beneath the land's surface in order to install a sewage system.

Easements usually are categorized as affirmative easements or negative easements. An affirmative easement gives the holder the right to do something on the land, such as to travel over another person's property. Negative easements, in contrast, prohibit the owner from doing something that an owner would normally be entitled to do. For example, a negative easement might prohibit an owner from building a structure of a certain height that would obstruct a neighbor's view. Negative easements, however, are not as common as affirmative easements.

IMPORTANT TIP

When buying real estate, it is important to identify whether any easements exist because they typically must be honored by future owners. While most easements are recorded at the county courthouse, they also may be scattered among different plats, deed books, and mortgage books. As a result, the best way to determine whether an easement exists is through a professional title search.

It is important to note that an easement creates a nonpossessory interest in another person's land. Essentially, an easement is merely a property interest that permits the holder of the easement to use property that does not belong to him or her. The easement holder does not have the right to occupy the land or to exclude others from the land, unless their use interferes with the easement holder's use. The person who owns the land, in contrast, also may continue to use the easement and may exclude all others except the easement holder from the land.

> ## Example
>
> Tom and Susan own adjoining parcels of land near a beach. Tom's land borders the lake, while Susan's property does not. Tom grants Susan an easement, created by a deed that has been delivered and recorded, that allows her to use his driveway to reach the beach. Susan may use the road but may not stop others from also using it unless their use interferes with her own use. In contrast, Tom may exclude everyone except Susan from crossing his property, while continuing to use the road himself.

Easements can be broken down further into two additional categories:

1. Appurtenant easements
2. Easements in gross

Appurtenant Easement

An appurtenant easement is annexed to the ownership of a particular piece of land and allows the owner to use a neighbor's land. To create this type of easement, two adjacent parcels of land must be owned by two different individuals.

The real estate that is subject to the easement often is referred to as the *servient estate.* For example, the property across which an easement has been granted for ingress and egress purposes would be considered the servient estate. The neighboring parcel of land that benefits from the easement is known as the *dominant estate.*

In the previous example, Susan's property is considered the dominant estate while Tom's property is considered the servient estate. Because an appurtenant easement is part of the dominant estate, the easement transfers with the property if the land is ever sold. This type of easement is said to run with the land, which means that it will transfer with the deed of the dominant estate forever unless the holder of the dominant estate releases that right.

For example, if Susan sells her property to her brother, Stan, the easement is automatically included, even if the deed does not mention it. Stan now has the right to cross Tom's property.

An appurtenant easement is also irrevocable, which means that the owner of the servient estate cannot cancel it or terminate it by conveying the property. For instance, if in the above example Tom sells his property to Abby, the property remains subject to the existing easement.

While an easement holder has a right to use the easement, he or she may not place an unreasonable burden on the servient land. Conversely, the owner of the servient land may not use the land in a way that unduly interferes with the easement holder's use of the easement. Over the years, the courts have held that what constitutes an undue burden depends on the facts of each case. For example, if a dominant estate's use is changed from residential to commercial and the traffic correspondingly increases, courts have found that an additional burden has been placed on the servient estate.

If the use of the easement unduly burdens the servient estate, the servient estate owner has several options:

◆ Obtain a court order requiring the easement holder to use the easement in an appropriate manner.
◆ Bring an action seeking monetary damages when the servient estate has been injured.
◆ Bring an action to terminate the easement.

Easement in Gross

An easement in gross is merely a personal interest in or right to use someone else's land. The easement exists without a dominant estate. For example, a right of way granted to a utility company to build an electric power line is considered an easement in gross, as is an easement granted to a railroad to build railroad tracks or to a state highway authority to construct a new road. Courts have held that because of the benefit that commercial easements bring to the public, these easements also may be assigned and conveyed to others. A utility company could therefore freely transfer an easement to another utility company.

Easements in gross also may be granted to individuals for noncommercial purposes. In this case, the easement generally cannot be transferred and terminates on the death of the easement holder. Some common examples of nontransferable easements include easements granting recreational rights such as hunting, camping, and fishing.

Profits *a Prendre*

Related to easements are profits *a prendre,* which are another type of interest in land. Profits *a prendre* usually are given to physically remove substances, such as minerals, timber, and gravel, from the soil. Easements allow a third party to use the land while profits *a prendre* permit the removal of a substance from the land. However, whenever a profit *a prendre* is granted, it is nearly always accompanied by an easement, since the ability to remove a substance requires having access to the land itself to reach and remove the substance.

Creating an Easement

An easement is most commonly created by a deed that describes the land and the location of the easement. Most courts will not uphold an easement that has been created orally because all states require that interests in real property be created by a written document. In a deed, an easement can be created by either:

Express grant: This means that an owner has expressly granted a right to another person to use the property in a deed or other written instrument.

> ### Example
>
> Sara owns two adjoining lots in Lake Meander and sells one of the lots to her sister, Beth. Sara's lot has a private road. In her deed to Beth, Sara expressly grants to Beth the use of this road.

◆ *Express reservation:* This occurs when the owner conveys title to another person by deed but specifically reserves an easement in his or her favor.

> ### Example
>
> Sara sells Beth the lot that has the private road and keeps the other lot. Sara's deed will include a provision that expressly reserves her right to use the road.

Easement of Necessity

In contrast to an express easement, a court may acknowledge the creation of an easement by implication in some circumstances. An easement that is commonly created this way is an *easement of necessity*. This type of easement arises when a property owner is landlocked and does not have access to a street or other roadway except by crossing another person's property. An easement of necessity is based on the general legal principle that a property owner should have the right to enter and exit his or her property, also known as the right of ingress and egress.

Easement by Prescription

An *easement by prescription* arises after a person has used another's property for a certain period of time as defined by statute. In some states, prescriptive rights can be obtained after a 20-year period. In others, the period is 10 to 15 years. In California, for example, 5 years is sufficient. Central to the creation of a prescriptive easement is the idea that an owner who does not take legal action against the illegal use of his or her property within a certain time period is estopped from later making a claim asserting his or her rights.

Example

If a person has been crossing over a neighbor's property for 10 years and the neighbor has never complained, the person may have acquired a prescriptive easement that would allow him or her to continue using the property in the same manner.

To acquire rights via a prescriptive easement, the claimant's use must have been:

◆ Continuous and uninterrupted
◆ Adverse to the owner's interest

If the user has the owner's permission to use the property, the requirement that the use be adverse to the owner's interest will not be met. No matter how long such use continues, it will not become an easement. If, however, an owner gives permission but revokes it, later use of the property becomes adverse. To create an easement by prescription, the use by the person seeking the easement must be continuous and uninterrupted. To reach the required number of years necessary to establish a claim for a prescriptive easement, the legal concept called *tacking* allows different parties to tack on one person's possession to that of another. The parties, however, must have been successors in interest, such as a seller and buyer or a parent and his or her heir.

Example

Pam lives in a state where a claimant must have used another person's property for 10 years before a prescriptive easement will arise. For the past 11 years, Joan has driven her car across part of Pam's front yard several times a day. In this case, Joan has an easement by prescription. If Sam has driven sporadically across Pam's driveway for the past 11 years only when he feels like taking a shortcut, a prescriptive easement will not arise because his use was not continuous.

Joan also started parking her car at the edge of Pam's property and then sold her house to Chris, who continued to park in the same spot for the next 10 years. In this case, the statutory period for acquiring a prescriptive easement will be met by tacking Joan's period of use with Chris's.

Terminating an Easement

An easement need not be indefinite in duration; a property owner may grant an easement only for a specific number of years or for the holder's life. At the end of the period, the easement terminates automatically. However, easements that may potentially last forever may be terminated in various ways, such as:

- The easement holder expressly releases his or her easement right to the owner of the servient estate; note that an oral release alone is not effective.
- The term of the easement has expired, provided the easement was limited to a definite time by its creating language.
- The owner of either the dominant or servient estate acquires title to both properties; this is called *termination by merger.*
- The easement holder has abandoned the easement—that is, the holder has stopped using the property and clearly intends to give up his or her right to the easement.

◆ By the destruction of a structure on the servient tenement in which the easement exists—for example, if an easement was granted to pass through a building and the building is destroyed by a fire.

◆ The purpose for which the easement was given no longer exists—for example, when a pipeline easement is granted for transporting coal, but the easement holder no longer has coal to transport.

If there are grounds for terminating an easement, the owner of the servient estate may be required to take legal action to ensure its termination; an easement does not automatically terminate. The owners of the servient and dominant estates also may execute an agreement using the same formalities required to grant an easement—generally a deed—in order to terminate it.

Licenses

Similar to an easement, a license also involves permitting a person to enter and use another's property. The main difference is that a license is terminable at will by the licensor—the person granting the license—whereas an easement typically exists for a determinate period of time or perpetually. Easements also are considered an interest in land while licenses are not. Instead, a license is considered a personal privilege given only to the licensee.

Typically, if a person makes an oral or informal promise to another person giving them the right to use his or her property, the promise will be considered to be a license rather than an easement in gross. In contrast, easements must be in writing.

Example

If Steve asks Harvey for permission to enter his 1,000-acre farm to hunt quail, and Harvey agrees, Steve merely has a license to hunt on Harvey's property. Harvey may, at any time, prevent Steve from entering his property to go hunting. If Harvey later dies, the license automatically ends. Similarly, if Harvey sells the property, Steve no longer has the right to enter it.

Encroachment

An encroachment occurs when part or all of a structure, such as a fence or shed, extends onto an adjacent piece of land owned by another person. For example, a person may build a shed at the edge of his or her property but accidentally place part of it on a neighbor's yard. That part of the shed is said to be encroaching illegally on the neighbor's property.

In the absence of an easement or agreement, no person has any right to erect buildings or other structures on his own land so that any part, however small, will extend beyond his boundaries, either above or below the surface, and thus encroach on the adjoining premises.

If an encroachment occurs, several legal remedies are available to the party adversely affected:

- ◆ *Action to quiet title:* an action to quiet title often is brought by a plaintiff seeking removal of an encroachment after the encroaching party seeks to gain title to the land—for example, by claiming an easement over the encroached-upon land. When a property owner brings an action to quiet title, he or she is affirming ownership of the land.
- ◆ *Action to abate a nuisance:* a property owner can bring this type of action when he or she seeks to have an encroachment that has been deemed to be a nuisance removed. In legal terms, a nuisance means a condition or situation—such as a loud noise or foul odor—that interferes with the use or enjoyment of property. For example, if the eaves from a house extend five feet over a boundary line, the overhanging eaves may interfere with the other owners' enjoyment of their property, and a court may order their removal.
- ◆ *Damages:* in many encroachment cases, a court may award damages—monetary compensation—in place of or in addition to other remedies. Damages generally are awarded in cases where the injured party will not suffer irreparable injury, financially or otherwise.

For example, in *Rothaermel v. Amerige,* the court denied injunctive relief but awarded monetary damages when it found that the plaintiff did not suffer irreparable injury from the defendant's foundation, which encroached onto his property by 1½ inches.

◆ *Injunctive relief:* in most encroachment cases, the party adversely affected will bring an action to remove the encroachment so that he or she can recover possession of the property.

In deciding whether to grant injunctive relief, the courts generally will consider three factors:

1. A court will examine whether the encroachment was the result of the defendant's willful act—that is, did he or she intentionally create the encroachment, or did the defendant act negligently or without good faith? A court typically will grant injunctive relief if the defendant acted willfully, even if there is a high financial cost of removing the encroaching structure.
2. The court will assess whether the adversely affected party will suffer irreparable injury, financially or otherwise. In cases where an encroachment will diminish the value of a person's property substantially and seriously affect its salability, the courts have upheld awards for injunctive relief.
3. The court will compare the cost and difficulty of removing an encroaching structure with the hardship suffered by the continuation of the encroachment. In other words, the court will assess whether the cost of removing the encroaching structure is proportionate to the actual benefit that will accrue to the plaintiff.

Real Estate Investor Insights

In some cases where issuing an injunction would adversely affect the public, the courts will grant monetary damages only. For example, in *Uktomski v. Tioga Water Co.*, a water reservoir was encroaching on a property owner's land by 0.15 of an acre. The court declined to issue an injunction, stating that over 500 people would be cut off from their only water supply as a result. The plaintiff was compelled to accept damages only, and the court granted the defendant an easement to prevent future litigation.

Typically, if a property owner fails to bring an action contesting an encroachment in a timely manner, the courts may refuse to issue an injunction compelling the removal of an encroachment. The time frame during which an action must be brought is called a *statute of limitations,* and it varies from state to state. If not timely filed, an easement by prescription may arise.

IMPORTANT TIP

If a piece of property is affected by an encroachment and the owner wishes to sell the property, the seller must disclose the encroachment in the listing agreement and sales agreement. Otherwise, the seller may be subject to legal action when the buyer discovers the problem. Buyers generally are advised to avoid properties with encroachment problems because sorting them out can be an expensive and time-consuming process.

Liens

A lien is a charge that has been placed on property to satisfy the owner's debt or other obligation. For example, a property owner may agree to have a lien placed on his or her real property in order to obtain a mortgage to purchase the property. In other cases, a lien may be placed on property as a result of the property owner's debts. For example, if an owner does not pay his or her property taxes, the taxing authority may place a lien on the taxpayer's property. In some states, unpaid child support may become a lien on a person's property.

Enter the Internet

Over the past decade, the world of information has changed considerably, particularly for real estate investors. Today, the Internet has created a wealth of property search and management resources that puts individuals in control of information as never before. Web resources are spread throughout this book, but here is a summary of some of the most useful real estate investment sites you can find on the Web:

Associations

National Association of Realtors
www.realtor.org
National Association of Housing Cooperatives
www.coophousing.org

Construction Assistance
RS Means® Quick Cost Calculator
www.rsmeans.com/calculator/index.asp

Hanley Wood (provider of specialized paid reports on specific
      home renovation and construction projects)
www.hanleywood.com

Credit Sites
FICO® Credit Score
www.myfico.com

Economic Information
UCLA Anderson Forecast
http://uclaforecast.com

U.S. Census Bureau Census of Housing
www.census.gov

Buying Smart from Offer to Closing

14

Financing Your Property

The multiyear boom in real estate flipping that took place in the late 1990s and early 2000s put the spotlight on a key industry shift: access to easy credit for large purchases, with many lenders catering to the subprime loan market (or borrowers with poor credit ratings). The real estate slowdown that started in 2006 and ultimately led to the demise of the subprime mortgage market has had a negative impact on the trend, although its lure is guaranteed to raise the interest of investors in the future.

 Earlier in this book we told you that 25 percent of the nation's second homes were purchased by investors. And while over 80 percent of those buyers were able to put 20 percent down when they took out mortgages, there is no question that a change in the attitude of lenders is making possible more second-home ownership and real estate investment in general.

Former Federal Reserve Chairman Alan Greenspan offered a name for a new class of home loans particularly loved by investors and subprime borrowers: exotic mortgages. According to Greenspan, borrowing against home values added $600 billion to consumers' spending power in 2004, equivalent to 7 percent of personal disposable income—compared with 3 percent in 2000 and 1 percent in 1994.

Greenspan attributed the increase to declining mortgage interest rates, an increase in the turnover of homes, the popularity of cash-out mortgage refinancing, and home-equity loans.

Growth of Mortgage Offerings

Today's borrowers have a much wider choice of loans to fund home ownership and outside investments. Most experts in the industry admit that this is both good and bad. Some examples:

- ◆ Standard 15-, 20-, or 30-year mortgages with regular principal and interest payments are still the way most homes are mortgaged, yet you hear far more about newer entries in the loan market. With fixed-rate mortgages, the interest rate remains the same throughout the loan term. Adjustable-rate mortgages made their debut nearly 20 years ago, allowing a fixed rate for one to seven years and afterward moving to an adjustable rate. Yet as home prices skyrocket and borrowers struggle to make down payments, lenders in a protracted lower-rate environment are coming up with newer alternatives to keep their business strong.
- ◆ A recent study by LoanPerformance, a San Francisco–based mortgage loan research firm, shows that one of every four new mortgages in the early 2000s was an interest-only loan (a loan that delays principal payments for three years or more to guarantee the borrower a lower monthly payment).
- ◆ Skyrocketing real estate values, other forms of high-rate consumer debt, and a trend toward get-rich-quick real estate investments are driving supply and demand for loans that allow lower monthly payments in exchange for slower or, in some cases, negative buildup of equity.

IMPORTANT NOTE

Talk about foresight, in July 2005 former Fed Chairman Alan Greenspan warned the House Financial Services Committee, "There's potential for individual disaster here," referring to the negative buildup of equity accumulating in so many U.S. households.

Alternative Loan Options

Whether they come from your current lender or a late-night infomercial, here is an overview of several nontraditional loan options on the market and their potential risks and rewards.

Interest-Only Loans

This immensely popular loan option allows a borrower to pay only the interest on the mortgage in monthly payments for a fixed term. After the end of that term of five to seven years (typically), the borrower can refinance, pay the balance in a lump sum, or start paying off the principal, in which case the payments can rise. These loans do work for some people, such as those who expect their income to jump considerably in the next few years. Some types of interest-only mortgages have been around for decades and have been used by wealthy borrowers who were sophisticated and disciplined enough to find profitable uses for money saved on monthly payments. But today's loan products are increasingly marketed to ordinary homebuyers and, in many cases, to subprime borrowers who in the past could not have qualified for standard loans. That is where the risk comes in.

Zero-Down Mortgages

An increasingly common option for investors, these loans allow borrowers to buy with no money down. It gets a borrower into a property, but any chances of acquiring equity in a home will have to come from rising market values, and that is not something every borrower can count on. It might be better to ask for a low-down-payment alternative—such as FHA financing—that allows a borrower to have some small amount of equity at the start.

40-Year Loans

A 40-year fixed rate mortgage allows a borrower to invest a smaller down payment and pay less monthly than he or she would with a conventional 15- or 30-year loan. The disadvantage is living with a loan where equity builds so slowly. It is best for someone who needs a break on payments at the beginning and is willing to refinance later.

Piggyback Loans

Some borrowers who cannot make a 20 percent down payment may consider taking out a first and second mortgage concurrently. Typically, a piggyback loan works as follows: The most common type is an 80/10/10 where a first mortgage is taken out for 80 percent of the home's value, a down payment of 10 percent is made and another 10 percent is financed in a second trust at possibly a higher interest rate. Some lenders may allow a piggyback loan for less than a 10 percent down payment.

100-Plus Loans

Also known as loan-to-value (LTV) mortgages, 100-plus loans are promoted by lenders willing to loan 100 percent or more of appraised market value as a way to draw in customers who cannot make a down payment. An overly high appraisal value in a sliding market, a loss of home value or, even worse, a loss of a job can lead quickly to rising debt and possible foreclosure.

Negative Amortization Loans

Negative amortization means that a loan balance is increasing instead of decreasing. With a negative amortization loan, if a payment does not cover the interest and principal payment, the shortage is added to the loan balance, which means you never really start paying off the loan. Again, this may work for people in short-term housing situations in markets with rising rates, but those conditions are never guaranteed.

Figure 14.1 helps you compare these loans.

Questions to Ask Loan Officers before You Borrow

If you plan to buy an investment property with this new crop of low-down-payment loans, you should ask your loan officer:

- ◆ How much will I have to pay each month?
- ◆ How much will I pay when (or if) this loan converts?
- ◆ What kind of credit will you give me for the rent I collect on this property?
- ◆ Is this a negative amortization loan and if so, how much will I owe on the loan balance when the super-low interest rate expires?
- ◆ What happens if rates rise?

Mortgage Shopping Worksheet

	Lender 1		Lender 2	
	Mortgage 1	**Mortgage 2**	**Mortgage 1**	**Mortgage 2**
Name of contact				
Date of contact				
Mortgage amount				
Basic Information about the Mortgage				
Type of mortgage: conventional or high-ratio				
If high-ratio, what is the insurance premium?				
Minimum down payment required				
Mortgage term (length of loan)				
Interest rate				
Estimated monthly mortgage payment				
Costs				
Application fee or loan processing fee				
Survey or title insurance fee				
Appraisal fee				
Attorney fees				
Mortgage broker fees (if applicable)				
Credit report fee				
Other fees				
Are any of the fees or costs waivable?				
Prepayment Penalties				
Is there a prepayment penalty?				
If so, how is it calculated?				
Are extra principal payments allowed?				
List all prepayment privileges				
Interest Rate Lock In Before Closing				
Is the lock in agreement in writing?				
Is there a fee to lock in?				
When does the lock in occur? At application, approval, or another time?				
How long will the lock in last?				
If the rate drops before closing, can you lock in at a lower rate? Is this automatic?				

*Different institutions may have different names for some fees and may charge different fees. These are some typical fees you may see on loan documents.

Figure 14.1 Mortgage Shopping Worksheet

Risky Mortgages or Risky Borrowers?

During the 2005 housing boom, Chart 14.1 shows the types of mortgages—long available to borrowers with pristine credit—that were increasingly being offered to a wider market of borrowers.

Seller Financing

This unconventional financing arrangement allows a borrower to avoid the paperwork and approval process of conventional financing by borrowing directly from the seller. It is an arrangement that requires the advice of an attorney or a financial advisor to see if it is right for the seller and the borrower. It also ensures that legal documents are properly filed.

At the very least, it is a transaction that requires a good deal of trust. Sellers might consider taking back a mortgage from a buyer who finds it tough to borrow through conventional means. The seller's incentive is possibly a quicker sale with an above-market interest rate or a higher down payment with a promissory note and trust deed in the seller's favor. Some families arrange seller financing on certain deals, and real estate investors may convince sellers to finance the amount owed in certain situations where it benefits both parties.

Hard Money

This is nonconventional or private financing with private funds, usually for commercial property. Because hard money loans are not backed by governmental safeguards, the typical stringent guidelines and documentation required by banks are not necessary. In exchange for the lack of documentation, the borrower pays a premium. Hard money loans are often arranged for properties that are difficult to fund, such as vacant land, or for those who desire to borrow with low documentation. Hard money lenders tend to be independent companies, not conventional banks, mortgage brokers, or other common lenders. Loan amounts start at a minimum of $300,000.

Mortgage Type	Description	Potential Risk	Best for
Interest Only	For the first 3 to 10 years, payments cover interest, not principal.	When the interest-only term is up, payments could rise substantially.	Those who plan to sell the property before the interest-only provision ends.
Option/Flex-Payment ARM	Borrower chooses what to pay every month (principal and interest, only interest, or a stated minimum that is less than the interest).	If you pay less than the stated interest, it will be tacked onto the loan balance, making your debt potentially more than your home is worth.	Borrowers who need only occasional payment flexibility.
40-Year Fixed	The loan term is 40 years instead of the usual 30 or 15.	Slower equity buildup and a much longer loan payoff time.	Borrowers who cannot afford a shorter-term loan but do not want to take on a lot of rate risk.
Piggyback Loans	When a borrower takes out a standard mortgage and a home-equity loan at the same time to cover the 20 percent down payment, thus avoiding PMI.	If home prices drop, you have already started drawing on your equity, so you could owe more than your home is worth.	Those who fall a little short of the 20 percent down payment but expect their income to rise over time.
No-Doc or Low-Doc Loan	These loans let you borrow without standard income or disclosure requirements, and sometimes without documenting your income at all. You do need a minimum credit score of 600 to 620.	You may be tempted to borrow more than you can afford. Also, the rates may be more than one-half to three points higher than a standard mortgage loan.	Self-employed people tend to use this option because they often have trouble proving steady income.

Chart 14.1 Types of Mortgages

The Future of Lending

Bank regulators began sounding the alarm bells about rising risks in the mortgage market in 2005, and acted on their assumptions in 2006 by investigating and effectively pulling the plug on the subprime mortgage market. This wound up affecting the availability of mortgage money, although interest rates stayed at historic lows. At press time, the shakeout in the subprime mortgage lending market was still in full force, and was affecting the "traditional" market as well. Many mortgage lenders were taking a more cautious approach to doling out money to homebuyers, while the U.S. banking system was suffering its own losses and casualties. Falling home prices and record numbers of foreclosures (good news for investors like yourself!) were partially to blame, as were the earlier, poor decisions regarding the granting of credit/mortgages to folks who just five years prior would have never qualified for a mortgage.

For investors, key goals should include maintaining a pristine credit rating, access to liquid assets for down payments, and a sharp eye for the many good values that are sure to be making their way onto the market over the next few years.

CHAPTER 15

Determining Value through Property and Investment Analysis

One of the most important aspects of real estate investing is determining the value of a property and ensuring that it is at (or lower than) market value, which is defined as the price that someone is willing to pay for the property, and not the price that the seller wants to get for the property.

As home prices climbed to record levels in the early 2000s, appraisers came under criticism for overvaluing the price of real estate, resulting in an increased number of risky loans. In mid-2005, news reports indicated that several leading banks began to change their policy of hiring outside appraisers, bringing many appraisers on as full-time staff with tighter restrictions on how aggressively they could value properties.

These developments are significant because they could have a long-term effect on how much real estate investors may be allowed to borrow in the future. They also signal what may be the beginning of the end for a relationship fraught with possible conflicts of interest. Though there are many capable independent appraisers working today, reports indicate that banks often hire those with the lowest fees. These appraisers are commonly under subtle pressure to help approve business in the busy market.

With tougher lending restrictions currently surfacing, there is some speculation that rising valuations—and rising loan values to accompany them—were finally slowing. Backing up these sentiments was a fairly expedient decrease in home prices in areas that just a few years earlier were seeing skyrocketing housing appreciation brought on by investor frenzy, easy access to credit, and very low interest rates. States like Florida and California were hit especially hard, and at press time were still watching their once-sky-high home prices level off and decrease.

With real estate once again proving itself to be a highly cyclical industry, it's important for investors to be keyed into the accurate value of their properties and—whenever possible—have at least some foresight as to the key drivers of the local market, how it has performed over the past few years and where it is headed over the next several years. We know you don't have a crystal ball, but the more educated you can be, the better.

Role of the Appraiser

Appraisers are a key part of the loan process because they are hired to serve as detectives who locate value—and lack of value—for their lender clients. Remember that appraisers are the lender's advocate, not the borrower's. Their job is to provide an independent estimate of the market value of a property, and their certified opinion protects the bank against charges that the mortgage is improperly valued.

Appraisers also provide buyer's protection. If a bank's appraisal comes in significantly lower than the agreed-upon selling price, it might mean that the seller was not completely honest with you, or simply overpriced her property. Assuming the appraiser did her job competently, you might have been saved from a large and expensive mistake.

Formalize your request for an appraisal by using an Appraisal Request Form, such as the one shown in Figure 15.1.

Landlord Insights

It [the appraisal] could come back and bite a lot of people. If the appraisal is above the market value, then the buyer is upside down in the loan, and these loans are more likely to default. If they cannot sell, they may have to go through foreclosure to get out.

—William Apgar, Harvard Joint Center for Housing Studies

Appraisal Request Form

Client/Lender: _____

Client/Lender Contact: _____

Client/Lender Address: _____

_____

_____

Client/Lender Phone: _____   Fax: _____

Lender File No. _____

Invoice and Mail Appraisal to: _____

Client/Lender

E-Mail Appraisal to: _____

Property Address: _____

_____

_____

Borrower: _____

Contact for entrance to property: _____

Home Phone: _____ Cell: _____ Work: _____

Type of Property:	❑ Single Familly	❑ Multi-Family	No. of Units _____
	❑ Vacant Land	❑ Commercial	

Owner's Name: _____

Occupant: _____

Listing Broker: _____

Appraisal Form:	❑ URAR	❑ 2055 Form	❑ Drive-by

Other: _____

Number of Requested Copies: _____ E-Mail Address: _____

Photographs Requested: Exterior _____   Interior _____

Additional Instructions: _____

Thank you for your order. We will contact you with a confirmation of your order and approximate time for completion

Figure 15.1 Appraisal Request Form

Current Marketplace

Federal banking regulators have weighed in on the issue of overvaluations, examining how some lenders are overseeing their appraisal operations as part of an increased focus on mortgage fraud. There are obvious concerns throughout the lending industry as the real estate bubble, accelerated by overly generous appraisals, added fuel to a speculative housing market. In some of the cases investigated, appraisers colluded with borrowers to submit inaccurate reports to lenders.

Once a higher appraisal on a property is in, the unlawful borrowers quickly sell the property, pocketing a wrongfully high profit. Those who bought from unlawful sellers are left holding the bag. However, the *Wall Street Journal* quoted a recent survey from October Research Corporation, a provider of news and information to the real estate services industry, saying that about 55 percent of appraisers felt pressure to give a higher value to property.

The question is where does the pressure come from? It could be from the borrower, the lender that hires him or her for the job, the mortgage broker, or the real estate agent. In hot markets, there is definitely a problem when appraisal rates go down.

How to Protect Yourself

There are several steps you can take to ensure that you are not the victim of overvaluation by an appraiser. Consider the following:

- ◆ Let your lender know that you would like a copy of your appraisal report—federal laws guarantee this, but customers rarely ask for it.
- ◆ Share relevant information with the appraiser to support your conclusions on the value of your property. Show him or her paperwork on recent remodelings or additions that may not have entered county records yet and comparables if you can find them.
- ◆ Do your own price survey if you think an appraisal is going to come in low. Look at local homes sold in the past six months that are similar to what you own or are prepared to buy, and then determine the price paid per square foot. A neighborhood real estate agent can get you details on the most recent closings—critical in hot markets where prices quickly rise.

In good times when values are headed up, buyers rarely consider the property appraisal process. But as markets level off and lenders become increasingly worried about their loan portfolios—as they have in the United States in recent years—appraisals often come under fire. Knowing this, all real estate investors should stand ready to defend their property's value if a wave of newfound conservatism endangers their future profit margin.

CHAPTER 16

Buying Rental Property: Reality Checks before Buying

One of the most important questions you should ask before purchasing property investment is: How much is this property worth, and how much should I invest in it to get the profit I want? Unlike the purchase of a primary home, which is intended to provide shelter and security for yourself and/or your family, a piece of rental property is meant to generate income for its owner(s). Because of this, real estate investing becomes more art than science. The good news is that there are tried-and-true strategies for making wise financial decisions—and making your long-term financial goals work—when buying.

One of the best ways to ensure that you are indeed searching for bargains and ready to add value to the properties that you purchase is by going through a complete "reality check" before buying. Next we discuss a few key points to review.

Reality Check No. 1: This Is Not Your Personal Space

A typical novice mistake is renovating a property to your own taste rather than a level the market will accept. When you are buying an inexpensive property for fix-up and sale, your focus should be on the buyer—the one who will walk in and see a fresh coat of paint, a refinished floor or new carpet, and sensible window treatments. Then, if needed, focus on the remodeling projects most buyers look for—a new or updated kitchen or bath that will meet the standards of the neighborhood.

The National Association of Home Builders provides a good guideline: Remodeling investments should not raise the value of your house more than 10 to 15 percent above the median sale price of other houses in your area.

IMPORTANT TIP

Before you make an offer on any property, spend a few Sundays at local open houses. Take a close look at what kitchen and bathroom features are common in this particular neighborhood, and ask the agent what improvements were made to the property before it went on the market. Remember that your goal is to appear interested in the property as a buyer, not a future competitor in the marketplace.

Reality Check No. 2: Numbers Never Lie—Unless You Want Them To

In previous chapters, we stressed the importance of calculating expenses, holding costs, and profit before you make an offer on a property. As part of this process, you may need to bring a trusted building inspector to a prospective property to project renovation costs, timetables for completion, and whether you are likely to meet the critical 20 percent profit margin when you sell (or rent recapture for a rental property).

First, add up the costs to renovate the property based on a thorough assessment of the condition of the house. Be brutal with this estimate, which should include materials and labor—your labor and the labor you have to hire. Next, subtract that from the home's likely market value after renovation, drawn from comparable real estate prices in the neighborhood. Then deduct at least another 5 to 10 percent for extras you may add and unforeseen expenses. What is left should be your offer.

It is essential that the real estate contract include an inspection clause. At best, the inspection will assure you that the house is a good investment; at worst, it will release you from the contract. The inspector will likely document a serious problem or two, and you can use the findings to persuade the seller to pay for repairs or negotiate the sale price downward.

If the house needs significant structural improvements, many real estate experts suggest walking away. It is often difficult to determine the extent of major repairs, such as plumbing and electrical system overhauls, foundation upgrades, and extensive roof and wall work, and pouring money into these types of repairs rarely nets a return at sale.

Reality Check No. 3: Looks Are Everything

First impressions are of prime importance when selling a house, and studies show that most buyers decide within the first few minutes of a showing whether the house is a possibility. With this in mind, plan renovations and updates for maximum appeal and minimum cost. Here are some inexpensive changes that will make a big difference:

- ◆ Paint all interior walls in neutral colors.
- ◆ Upgrade lighting fixtures or install new ones in areas that appear dark.
- ◆ Add simple shutters or blinds to windows.
- ◆ Replace dated carpeting or refinish hardwood floors.
- ◆ Replace or repair/refinish the front door.

In terms of larger projects, kitchen and bathroom renovations generally produce the largest return on your investment, and will also help sell the property more quickly. Beware of over-improving, however. Consider the standard set by other homes in the area and proceed accordingly.

Reality Check No. 4: Do-It-Yourself Means Exactly That

If you have the time and know-how, you can save considerably on your investment by handling many tasks yourself. Perhaps the most common task owners take on is renovation. If you have the skills to paint, hang cabinets, install trim, or replace windows, you will save considerably in the renovation process. If not, plan on subtracting anywhere from 15 to 40 percent of your selling price to get the work done by professionals.

Reality Check No. 5: Be Prepared to Walk Away

If any aspect of the property you are considering fails to conform to your financial projections or gives you pause in other respects, walk away. Do not try to rework your numbers or, worse, ignore warning signs of bigger problems that may arise later. Successful real estate investors pass up far more properties than they acquire.

Do Your Homework

Searching for real estate values doesn't necessarily mean finding the most run-down, antiquated properties and buying them at a cheap price. In fact, not every fixer-upper is a diamond in the rough; many properties simply require too much time and money to be considered a solid investment opportunity. Those properties that are worth the effort should not become money pits, as long as you do your homework.

All sellers are looking for a quick sale and a healthy profit, but not all are honest in their efforts to meet those ends. *Caveat emptor,* Latin for let the buyer beware, is especially good advice when buying real estate. It is often a challenge to get full disclosure on a residential home purchase, but when it comes to investment property, you may have to be the IRS, SEC, and FBI rolled into one.

Sellers naturally want to show their property in the best light, and they are counting on you—the buyer—to believe the information provided without asking too many questions. But sellers can distort, withhold, or simply lie about information vital to buyers' informed decision making.

Remember, however, when reviewing financial information provided by a seller, you are not bound to adapt their business practices to yours after you close. Your goal is to examine closely how, or if, they have profited from their ownership, devise a way to do it better and build that into the formula of what you will ultimately pay for the property. It is also crucial to consider how involved you want to be as a landlord, and how much support or assistance you will need in this area.

The key to success lies in knowing when to pass on homes that are actionable—meaning homes you know would not pass a buyer's inspection because of major problems, such as foundation damage and other serious repairs. Properties that require only cosmetic improvements to bring them in line with other properties in the area are generally your best investment.

CHAPTER 17

Residential Income Property Due Diligence

Long before you make your way to the closing table to get the keys to your new real estate investment you'll want to conduct a thorough due diligence on the property that you intend to buy. This is especially important for new investors who don't always have the instincts necessary to "catch" problems with properties on the first walk-through for a potential investment.

 There are several ways to make sure that you and the seller are working on the same page when considering the option of investing in a property that has tenants:

- *Do an outside tour:* Get to know the neighborhood's rent base block-by-block. Check posted For Rent signs for average area rental rates and get a feel for the neighborhood demographics and culture. Think like a landlord and a tenant on these walks. Look over the existing apartment stock in the neighborhood and decide if this is a place where you would consider living. If you are unsure, build that factor into your offering price. Today's struggling neighborhood could be tomorrow's gold mine if you time it right.
- *Do an inside tour.* Ask to see all units and common areas inside and out, and bring a contractor with you if you can. Do this before you make an offer; problems discovered early in the process are easier to handle.

◆ *Check local demographics.* Chapter 5 lists several web sites offering demographic and pricing information on specific areas. Check that research to gain a better understanding of your market before you invest.

◆ *Ask for the property's income statement.* If you are serious about buying the property, you will need to have the owner's income statement to make your own financial projections. Though there is no guarantee that the information will be accurate or complete, an upfront seller should readily provide you with this information. Once you have the income statement and have inspected the property, check the accuracy of those numbers, if possible. For instance, if there are income streams from parking and laundry, verify those numbers with tenants and any vendors who service those areas. It may also be useful to find a tenant willing to answer a few questions. Ask if there are any known problems with other tenants defaulting on rent payments. You need to make sure that the current owner is able to collect rents in a timely fashion if you will inherit the tenants.

◆ *Ask for their Schedule E.* Schedule E is the IRS form for Supplemental Income and Loss (from rental real estate, royalties, partnerships, S corporations, estates, trusts, and other businesses). Again, ask for this only if you are serious about the property. Because your seller is likely to be more honest with the IRS than with potential buyers, they may be reticent to hand it over, but politely persist.

◆ *Ask for copies of current leases.* If buying a property with tenants, you need to know all that you can about current tenants— what they are paying, how long they have been there, whether they have pets, and how many family members are living with them.

◆ *Ask to talk to tenants.* Honest sellers will provide you a list of tenant names and phone numbers. If there is any hesitation, beware. If you really want the property, copy tenant names off the mailbox, locate their phone numbers by name and address, and contact them that way. Be friendly, but ask important questions, including, "What do you least like about living here?"

◆ *Consider new income streams.* You may find that the current owner is undercharging for parking compared with other buildings in the neighborhood. Or perhaps he or she is providing no-cost cable access. Of course, you do not want to upset current tenants—unless you are ready to replace them with new ones—but you should also be charging what the market will bear.

◆ *Watch for new home and condo development.* As long as interest rates remain low, potential renters may opt for a low down-payment loan and buy instead. Beware of neighborhoods filled with new condo construction or conversions. They may end up being your competition.

◆ *Watch for new amenities under construction.* Do you see tasteful new shopping areas opening nearby? A satellite medical center for a respected local hospital? A Starbucks? These are all signs of good development that will gentrify your neighborhood and send your property values up.

◆ *Talk to other owners.* Choose several properties similar to the one you are considering in the immediate neighborhood, copy the names off the mailboxes, find their numbers, and try to contact the owners. Find out as much as you can about their experience renting in the neighborhood. Ask if they know of any major construction or street repair projects coming up; noisy, dusty neighborhoods are not terribly renter-friendly.

◆ *Call city hall.* Ask your alderman or councilperson about parking restrictions, major public works projects, or any other issues in the immediate neighborhood that landlords should be aware of.

◆ *Call the tax assessor.* Check average neighborhood tax increases over the past 10 years, and stay on top of recent news stories about local property taxes. Increases will affect your bottom line. You may be able to find this information online.

◆ *Call the police.* Talk to a nonemergency contact at the local police department and ask him or her to point you in the direction of neighborhood crime statistics. If there are specific types of crime occurring in the neighborhood, you want to know what, if anything, is being done about it. Another source for crime statistics and stories is the online version of your local newspaper.

◆ *Check public transportation.* Do more than simply check the building's proximity to public transportation, find out how safe it is (make that a focal point of your crime statistics search), and how many local residents make use of it. If public transportation is being extended to the neighborhood you are looking in, see when it will be up and running.

◆ *Recalculate.* Consider all of the information you have gathered and recalculate your expectations for the property. If everything looks good, make an offer.

At CompleteLandlord, we feel that the best real estate investors become neighborhood anthropologists, thoroughly researching the neighborhood's demographics and economic potential. Imagine what it is like to live in the neighborhood and the building you want to buy into, asking local residents to share their experiences, good and bad, with you. In this way, you will have a clearer picture of the management issues you are likely to face.

Fix It: What the Successful Fixer-Upper Needs to Know

18

Creating Curb Appeal

You've already learned from this book that renovating a home for rental or sale does not have to cost an arm and a leg. In fact, if you are going to make your investment work, renovation expenses should be kept to a minimum.

How can you do this? Start by using the presale inspection to make a list of improvements that could be made to the property. When making the list, think about "curb appeal," or, the first impression that people get when viewing your home from the street. By opting for affordable interior and exterior improvements, you can enhance a home's curb appeal in a way that pays off when it comes time to sell.

In this chapter, we walk you through some of the ways that you can improve a property both for your prospective tenants, and for future buyers.

The Home's Exterior

Landscaping

Though all of us have at one time admired the landscaping in front of a beautiful house, it is in fact a tricky expenditure for investment property. Why? Because landscaping is a highly individual investment, and though it can increase the curb appeal of a home, it may not increase the final sale price.

You do, however, want the home's landscaping to appear neatly trimmed and maintained. Though elaborate landscaping may not increase a home's value, overgrown or outdated landscaping can certainly decrease the value. Find a middle ground and stick with common shrubs that provide neat and clean coverage. Trim any overgrown shrubs, cleanly edge planting beds, add simple annuals for color, and include a thorough covering of mulch. Potential buyers will see a well-cared-for yard, and that is a selling point. A landscaping budget of $400 to $600 should suffice for most homes.

Painting

Inside and out, painting is one of the cheapest and most effective ways to freshen the look of a property. It's also the single household fix-up chore that most anyone can do without any training, and it allows you to instantly change the visual appearance of the property—making it look bigger or brighter. A nice coat of interior and/or exterior paint can do wonders for a property, and costs as little as a few hundred dollars (if you do it yourself) or as much as a few thousand (if you hire a contractor to handle it).

Replace Damaged Hardware, Doors, and Screens

Anything that can be "seen" on a home represents an opportunity to improve the selling price of the property. Buyers who are faced with torn screens, rusty hardware, or broken doorknobs are probably discounting the price of the property in their head. Avoid this issue by replacing or repairing these items before you sell.

Lighting and Electrical Wiring

Try to find a property that is nearly up to code because rewiring or replumbing a property can be costly. Smaller steps can include adding new lighting fixtures where there is an opportunity to make a room larger or brighter, or repairing any electrical face plates that might be broken or missing.

Have Windows and Gutters Cleaned

Noticeable dirt anywhere in a home indicates neglect, but dirty windows are especially noticeable to buyers. Get them washed. Do it yourself or hire the job out to get it done—costs range from $150 to $300 if you hire out. The same holds true with gutters, though for a different reason. Buyers are unlikely to notice debris built up in gutters, but an inspector will. You can be sure that this information will be passed along to the buyer.

The Home's Interior

Do a Deep Cleaning

You can hire this to be done or tackle it yourself, but make sure everything—right down to the corners—is clean. Cabinets, appliances, bathroom grout, and baseboards should shine. The result will be a clean and fresh-smelling home, which is an important selling point.

Replace Worn or Stained Carpeting

There is no easy way to disguise a worn carpet, and stained carpets and rugs suggest a poorly cared-for home. Carpets are relatively inexpensive to replace and add immediate value to the look and feel of a home.

Bigger Projects

If you buy a property that looks like it could use substantial updating, it makes sense to look at national averages of what the most popular renovation projects are and what they return at sale time. You should never approach a major renovation unless you know it will return at least 70 percent of the cost at sale.

Cost versus Value

Remodeling magazine produces an annual study, the "Cost versus Value Report," that includes cost information collected quarterly from a

(continued)

Cost versus Value (*Continued*)

nationwide network of remodeling contractors based on a 40 percent margin—a very conservative estimate. Costs are also adjusted for city-to-city pricing variations. This information can be found at http://costvalue.remodelingmagazine.com/index.html, which shows renovation projects ranked in terms of best return.

Renovating your investment property should be part of your early valuation process before you purchase a home. It is crucial to devise accurate remodeling estimates to improve the value of the property while ensuring the minimum profit you need to produce from your investment.

By taking these steps, you'll avoid the problem that many investors run into when they buy properties that require an exorbitant amount of work to make them appealing to tenants and future buyers.

CHAPTER 19

Handling the Competition

The real estate investment field is highly competitive, and finding the right properties to invest in requires a solid strategy and self-education. It also helps to know about the cyclical nature of the real estate market because it's relatively easy for inexperienced investors to get a toehold in the foreclosure and fix-up movement when the market is hot. When markets cool, however, those still in the game tend to be people with deep pockets and good information networks.

In this chapter, we show you how to navigate the sometimes-murky waters of real estate investment, particularly when it comes to purchasing fix-up properties at a value rate and either renting them out or reselling them.

Prepare Yourself with Knowledge

If the newspaper headlines are screaming "Buy Property Now," it may be time to read a book on real estate or a newspaper's classified section. Or perhaps you should sign up for a real estate agents class or take a drive to see what properties are available in various neighborhoods. Review the market carefully before you buy; an unprepared investor is the one most likely to lose money.

A real estate course at a community college might give you an overview of marketplace information and let you in on what most real estate agents and other professionals already know. If you are not a regular reader of local newspapers or real estate web sites, read the fine print in classified ads to find out what types of properties are available for purchase. If you have questions, write them down and call the contacts to ask questions. You should feel no pressure to buy; just gather the information.

Change Your Spending Lifestyle

When you start investing in real estate, you make a new best friend: the almighty dollar, or more simply, "cash." If you are preparing to enter the real estate market, downsize your spending wherever you can, reduce or eliminate your nondeductible debt, and start saving. The most successful real estate investors have cash reserves to cover emergency needs, prepay mortgage payments, or take advantage of new investment properties. You may decide at some point to make real estate investing a full-time career, so prepare by saving now.

Key Competitive Strategies

Now let's look at some of the top strategies that you, as a real estate investor, can use to stand out from the competition and wind up with the properties that will produce the best returns.

Build Cash, Not Debt

You've already learned about the importance of cash to real estate deals. The plain truth is that cash always wins out over financing, which takes time to secure. Cash is particularly vital in foreclosure acquisitions or auctions, when it may be the only way to close the deal. As much as you can, work toward building a sizable cash cushion as your real estate investment career progresses.

Start Your Fix-Up Training

Not every real estate investor spends his or her weekends plastering wallboard or hanging new doors, but knowing how to do so when needed will better prepare you to hire qualified workers. If you plan to pay others to do renovation work, you need to make sure they are charging you fairly for labor and supplies and to judge the quality of their workmanship. So

(continued)

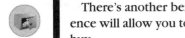

Start Your Fix-Up Training (*Continued*)

unless your chosen contractor is your father or brother who has been in the construction business for decades, you have to develop some knowledge of what they do and how quality work gets done.

There's another benefit to the do-it-yourself approach: Hands-on experience will allow you to spot quality (or shoddy) work in the properties you buy.

IMPORTANT NOTE

Be sure to check every contractor's license, insurance coverage, and references (from past customers) before having him or her perform any work on your properties.

Consider the Worst Homes in the Best Neighborhoods

Desirable areas appreciate faster in good times and hold their value better in bad times. It is possible to earn a good investment return in these neighborhoods by making upgrades on those homes that need renovation. This will put those homes on par with other properties in the area.

Where Is the Nearest Starbucks?

Smart investors follow some of the biggest names in retail to see where the next hot neighborhood may be. Starbucks, Borders, and Barnes and Noble are good companies to follow. Their track record in site selection over the past 20 years has been legendary. These are among top companies that move into an area when prices are low, and they almost immediately create the kind of foot traffic and patronage that gentrify neighborhoods. Keep a sharp eye on where they are going, and use their site-selection professionals as your own.

Understand the Courts and Public Agencies

As stated before, take the time to learn how public auctions and preforeclosure and foreclosure filings are handled in your community.

Though your contacts at banks will certainly help you, it also helps to know government clerks who have a sense of whether bankruptcy and liquidation filings are heavy or light. Bargain homes do not sit long in bankruptcy court, and they may be disposed of in probate court as well. Tax lien properties (buying tax-delinquent properties from local governments) can be risky, but they can also end up being lucrative investments.

Build Smart Relationships with Agents or Brokers

As you already read in Chapter 10, real estate professionals not only help you manage deals, but they sometimes share crucial information about individuals who are going through transitions—divorce, widowhood, illness, relocation, and foreclosure. If you are an interested, informed, and qualified buyer, agents are always willing to work with you.

Get Preapproved

Preapproval is preferred over prequalification by all sellers. Prequalification is a simple calculation of what you may qualify for based on your income; preapproval requires a more thorough look at your personal financial picture and all but guarantees the seller that you are creditworthy. It's just a step away from a loan approval, which means that when it comes time to apply for a loan you'll already have many of the documents and information organized for the loan officer.

IMPORTANT NOTE

A preapproval is particularly important in a hot market: when it's time to make your offer, you want to be able to tell the seller that a lender has already committed to loan the money to you. This can give you an advantage over a buyer who is less prepared to close the deal.

Reach Potential Contacts by Mail

Many investors mail postcards to people in foreclosure indicating their interest in the property. This is a safe and unobtrusive means of making contact with sellers. There is also potential contact information in divorce, probate, and eviction court. Widen your mailing list at no cost with this public, easy-to-find information that may be on the Internet in some communities.

Approach Foreclosure Sellers Directly

Many investors feel uncomfortable approaching people in trouble personally, but doing so might give you an advantage. When you know the foreclosure process has begun at a particular home, start with a letter to the owner first. Follow up by stopping by and letting him or her know that you have done your research and noticed a pending problem with their property. If you are met with a blank stare or claims of denial, simply offer your business card and a written description of what you can do for him or her. The owner may decide to do business with you sometime in the future.

Use Newspaper Ads

Place ads under the "Money to Lend" section of your local newspaper. Here, many property owners in trouble look for last-ditch ways to get money to save their homes. You can offer your services with the promise that they will not have a bankruptcy blot on their record.

Success in real estate investment depends on personal relationships and networking. As you begin to discover contacts and information resources, you are bound to find more. Give yourself adequate time to learn and do the job properly and the returns will come.

CHAPTER 20

The Limits of Do-It-Yourself

The level of confidence individuals have in their ability to fix up property on their own or with professional help is bigger than it has ever been. Although the slowdown in the real estate market that started in 2006 also put the brakes on the remodeling market, the percentage of U.S. homeowners who decide to manage their own home renovation projects is climbing.

The do-it-yourself approach isn't easy. Typical problems include organizing the work, ensuring quality workmanship, or simply getting subcontractors to show up. Overconfidence and poor planning could put a serious dent in your investment projections.

> **Landlord Insights**
>
> I would never attempt to do major plumbing or electric by myself. I can do minor stuff, but anything bigger than that, I go to someone who knows what he or she is doing.
>
> —Will Creaney, general contractor/carpenter

A general contractor and carpenter by training, even Will Creaney knows his limitations. He knows, for example, that certain projects are better handled by someone who specializes in a certain aspect of construction (such as electrical installation or carpet-laying).

All real estate investors can learn a lesson from Creaney, for when it comes to home renovation from a do-it-yourself perspective, don't be afraid to take on a project that you can handle, but never take a chance with complicated tasks if you have no experience—at least not without some guidance.

That's a tough pill for some real estate owners to swallow, given the raging do-it-yourself movement spurred on by the development (and millions of dollars spent on advertising) of mammoth home improvement chains like Home Depot and Lowe's.

Will Creaney invests in property for himself, and he knows the first step in any renovation/sale strategy is identifying potential problems during open houses. He has the skills to see foundation trouble and evidence of other potentially expensive repairs. That is why he encourages investors to tour properties with trusted contractors or licensed inspectors at an early stage.

IMPORTANT TIP

Make friends with real estate agents in your neighborhood. Local agents know contractors and they know the going rates for various renovation jobs. They can also pass along the wisdom they have gained from working with other clients—such as the woman two blocks down from you who put $60,000 into a kitchen for a two-bedroom, one-bath house and never got her money back. Collect facts, figures, and these all-important cautionary tales.

Adding Up the Expenses

Here are some general tips to consider at the start of your home search for minimizing renovation expenses:

♦ *Write down everything you think needs to be updated; you can always eliminate items later on.* Experienced investors know to put aside their personal tastes when estimating renovation expenses for property. Review Chapter 18 to evaluate which renovation jobs have the best chance of recovering expenses and stick to them.

◆ *Always check on construction loans and mortgages at the same time.* A construction loan should never be an afterthought. Make sure lenders who are competing for your mortgage business know that you will also need a construction loan. You may be offered a more favorable package.

◆ *Do not buy too much square footage.* Smaller properties in popular neighborhoods generally sell more quickly than larger ones because they are less expensive to buy and less costly to renovate. Smaller areas also take less time to repair, paint, and generally fix up.

◆ *Assemble a renovation team and stick with it.* Some investors hire a rotating cast of laborers for renovation projects, which may work fine from an expense and quality standpoint. But if you plan on investing in multiple properties over the long term, find a consistent, quality-conscious team that will work for a reasonable market rate and stick with them. An ongoing relationship with one group of workers may ensure higher-quality work, and your projects may be given priority if there are time limitations. Delays cost time and money.

◆ *Consider permit costs and other related expenses.* Local building codes and requirements will vary, so before you begin any project check with the local village or city hall for the necessary permits. Failing to do so may cause serious setbacks in your schedule and finances.

◆ *Find quality stock fixtures and equipment and stick with them.* Unless you are renovating in a high-end neighborhood, bypass top-of-the-line appliances and custom-made cabinets when choosing products for your remodel. The midrange choices available from many well-known manufacturers will save you money and still look stylish. You may be able to save even more by negotiating a volume discount with the manufacturer or a particular local supplier.

◆ *Make economic renovations.* Make this your mantra. If you walk into a property that needs more than this, make sure you can justify making the investment and the renovation costs.

◆ *Keep cash reserves for contingencies.* Each property budget projection should allow room for unforeseen problems or possible delays. Make sure you have the cash reserves to handle contingencies.

Becoming Your Own Contractor

Though the temptation to direct your own home renovation may be strong—after all, you may save between 10 and 25 percent of your project costs by doing so—consider carefully what is involved before you make this decision. Directing a home renovation requires knowledge of construction, plenty of time, and the ability to calmly resolve conflicts. You also need to have a good idea what certain jobs should cost and the potential for cost overruns in each.

For your first project, it may make sense to hire a good contractor and spend as much time as possible working alongside him or her learning the job. You will get a sense of what a day on a job site is like, what a renovation entails, what problems crop up, and what you can reasonably handle to do by yourself in the future. Consider it paid training.

If you do plan to handle the task of contracting, here is a general overview of what a contractor does:

◆ Communicates with the owner to see what jobs are necessary
◆ Oversees all details of the project
◆ Hires and schedules subcontractors
◆ Inspects the subcontractors' work
◆ Orders all supplies and oversees their installation
◆ Helps to resolve design or logistical issues and any other problems

Ask yourself the following questions before you consider overseeing a large project:

◆ Can you be available at all hours of the day to direct the project? Can you work full-time or part-time on a project if you need to?
◆ Are you a good supervisor?
◆ Are you a calm problem solver?
◆ Can you multitask?
◆ Can you learn new skills quickly?
◆ How good are you with figures and budgets?
◆ How well do you handle a crisis? What if something expensive goes wrong? What if someone gets hurt on the job?

Your answers should help you determine whether you are cut out to oversee a large project, or if you'd be better off if you outsourced it to an experienced professional.

Handling Stress

Some people love the challenge of overseeing complex tasks. They like the work, they like learning, and they like dealing with people. Granted, saving money is a strong incentive to become your own general contractor, but if it is the only reason you are interested in the job, that may be a problem. Running a renovation project takes a tremendous amount of your time over a period of weeks or months, and you have to want to be there. Handing it over to a professional in midstream to repair what you have done could easily double the cost of the project. Be sure you have the willingness and skill to do it the right way.

Think before You Leap

As you've learned in this chapter, acting as your own general contractor can be an attractive proposition made somewhat easier by the proliferation of giant home improvement retailers who cater to the do-it-yourself crowd. As many before you have already learned, doing it yourself can save you money and get you exactly what you want—that is, if you know exactly what you want.

Rather than jumping into the do-it-yourself waters feet first, you may want to train under a good contractor on a first-time investment to see if this is what you really want to do. Remember: Your budget and profit depend on it.

CHAPTER 21

Creating an Exit Strategy

Exit strategies are growing in popularity, particularly in the business world, where anyone who is just starting up is being urged to think about the future and how they can walk away from the investment should it sour, become uninteresting, or be replaced by something better.

It's perfectly fine to consider exit strategies in our work, and sometimes even in our relationships. After all, no one likes to be caught by surprise when the unexpected happens. As a real estate investor, you'll want to be thinking about an exit strategy from day one. Why is this so important? Because market conditions fluctuate, personal situations change, and, most importantly, tax conditions morph over time.

 To best deal with these changes, you'll want to make sure that you always have an accessible escape route. In this chapter, we look at how to go about creating this all-important aspect of your real estate investment business.

Once you have this part of your strategy worked out, you'll be much better positioned to maximize value without a holding period (if so desired) because you'll be equipped with an exit strategy that will work in any market conditions.

> **IMPORTANT NOTE**
>
> Sometimes having a well-thought-out exit strategy is a simple matter of having the freedom to do things with your money when you want to do them.

Establish Your Goals

The first step to a successful exit strategy is to establish whether your goals in real estate investment are long-term or short-term. Flippers are not long-term thinkers, but that is due to the nature of their game. For everyone else, it is good to have a plan.

Some critical questions you need to consider before you start investing, even if you do not have the answers right now, are these:

♦ What motivates you to invest in real estate?
♦ Do you want to be a landlord for the rest of your life?
♦ Do you envision pulling your money out of the property at some point? Will it be when your kids go off to college or when you retire?
♦ Given all the effort and expense rental property may require, could you get better returns somewhere else?
♦ What is the minimum price you want to get for your property if you do decide to sell?

There are dozens of questions beyond these, but the critical issue in real estate investment is knowing yourself and your motivations. You have to bring a broad range of skills to the process if you plan to make money.

For long-term investors, knowing when to sell is often as important as knowing when and what to buy. Here are several factors to consider when making the decision to unload a property:

♦ Is the economic health of the neighborhood improving or is it deteriorating?
♦ Are local regulations making it tough to operate this investment, and are they going to get tougher?
♦ What is happening with property taxes and are you getting your money's worth from city services?
♦ How is the wear and tear on the building and what investment will be necessary in future years to keep it in good repair?
♦ What are the tax implications of selling outright?

We explored the topic of real estate bubbles and various indicators to spot the top of a market. Here are some key indicators that you'll want to include in a reminder file that you can refer to on a regular basis and integrate into your exit strategy.

Tax Implications

Because tax implications are so important, you might want to develop an alternate strategy like a 1031 exchange with the help of your tax professional. Capital gains tax after a long ownership may be a rude surprise, so you will need expertise to deal with it.

There is another tax trigger that may influence a decision to sell: the end of your property's depreciation allowance. Investors are allowed 27.5 years to depreciate property, which means that after that time, they lack tools to reduce their tax burden. These details are available in IRS Publication 946. Once you hit maximum depreciation, it may be a signal to sell.

IMPORTANT TIP

Stay on top of the current tax codes. Even investors with less expertise in tax issues than the average CPA or real estate attorney need to have a basic understanding of how taxes affect real estate transactions. The IRS web site (www.IRS.gov) is a good bookmark to help investors start that education.

Figuring Your Capital Gains Impact

Most experts advise you to hold an investment property for at least a year so that it is possible to qualify for long-term capital gains tax on the profit. However, if you decide to move into the property, you could potentially keep it tax-free. It makes sense to call in your tax advisor to work various scenarios based on your term of ownership and residency to determine whether an offer on the property is truly a good deal for you.

Basically, you will be subtracting your total selling costs (title and transfer fees, broker commissions, legal fees, survey fees, and so on) from your gross sale price as a start. Then you will subtract the cost of your various improvements to the property over the life of your ownership.

The 1031 Exchange Alternative

There is another way that property investors in for the long haul can delay the tax impact on their purchase and sale of investment property over the years. It is called a 1031 exchange, or a like-kind exchange. This is now a popular part of many property owners' long-term business or asset strategies, but it requires good advice and careful execution. See Chapter 3 for a more detailed discussion on 1031 exchanges and how they can work for you.

Leave Your Emotions Out

The buyer who is purchasing a single-family home for himself, his wife, and three children could conceivably get emotional about the purchase, knowing just how much those kids will enjoy the backyard pool and how fun it will be to barbecue on the patio. Investment purchases are quite different and shouldn't be based on emotions or a "feel good" sentiment that comes from looking at or walking through the property.

Developing an exit strategy in any investment is important because it takes emotion out of the question of making good financial decisions. Always consider potential and unforeseen life events when buying a property—it will help you buy real estate with more value, and possibly more liquidity. Any transaction requires plenty of study and the benefit of good tax advice. There are measuring sticks to follow, and the best way to get the timing right is to consult a qualified tax expert who can guide you through the process.

Hold versus Sell: Owning Property as a Long-Term Investment

CHAPTER 22

Life as a Landlord: Is There Equity without Sweat?

We live in a world fraught with bad plumbing, leaky roofs, cracked foundations, and tenants who may not pay their rent. We're also operating in an increasingly litigious society, where lawsuits are filed daily for a number of reasons that in the past may have been inconceivable . . . some of them against landlords.

Knowing this, no one should be surprised that landlording is tedious work. In fact, most of us have rented at one point or another in our lives, and the best landlords are worth their weight in gold. The worst ones are fairly memorable as well.

Now put yourself in their position. How good would you be at this job? When you own real estate outright, there really is no such thing as passive investment. Unless you possess a significant amount of wealth and can afford a management company to take the midnight calls and the flak, all tenant relationships are going to be personal.

IMPORTANT TIP

If you live near a college or a university with a substantial number of students in rental housing, call their administrative office to find out if they offer seminars in local tenant law. You may need a student ID to get in, but these seminars are usually free and allow you to get the opposing viewpoint on dealing with landlords.

As a landlord, you must be a diplomat and a taskmaster at the same time. Most importantly, you have to watch every nickel you put into your property and every nickel your tenant takes out of it.

As of the first quarter of 2008, the U.S. Census Bureau reported national vacancy rates of 10.1 percent for rental housing and 2.9 percent for homeowner housing. The Census Bureau said the rental vacancy rate was not statistically different from the first quarter rate the year prior, but was higher than the previous quarter. That relatively high rental vacancy rate is a result of low interest rates turning renters into buyers—another vexing problem for landlords.

Some experts have speculated that residential landlords would catch a break from high home prices that were beginning to put some potential buyers out of the game and back into the rental economy. The residential real estate market bust that took hold of the country in 2006 and continued well into 2008 supported these assumptions and at press time was helping to chip away at high appreciation rates, all while the subprime mortgage fallout was turning more would-be homeowners into renters.

The Basics

Whatever the economic environment, landlords need to be on top of their game to make a rental property investment work. Here are some tips that you can use to maintain an edge in this competitive industry.

Get an Early Handle on All of Your Costs

Years or months from now, when you finally try to sell your property (see Chapter 21), you will be totaling up all your expenses from the day you got the keys to see if the offer on the table is worthwhile. So think about your spending this way—every wasted dollar is a dollar out of your potential profit when you decide to stop being a landlord. Start by doing your homework before you buy. Talk to people who are currently landlords. Ask them the five worst things they hate about the job and then the best tricks they learned to help them save money.

Most new landlords grossly underestimate their expenses at the outset. Consider putting your spending on a spreadsheet or bookkeeping computer program so that you can track where your money is going. It is quite possible that your monthly expenses will eat up half your rental income. If you are depending on that rent check to pay most of or your entire mortgage, that is not a welcome surprise.

Costs include obvious expenses, such as insurance, maintenance, and property taxes, but they also include items that some landlords overlook, such as periods of vacancy, bad debts, the occasional need to replace expensive items like roofs or furnaces, and time spent managing the properties. Considering using a form similar to Figure 22.1 to track expenses.

IMPORTANT TIP

Try and keep your rental income at least 25 percent higher than your mortgage cost. This will not only help pay for any unforeseen expenses, it can help pay off your mortgage quicker or put you in a better position to buy additional property.

Price Your Property Right

Rental units should be priced competitively for the market, based on their features and location. Avoid setting your rent too high or too low. In a tough rental market, consider tenant incentives, such as an early payment discount, to keep good tenants in your building and your cash income flowing.

Understand the Fair Housing Act

This 1968 law prohibits discrimination in the renting of housing based on race, color, national origin, religion, gender, family status, or disability. Talk to your attorney about this law and the proper way to interact with prospective tenants so you are not demonstrating bias.

Screen Tenants Thoroughly

The Internet provides subscription-based services that will allow you to check credit reports of various applicants. At CompleteLandlord.com,

Monthly Budget Planner

	Party 1	Party 2	
Average Salary	_____	_____	
Average Commission	_____	_____	
Benefits	_____	_____	
Investment Dividends	_____	_____	
Retirement Plans/Profit Sharing	_____	_____	
Other (_____)	_____	_____	
Total Monthly Income	_____	_____	_____
			Joint Total

	Present	Proposed	
Rent/Mortgage Payment	_____	_____	
Electricity	_____	_____	
Water	_____	_____	
Phone	_____	_____	
Cable	_____	_____	
Trash Pickup	_____	_____	
Lawn Service	_____	_____	
Property Tax	_____	_____	
Homeowner's Insurance	_____	_____	
Auto Payments	_____	_____	
Auto Maintenance	_____	_____	
Auto Insurance	_____	_____	
Food	_____	_____	
Clothing	_____	_____	
Child Care	_____	_____	
Education	_____	_____	
Child Support	_____	_____	
Alimony	_____	_____	
Entertainment/Vacation	_____	_____	
Pet Expenses	_____	_____	
Life/Health Insurance	_____	_____	
Medical/Dental/Optical	_____	_____	
Credit Cards	_____	_____	
Loans	_____	_____	
Other (_____)	_____	_____	
Other (_____)	_____	_____	
Total Monthly Spending	_____	_____	_____
			Joint Total

Figure 22.1 Monthly Budget Planner

you'll find a comprehensive tool for thoroughly screening prospective tenants. You'll also want to talk to your attorney, tax professional, and fellow landlords to see whom they use to screen applicants, and follow these tips:

Create a form you can have by the phone to fill out when a prospective tenant calls. Keep this information on file. It should include the following:

- ◆ Prospective tenant's name
- ◆ Occupancy date
- ◆ Reason for moving
- ◆ Smoking preference
- ◆ Referral/reference
- ◆ Phone
- ◆ Number of children and their ages
- ◆ Pets
- ◆ Number of people living in the unit

What Is the Difference between a Rental Agreement and a Lease?

A lease is an agreement between a landlord and renter to occupy a rental property for a set period of time, usually six months or a year. This agreement holds the amount of rent and other terms of the lease in place for the term of the signed agreement.

A rental agreement typically covers a shorter term of 30 days and allows the landlord and tenant to rent the property month to month. The terms, however, can be changed by the landlord with 30 days notice. Always use formal, written rental agreements and leases like the ones shown in Figures 22.2 and 22.3.

While You Are Showing the Property

Keep in the mind the following as you show prospective tenants around the building:

- ◆ *Their appearance:* Good tenants want to make a good impression. Unkempt people tend to keep unkempt homes.
- ◆ *Their car's appearance:* If you have the chance to take a look at their car, it may serve as another indicator of how they might

Residential Lease

Apartment–Condominium–House

By this agreement made and entered into on _____, 20_____,
between _____ herein referred to as Lessor,
and _____ herein referred to as Lessee.
Lessor leases to Lessee the premises situated at _____, in the City
of _____, County of _____, State of
_____, and more particularly described as follows: _____
_____
_____
_____

together with all appurtenances, for a term of _____ years, to commence on _____, 20_____,
and to end on _____, 20_____, at _____o'clock ___. m.

1. Rent. Lessee agrees to pay, without demand, to Lessor as rent for the demised premises the sum of _____
_____ Dollars ($_____) per month in advance on the _____
day of each calendar month beginning _____, 20_____, at _____, City of
_____, State of _____, or at such other place as Lessor
may designate.

2. Form of Payment. Lessee agrees to pay rent each month in the form of one personal check, OR one cashier's
check, OR one money order made out to _____.

3. Late Payments. For any rent payment not paid by the date due, Lessee shall pay a late fee in the amount of
_____ Dollars ($_____).

4. Returned Checks. If, for any reason, a check used by Lessee to pay Lessor is returned without having been paid,
Lessee will pay a charge of _____ Dollars ($_____) as
additional rent AND take whatever other consequences there might be in making a late payment. After the second
time a Lessee's check is returned, Lessee must thereafter secure a cashier's check or money order for payment of rent.

5. Security Deposit. On execution of this lease, Lessee deposits with Lessor_____
Dollars ($_____), receipt of which is acknowledged by Lessor, as security for the faithful
performance by Lessee of the terms hereof, to be returned to Lessee, without interest, except where required by law,
on the full and faithful performance by him of the provisions hereof.

6. Quiet Enjoyment. Lessor covenants that on paying the rent and performing the covenants herein contained,
Lessee shall peacefully and quietly have, hold, and enjoy the demised premises for the agreed term.

7. Use of Premises. The demised premises shall be used and occupied by Lessee exclusively as a private single
family residence, and neither the premises nor any part thereof shall be used at any time during the term of this
lease by Lessee for the purpose of carrying on any business, profession, or trade of any kind, or for any purpose
other than as a private single family residence. Lessee shall comply with all the sanitary laws, ordinances, rules, and
orders of appropriate governmental authorities affecting the cleanliness, occupancy, and preservation of the demised
premises, and the sidewalks connected thereto, during the term of this lease.

8. Number of Occupants. Lessee agrees that the demised premises shall be occupied by no more than _____
_____ persons, consisting of _____ adults and _____
children under the age of _____ years, without the written consent of Lessor.

Figure 22.2 Residential Lease

Figure 22.2 *(Continued)*

9. Condition of Premises. Lessee stipulates that he or she has examined the demised premises, including the grounds and all buildings and improvements, and that they are, at the time of this lease, in good order, repair, and in a safe, clean, and tenantable condition.

10. Keys. Lessee will be given _____ key(s) to the premises and _____ mailbox key(s). If all keys are not returned to Lessor following termination of lease, Lessee shall be charged _____ Dollars ($_____).

11. Locks. Lessee agrees not to change locks on any door or mailbox without first obtaining Lessor's written permission. Having obtained written permission, Lessee agrees to pay for changing the locks and to provide Lessor with one duplicate key per lock.

12. Lockout. If Lessee becomes locked out of the premises after management's regular stated business hours, Lessee will be required to secure a private locksmith to regain entry at Lessee's sole expense.

13. Parking. Any parking that may be provided is strictly self park and is at owner's risk. Parking fees are for a license to park only. No bailment or bailee custody is intended. Lessor is not responsible for, nor does Lessor assume any liability for, damages caused by fire, theft, casualty, or any other cause whatsoever with respect to any vehicle or its contents. Snow removal is the responsibility of the vehicle owner. Any tenant who wishes to rent a parking space or garage must sign a Parking Space or Garage Rental Agreement.

14. Assignment and Subletting. Without the prior written consent of Lessor, Lessee shall not assign this lease, or sublet or grant any concession or license to use the premises or any part thereof. A consent by Lessor to one assignment, subletting, concession, or license shall not be deemed to be a consent to any subsequent assignment, subletting, concession, or license. An assignment, subletting, concession, or license without the prior written consent of Lessor, or an assignment or subletting by operation of law, shall be void and shall, at Lessor's option, terminate this lease.

15. Alterations and Improvements. Lessee shall make no alterations to the buildings on the demised premises or construct any building or make other improvements on the demised premises without the prior written consent of Lessor. All alterations, changes, and improvements built, constructed, or placed on the demised premises by Lessee, with the exception of fixtures removable without damage to the premises and movable personal property, shall, unless otherwise provided by written agreement between Lessor and Lessee, be the property of Lessor and remain on the demised premises at the expiration or sooner termination of this lease.

16. Damage to Premises. If the demised premises, or any part thereof, shall be partially damaged by fire or other casualty not due to Lessee's negligence or willful act or that of his employee, family, agent, or visitor, the premises shall be promptly repaired by Lessor and there shall be an abatement of rent corresponding with the time during which, and the extent to which, the leased premises may have been untenantable; but, if the leased premises should be damaged other than by Lessee's negligence or willful act or that of his employee, family, agent, or visitor to the extent that Lessor shall decide not to rebuild or repair, the term of this lease shall end and the rent shall be prorated up to the time of the damage.

17. Dangerous Materials. Lessee shall not keep or have on the leased premises any article or thing of a dangerous, inflammable, or explosive character that might unreasonably increase the danger of fire on the leased premises or that might be considered hazardous or extra hazardous by any responsible insurance company.

18. Utilities. Lessee shall be responsible for arranging for and paying for all utility services required on the premises, except that _____ shall be provided by Lessor.

(continued)

Figure 22.2 *(Continued)*

19. Right of Inspection. Lessor and his or her agents shall have the right at all reasonable times during the term of this lease and any renewal thereof to enter the demised premises for the purpose of inspecting the premises and all building and improvements thereon.

20. Maintenance and Repair. Lessee will, at his sole expense, keep and maintain the leased premises and appurtenances in good and sanitary condition and repair during the term of this lease and any renewal thereof. In particular, Lessee shall keep the fixtures in the house or on or about the leased premises in good order and repair; keep the furnace clean; keep the electric bells in order; keep the walks free from dirt and debris; and, at his sole expense, shall make all required repairs to the plumbing, range, heating, apparatus, and electric and gas fixtures whenever damage thereto shall have resulted from Lessee's misuse, waste, or neglect or that of his employee, family, agent, or visitor. Major maintenance and repair of the leased premises, not due to Lessee's misuse, waste, or neglect or that of his employee, family, agent, or visitor shall be the responsibility of Lessor or his assigns. Lessee agrees that no signs shall be placed or painting done on or about the leased premises by Lessee or at his direction without the prior written consent of Lessor.

21. Painting. Lessor reserves the right to determine when the dwelling will be painted unless there is any law to the contrary.

22. Insurance. Lessor has obtained insurance to cover fire damage to the building itself and liability insurance to cover certain personal injuries occurring as a result of property defects or Lessor negligence. Lessor's insurance does not cover Lessee's possessions or Lessee's negligence. Unless the opt-out clause below is initialed by both Lessee and Lessor, Lessee must obtain a renter's insurance policy to cover damage or loss of personal possessions as well as losses resulting from Lessee's negligence.

    Opt-Out Clause:

    _____ Lessee and Lessor must both initial and date here if the requirement that Lessee obtain renter's insurance is waived. If the requirement is waived, Lessee will not be required to obtain renter's insurance. Lessor's insurance policy does not cover damages or loss of Lessee's personal possessions as well as losses resulting from Lessee's negligence.

23. Pets. Pets shall not be allowed without the prior written consent of the Lessor. At the time of signing this lease, Lessee shall pay to Lessor, in trust, a deposit of _____ Dollars ($_____), to be held and disbursed for pet damages to the Premises (if any) as provided by law. This deposit is in addition to any other security deposit stated in this lease. Any Lessee who wishes to keep a pet in the rented unit must sign a Pet Agreement Addendum.

24. Display of Signs. During the last _____ days of this lease, Lessor or his or her agent shall have the privilege of displaying the usual "For Sale" or "For Rent" or "Vacancy" signs on the demised premises and of showing the property to prospective purchasers or tenants.

25. Rules and Regulations. Lessor's existing rules and regulations, if any, shall be signed by Lessee, attached to this agreement and incorporated into it. Lessor may adopt other rules and regulations at a later time provided that he or she has a legitimate purpose, not modify Lessee's rights substantially and not become effective without notice of at least two (2) weeks.

26. Subordination of Lease. This lease and Lessee's leasehold interest hereunder are and shall be subject, subordinate, and inferior to any liens or encumbrances now or hereafter placed on the demised premises by Lessor, all advances made under any such liens or encumbrances, the interest payable on any such liens or encumbrances, and any and all renewals or extensions of such liens or encumbrances.

Figure 22.2 (*Continued*)

27. Holdover by Lessee. Should Lessee remain in possession of the demised premises with the consent of Lessor after the natural expiration of this lease, a new month-to-month tenancy shall be created between Lessor and Lessee, which shall be subject to all the terms and conditions hereof but shall be terminated on _____ days' written notice served by either Lessor or Lessee on the other party.

28. Notice of Intent to Vacate. *[This paragraph applies only when this Agreement is or has become a month-to-month Agreement.]* Lessor shall advise Lessee of any changes in terms of tenancy with advance notice of at least 30 days. Changes may include notices of termination, rent adjustments, or other reasonable changes in the terms of this Agreement.

29. Surrender of Premises. At the expiration of the lease term, Lessee shall quit and surrender the premises hereby demised in as good state and condition as they were at the commencement of this lease, reasonable use and wear thereof and damages by the elements excepted.

30. Default. If any default is made in the payment of rent, or any part thereof, at the times hereinbefore specified, or if any default is made in the performance of or compliance with any other term or condition hereof, the lease, at the option of Lessor, shall terminate and be forfeited, and Lessor may reenter the premises and remove all persons therefrom. Lessee shall be given written notice of any default or breach, and termination and forfeiture of the lease shall not result if, within _____ days of receipt of such notice, Lessee has corrected the default or breach or has taken action reasonably likely to effect such correction within a reasonable time.

31. Abandonment. If at any time during the term of this lease Lessee abandons the demised premises or any part thereof, Lessor may, at his or her option, enter the demised premises by any means without being liable for any prosecution therefor, and without becoming liable to Lessee for damages or for any payment of any kind whatever, and may, at his or her discretion, as agent for Lessee, relet the demised premises, or any part thereof, for the whole or any part of the then unexpired term and may receive and collect all rent payable by virtue of such reletting, and, at Lessor's option, hold Lessee liable for any difference between the rent that would have been payable under this lease during the balance of the unexpired term, if this lease had continued in force, and the net rent for such period realized by Lessor by means of such reletting. If Lessor's right of reentry is exercised following abandonment of the premises by Lessee, then Lessor may consider any personal property belonging to Lessee and left on the premises to also have been abandoned, in which case Lessor may dispose of all such personal property in any manner Lessor shall deem proper and is hereby relieved of all liability for doing so.

32. Binding Effect. The covenants and conditions herein contained shall apply to and bind the heirs, legal representatives, and assigns of the parties hereto, and all covenants are to be construed as conditions of this lease.

33. Radon Gas Disclosure. As required by law, (Landlord) (Seller) makes the following disclosure: "Radon Gas is a naturally occurring radioactive gas that, when it has accumulated in a building in sufficient quantities, may present health risks to persons who are exposed to it over time. Levels of radon that exceed federal and state guidelines have been found in buildings in every state. Additional information regarding radon and radon testing may be obtained from your county public health unit."

34. Lead Paint Disclosure. "Housing built before 1978 may contain lead-based paint. Lead from paint, paint chips, and dust can pose health hazards if not managed properly. Lead exposure is especially harmful to young children and pregnant women. Before renting pre1978 housing, lessors must disclose the presence of known lead-based paint and/or lead-based paint hazards in the dwelling. Lessees must also receive a federally approved pamphlet on lead poisoning prevention."

35. Severability. If any portion of this lease shall be held to be invalid or unenforceable for any reason, the remaining provisions shall continue to be valid and enforceable. If a court finds that any provision of this lease is invalid or unenforceable, but that by limiting such provision it would become valid and enforceable, then such provision shall be deemed to be written, construed, and enforced as so limited.

(continued)

Figure 22.2 (*Continued*)

36. Other Terms: _____

_____

_____

_____

_____

_____

_____

_____

_____

_____

_____

_____

_____

_____

_____

_____

_____

_____

_____

_____

_____

_____

_____

IN WITNESS WHEREOF, the parties have executed this lease the day and year first written above.

Lessor: _____   Lessee: _____

Lessor: _____   Lessee: _____

NOTICE: State law establishes rights and obligations for parties to rental agreements. This agreement is required to comply with the Truth in Renting Act or the applicable Landlord Tenant Statute or code of your state. If you have a question about the interpretation or legality of a provision of this agreement, you may want to seek assistance from a lawyer or other qualified person.

NOTICE: Contact your local county real estate board for additional forms that may be required to meet your specific needs.

Monthly Rental Agreement

THIS AGREEMENT, entered into this _____ day of _____ , 20____, by and
between_____, hereinafter Lessor,
and _____, hereinafter Lessee.

WITNESSETH: That for and in consideration of the payment of the rents and the performance of the covenants
contained on the part of Lessee, said Lessor does hereby demise and let unto Lessee, and Lessee hires from Lessor
those premises described as: _____
_____,
located at: _____
_____,
for a tenancy from month-to-month commencing on the _____ day of _____,
20____, and at a monthly rental of _____ Dollars
($_____) per month, payable monthly in advance on the _____
day of each and every month, on the following **TERMS AND CONDITIONS:**

1. Form of Payment. Lessee agrees to pay rent each month in the form of one personal check, OR one cashier's
check, OR one money order made out to _____.

2. Delivery of Payment. Rent will be paid:
      ❑ in person, at _____
      ❑ by mail, to _____

3. Returned Checks. If, for any reason, a check used by Lessee to pay Lessor is returned without having been paid,
Lessee will pay a charge of _____ Dollars
($_____) as additional rent AND take whatever other consequences there might be in
making a late payment. After the second time a Lessee's check is returned, Lessee must thereafter secure a cashier's
check or money order for payment of rent.

4. Late Payments. For any rent payment not paid by the date due, Lessee shall pay a late fee in the amount of
_____ Dollars ($_____).

5. Prorated First Month. For the period from Lessee's move-in date, _____ 20_____,
through the end of the month, Lessee will pay to Lessor a prorated monthly rent of _____
Dollars ($_____). This amount will be paid on or before the date the Lessee moves in.

6. Occupants. The said premises shall be occupied by no more than _____ adults and _____
children.

7. Pets. Pets shall not be allowed without the prior written consent of the Lessor. At the time of signing this lease,
Lessee shall pay to Lessor, in trust, a deposit of _____ Dollars
($_____), to be held and disbursed for pet damages to the Premises (if any) as
provided by law. This deposit is in addition to any other security deposit stated in this lease. Any Lessee who wishes
to keep a pet in the rented unit must sign a Pet Agreement Addendum.

8. Parking. Any parking that may be provided is strictly self park and is at owner's risk. Parking fees are for a
license to park only. No bailment or bailee custody is intended. Lessor is not responsible for, nor does Lessor assume
any liability, for damages caused by fire, theft, casualty, or any other cause whatsoever with respect to any vehicle or
its contents. Snow removal is the responsibility of the vehicle owner. Any tenant who wishes to rent a parking space
or garage must sign a Parking Space or Garage Rental Agreement.

Figure 22.3 Monthly Rental Agreement   *(continued)*

Figure 22.3 (*Continued*)

9. Ordinances and Statutes. Lessee shall comply with all statutes, ordinances, and requirements of all municipal, state, and federal authorities now in force, or which may hereafter be in force, pertaining to the use of the premises.

10. Repairs or Alterations. Lessee shall be responsible for damages caused by his or her negligence and that of his or her family or invitees and guests. Lessee shall not paint, paper, or otherwise redecorate or make alterations to the premises without the prior written consent of Lessor. All alterations, additions, or improvements made to the premises with the consent of Lessor shall become the property of Lessor and shall remain and be surrendered with the premises.

11. Painting. Lessor reserves the right to determine when the dwelling will be painted unless there is any law to the contrary.

12. Keys. Lessee will be given _____ key(s) to the premises and _____ mailbox key(s). If all keys are not returned to Lessor following termination of lease, Lessee shall be charged _____ Dollars ($_____).

13. Locks. Lessee agrees not to change locks on any door or mailbox without first obtaining Lessor's written permission. Having obtained written permission, Lessee agrees to pay for changing the locks and to provide Lessor with one duplicate key per lock.

14. Upkeep of Premises. Lessee shall keep and maintain the premises in a clean and sanitary condition at all times, and upon the termination of the tenancy shall surrender the premises to Lessor in as good condition as when received, ordinary wear and damage by the elements excepted.

15. Assignment and Subletting. Lessee shall not assign this Agreement or sublet any portion of the premises without prior written consent of Lessor.

16. Utilities. Lessee shall be responsible for the payment of all utilities and services, except _____ _____, which shall be paid by Lessor.

17. Default. If Lessee shall fail to pay rent when due, or perform any term hereof, after not less than three (3) days written notice of such default given in the manner required by law, Lessor, at his option, may terminate all rights of Lessee hereunder, unless Lessee, within said time, shall cure such default. If Lessee abandons or vacates the property, while in default of the payment of rent, Lessor may consider any property left on the premises to be abandoned and may dispose of the same in any manner allowed by law.

18. Security. The security deposit in the amount of _____ Dollars ($_____), shall secure the performance of Lessee's obligations hereunder. Lessor may, but shall not be obligated to, apply all or portions of said deposit on account of Lessee's obligations hereunder. Any balance remaining upon termination shall be returned, without interest, to Lessee. Lessee shall not have the right to apply the security deposit in payment of the last month's rent.

19. Right of Entry. Lessor reserves the right to enter the demised premises at all reasonable hours for the purpose of inspection, and whenever necessary to make repairs and alterations to the demised premises. Lessee hereby grants permission to Lessor to show the demised premises to prospective purchasers, mortgagees, tenants, workmen, or contractors at reasonable hours of the day.

20. Deposit Refunds. The balance of all deposits shall be refunded within two (2) weeks (21 days in California and Wisconsin) from date possession is delivered to Lessor, together with a statement showing any charges made against such deposits by Lessor.

Figure 22.3 *(Continued)*

21. Termination. This Agreement and the tenancy hereby granted may be terminated at any time by either party hereto by giving to the other party not less than one full month's prior notice in writing.

22. Insurance. Lessor has obtained insurance to cover fire damage to the building itself and liability insurance to cover certain personal injuries occurring as a result of property defects or Lessor negligence. Lessor's insurance does not cover Lessee's possessions or Lessee's negligence. Unless the opt-out clause below is initialed by both Lessee and Lessor, Lessee must obtain a renter's insurance policy to cover damage or loss of personal possessions as well as losses resulting from Lessee's negligence.

Opt-Out Clause:

_____ Lessee and Lessor must both initial and date here if the requirement that Lessee obtain renter's insurance is waived. If the requirement is waived, Lessee will not be required to obtain renter's insurance. Lessor's insurance policy does not cover damages or loss of Lessee's personal possessions as well as losses resulting from Lessee's negligence.

23. Attorney's Fees. The prevailing party in an action brought for the recovery of rent or other moneys due or to become due under this lease or by reason of a breach of any covenant herein contained or for the recovery of the possession of said premises, or to compel the performance of anything agreed to be done herein, or to recover for damages to said property, or to enjoin any act contrary to the provision hereof, shall be awarded all of the costs in connection therewith, including, but not by way of limitation, reasonable attorney's fees.

24. Rules and Regulations. Lessor's existing rules and regulations, if any, shall be signed by Lessee, attached to this agreement and incorporated into it. Lessor may adopt other rules and regulations at a later time provided that they have a legitimate purpose, not modify Lessee's rights substantially, and not become effective without notice of at least two (2) weeks.

25. Radon Gas Disclosure. As required by law, (Landlord) (Seller) makes the following disclosure: "Radon Gas is a naturally occurring radioactive gas that, when it has accumulated in a building in sufficient quantities, may present health risks to persons who are exposed to it over time. Levels of radon that exceed federal and state guidelines have been found in buildings in every state. Additional information regarding radon and radon testing may be obtained from your county public health unit."

26. Lead Paint Disclosure. "Housing built before 1978 may contain lead-based paint. Lead from paint, paint chips, and dust can pose health hazards if not managed properly. Lead exposure is especially harmful to young children and pregnant women. Before renting pre-1978 housing, lessors must disclose the presence of known lead-based paint and/or lead-based paint hazards in the dwelling. Lessees must also receive a federally approved pamphlet on lead poisoning prevention."

27. Additional Terms and Conditions. _____
_____
_____
_____
_____
_____
_____
_____
_____
_____
_____

(continued)

Figure 22.3 (*Continued*)

IN WITNESS WHEREOF, the parties hereto have executed this Agreement in duplicate the day and year first written above.

Signed in the presence of:

Witness _____   Lessee _____

Witness _____   Lessor _____

NOTICE: State law establishes rights and obligations for parties to rental agreements. This agreement is required to comply with the Truth in Renting Act or the applicable Landlord Tenant Statute or code of your state. If you have a question about the interpretation or legality of a provision of this agreement, you may want to seek assistance from a lawyer or other qualified person.

treat your property. Regardless of the make and model, if it is neat and clean, you may have neat and clean tenants.

◆ *Their attitude:* Are the people respectful of you, and are their questions intelligent and fair without undue criticism? Did they wipe their feet before coming in? Were they smoking on the way in? The way they treat your property the first time they see it says a lot about how they will treat it as tenants.

◆ *Prepared to rent:* If the prospects are ready to fill out an application and provide a check for the application fee, the process should move along quickly.

Application Process

If a prospective tenant is interested in renting a unit after a showing, be ready to hand over an application and the information necessary to get the process moving smoothly. Be ready to do the following:

◆ Use a quality rental application that conforms to local laws and explain it carefully to each prospective tenant. Inform them you will be running a credit check, and that their application fee will pay for the cost.

- ◆ Provide them a fax number and encourage them to return the application quickly.
- ◆ Start the credit check immediately. Require each prospective tenant to fill out a credit application.

Lease Signing

Make sure your lease conforms to local laws and clearly states your requirements for the tenant relationship. Your attorney should review the lease language every year to see if any changes should be made.

Also, make sure you set a deadline for the signed lease to be returned with the security deposit. The lease signing is a good time to review all rental policies with your new tenant. Provide a written copy of these policies and make sure your tenants understand the logic behind the property rules and regulations. In addition:

- ◆ *Set firm boundaries with problem tenants and late payers.* If your lease has set specific terms for dealing with late payments or disruptive behavior on the property, enforce them. It might not hurt to go over your planned conversation with your attorney.
- ◆ *Inspect your property regularly.* Check every square inch of each unit at least once every six months. But there are limits; a tenant has a right to privacy. Some state laws allow landlords to enter to make health and safety inspections. However, in nearly all cases, the tenant must have notice that the landlord plans to enter or has entered the premises.

Managing Risk

The possibility of losing some or all of their hard-earned real estate investments is something most landlords do not want to even consider. Unfortunately, the possibility of this happening is real, and it can occur in unforeseen ways. As a landlord, you face countless risks associated with property management and maintenance. Damage from lightning, fire, water, wind, and hail—not to mention personal injury claims from a tenant or even from visitors to your properties—costs building owners and managers hundreds of millions of dollars each year.

How do you manage these risks without spending huge sums annually? How do you ensure that your own personal finances and property are protected? How do you ensure that you and your family or heirs are protected from unexpected losses? Managing these risks and balancing the cost benefit equation requires you to take action on several fronts.

First, incorporate as your principal means of asset protection in the event of a lawsuit. The proper incorporation plan keeps personal assets (home, cars, savings, and investments) free from any claim should rental properties experience unreasonable and unexpected claims. The added tax benefits of incorporation are a bonus. Second, establish a well-defined and cost-effective risk management program with these four steps:

1. Purchase a variety of insurance plans to reduce the risk of loss for specific perils.
2. Transfer some risk to a third party (e.g., your tenant) by insisting that each tenant carry renter's insurance or sign tenant's self-insured responsibility forms. For more information and help on renter's insurance, visit www.completelandlord .com, where you can also learn about the Minotaur Insurance Renter's Insurance Program for Landlords.
3. Use higher deductible levels on your insurance policies to reduce premiums.
4. Practice good loss reduction strategies—keeping the building in good repair and leasing to quality tenants.

Four Types of Insurance Coverage Landlords Should Carry

At a minimum, residential rental property owners should carry the following four types of insurance coverage:

1. *Property and casualty insurance:* A P&C policy, as it is called in the trade, in its most basic form will provide you with protection against damage to the property from events as diverse as civil commotion, glass breakage, and vandalism to lightning, fire, smoke, or damage resulting from a car running into your building. P&C insurance also provides protection against lost income if a unit is uninhabitable due to a peril covered under your policy.

Four Types of Insurance Coverage Landlords Should Carry (*Continued*)

2. *General liability insurance:* This kind of coverage insures you against claims by third parties (e.g., tenants or visitors) for negligence, damage caused to the property of a tenant or visitor to your property, injury to someone on the premises, or damage or harm to a third party who may be working on your property. Falling on a slippery stair and physical harm to a visitor or tenant due to a faulty handrail are examples of the kinds of risks managed by a general liability insurance policy.

3. *Flood insurance and/or water damage insurance:* As the name implies, this coverage protects against any sort of water damage except sewer back-up. Such insurance takes in a considerable range: accidental damage as a result of malfunctioning plumbing, heating, refrigeration, or air conditioning systems, as well as water damage caused by nature, such as rain or snow. Normally this sort of coverage is in addition or an endorsement to a basic property insurance policy. A provision in most property insurance policies excludes water damage caused by floods. Often people in areas susceptible to floods (or to hurricanes) must rely on federal government backed insurance programs to cover this sort of risk.

4. *Umbrella liability insurance:* For most businesses—and landlording should be treated as a business—this is coverage beyond that which a basic liability insurance policy provides and comes into force after the basic policy has paid the maximum it will pay. In other words, this is insurance against an unexpected, even catastrophic loss; a basic policy is sufficient only for basic needs and losses.

Depending on whether you have employees, your P&C policy and general liability insurance coverage should include:

♦ A dwelling policy that will protect your property against: riot, civil commotion, vandalism, theft, glass breakage, lightning, wind, hail, volcanic eruption, fire, smoke, explosion, and damage from an automobile or airplane impact.

♦ Liability for tenant and guest injuries.

♦ Crime policy and a fidelity bond to protect against employees and other burglary and theft.

♦ Loss of rental income.

♦ Beyond the mandatory workmen's compensation insurance required of all employers, additional coverages to consider if you have employees include: libel and slander by employees against tenants; discrimination lawsuits filed by disgruntled employees; and allegations of fraud, misrepresentation, and other intentional acts by employees.

Insured and Bonded

To reduce general liability insurance premiums, you should require a certificate of insurance from any contractor or repairman working on your rental properties. The certificate of insurance will give you proof that these contractors have adequate levels of liability insurance and are up-to-date on their workmen's compensation insurance. If they do not have adequate insurance, any damages become your liability and will increase both your risk exposure and insurance premiums.

As added insurance that your contractors will complete a job, require a surety bond that will allow you to hire another contractor to complete the work at the surety bonding company's expense should your contractor leave your job unfinished.

Renter's Insurance or Self-Insured Responsibility

As part of your risk management program, require tenants to provide proof of renter's insurance coverage prior to taking possession and occupying the premises. Should you decide not to require renter's insurance, you and your tenants may initial the decline option to opt out of this requirement. Minotaur Insurance Agency provides easy access to a basic renter's insurance policy that is backed by A. M. Best A-rated national insurance underwriter and accepts all applicants. Most renter's insurance policies provide coverage against everything from fire and theft to personal property and personal liability coverage for injuries and damages caused by tenant neglect. In essence, this provides an extra layer of liability protection for you as a landlord—at no cost to you. An added benefit is the natural inclination of tenants to take greater care of your property when they are required explicitly to take responsibilities for their actions.

Four Ways to Reduce Risk and Limit Personal Liability

Here are four ways to reduce your risks and limit your personal liability as a landlord:

1. Maintain adequate P&C coverage and general liability insurance coverage on your rental property.
2. Use the CompleteLandlord Incorporation Kit to form a separate business entity to hold the title to your rental property, with a separate corporation for each property to provide maximum protection. Talk to your accountant or lawyer to ensure you maintain a separate identity for the company in practice by not commingling funds and to learn about other easy-to-avoid traps.
3. Practice risk management techniques that reduce your risks and personal liability as a landlord, such as requiring scheduled maintenance and inspections.
4. Use the tools like those available on www.Completelandlord.com to screen prospective tenants for credit history, criminal background, eviction history, and other determining factors to ensure you accept only high-quality tenants.

IMPORTANT TIP

Tenants who pay their rent on time, show respect for the property, and are pleasant to deal with are what every landlord hopes for. If you have tenants such as this, do your best to keep them happy even consider rewarding them with a rent discount.

Important Deductions for Landlords

- *Interest expenses:* Landlords can deduct mortgage interest payments and interest on construction loans used to acquire or improve rental property. Credit card interest on expenditures for goods or services used in a rental activity is also deductible.
- *Property depreciation:* Residential rental property must be depreciated over 27.5 years.
- *Property repairs:* The costs of repairs to rental property are fully deductible during the year they happen. Replacing broken

(continued)

Important Deductions for Landlords (*Continued*)

windows, security equipment, floors, gutters, and other structural features are examples of repairs that can be deducted.

- *Local travel:* Landlords are allowed to deduct the cost of travel related strictly to their rental activity. Landlords have the option of using the standard mileage rate deduction or actual expenses, which include vehicle repairs, upkeep, and gasoline, whichever is more advantageous.
- *Out-of-town travel:* Any landlord traveling overnight for their rental activity can deduct airfare, hotel bills, meals, and other expenses. Remember to document these expenses carefully.
- *Insurance related to the rental business:* Fire, theft, liability, and flood insurance related to the rental property are possible deductions. Likewise, health and workmen's compensation insurance may also be eligible for deduction.
- *Home office:* Landlords may deduct their home office expenses from their taxable income if they meet requirements for doing so. This deduction may also apply to workshops or other workspace exclusive to the rental business.
- *Employees/independent contractors:* Any formal hires of full-time, part-time, or contractor labor for the real estate business can be deducted as a rental business expense.
- *Casualty/theft losses:* If rental property is damaged or destroyed by a weather event or foul play, it is possible to get a tax deduction for all or part of the loss. However, the amount of the deduction depends on how much property was destroyed and how much of the loss was covered by insurance.
- *Legal/professional services:* Fees to attorneys, accountants, property management companies, real estate investment advisors, and other property-related professionals can be deducted as operating expenses as long as they relate solely to rental activity.

IMPORTANT TIP

Some landlords have been known to withhold a renter's security deposit when he or she is moving out to cover house cleaning, carpet cleaning, and perhaps repainting. But unless these chores were necessary because of the tenant's unreasonable use of the rental, such deductions are not

---

IMPORTANT TIP (*Continued*)

proper. A renter can argue that the security deposit should not be used toward ordinary wear and tear during his or her occupancy. You might consider producing a checklist (included with the lease agreement) of how you expect the unit to be left when the tenant moves out so there is no confusion at the end of the tenant's stay.

It's Your Choice

The decision to become a landlord should begin with a personal assessment and end with a business assessment. Some workdays may be 24/7, and the battle to monitor costs is constant. Investors need to be ready for this lifestyle change, or consider a passive investment in real estate instead. Not everyone is up for the stress, strain, and time commitment that active real estate investment brings. But that does not mean real estate should not be part of your total investment portfolio. You can own real estate properties through investment vehicles such as individual real estate stocks, limited partnerships, real estate mutual funds, REITs, and others.

The advantage of this market approach to real estate investment is clear: You carry no mortgage debt and spend no time examining individual properties and then jockeying to get your hands on them. You are basically turning your real estate investment decision over to professionals—management is out of your hands. The disadvantage of this strategy is that if you fail to pick successful funds or REITs, or you fail to diversify your choice of individual stocks, you stand to lose at least a portion of your investment. It is also likely that your dollar returns will be lower than those you might reap in an individual real estate deal, providing it is successful. But diversification provides protection from the market's severe highs and lows, so it is an investment path worth considering.

Remember, whether you own investment real estate by yourself or through stocks or structured investment products, when the real estate market is up, it is likely that all your picks will be doing well; if it is down, only the quality choices will survive.

CHAPTER 23

When the Rent Check Does Not Arrive: A Primer in Cash Flow Management

Take a look around at your friends, family, and colleagues, and it's not hard to see that cash flow management comes easier for some than others. Your parents, for example, may have managed cash by saving like crazy and spending cautiously. Your best friend, on other hand, may be up to his ears in debt thanks to his new sports car and 5,000-square-foot home. Both are probably pretty happy with their financial situations, yet neither would approve of the other's cash management tactics.

As a landlord, you'll want to take an in-depth look at your own financial management skills and come up with a way to deal with income fluctuations, unexpected expenses, and other issues that can put a dent in your cash reserves. Ensuring a steady cash flow from your rental investment involves more than simply hanging out the For Rent sign. The reality is that apartments can go unrented for three to six months at a time, and many tenants leave their units in serious disrepair, costing owners time and money to fix.

One way to make sure that rent check arrives on time, every time, is by using monthly rental agreements. Visit www.completelandlord.com/store/monthlyrental-agreement.aspx to get your hands on agreements for all 50 states. The forms are legally approved and up to date.

Cash flow is the lifeblood of any business, and smart real estate investors plan for the inevitable surprises inherent in the business. The common lags between income received and payments due to others, including mortgage, utilities, and other basic expenses of real estate ownership, are the problem. The solution is cash flow management.

Cash Flow Management

The time to focus on the issue of cash flow is before closing. It should be a key part of your investment planning in the weeks and months before you buy. Here are some issues you need to consider:

- ◆ *Budget for the good, bad, and ugly.* Good means that all units are rented to considerate tenants who pay their rent in full on the due date. Bad is when the economy is a little off, and perhaps the rent checks do not all arrive on time. Ugly is the perfect storm of deadbeat tenants and poor treatment of your property. Envisioning the best—and worst—case scenarios of your particular situation may force you to reevaluate your philosophy about having money in the bank. You need to create a financial contingency plan, even if you never have to use it.
- ◆ *Forecast what you will need going forward.* As a first-time real estate investor, your business is a start-up. As the owner of this new business, you need to know how much cash you will need to pay expenses throughout each month and over an entire year. Now is the time to find out what other property owners in your target neighborhood are charging.
- ◆ *Plan the major expenditures in advance.* If you know your 15-year-old roof is on year 13, it is time to start setting money aside for a new roof. Cash flow management involves more than just getting by month-to-month. Larger expenses should be built into your rent structure as well.
- ◆ *Boost your receivables.* Receivables comprise all of the money that's coming into your landlording business. As a goodwill gesture to tenants, consider giving them a 3 to 5 percent discount off their rent if they pay five days early. You might also consider charging a late fee, which can always come out of their security

deposit. You want to create incentives for steady, predictable money coming in the door.

◆ *Watch your expenses.* Avoid sinking a lot of money into cosmetic items for your property, and keep a close eye on the maintenance and working order of appliances, plumbing, and electrical service in the tenant units. Negotiate firm fees and scheduling issues with repairmen and other service providers so you are not paying for excess time.

◆ *Pay bills carefully.* Do not pay bills early unless you are offered a discount for doing so. Pay bills exactly on the day you need to get them in the mail to arrive on time. Better yet, convert to automatic bill payment so you save postage and time.

◆ *Start your emergency fund first.* A cash cushion during your business start-up is essential until you get the rhythm of property management down. If a few years pass and you never quite get the hang of it and property values are up, consider selling. The life of a landlord may not be for you—or your wallet.

◆ *Do an annual checkup.* Your cash flow issues will vary, perhaps considerably, from one year to the next. Though rent levels may rise over the years, you may be faced with large capital expenditures in some years. Designate a time each year to review your financial situation and make necessary adjustments.

IMPORTANT TIP

If dealing with numbers makes you nervous, hire professional help. As you interview tax professionals or bring your investment goals to a financial planner, ask them to help you work out key cash flow issues for your investment property. That is, after all, what you are paying them for.

Crucial Calculation: The Cap Rate

To determine whether a property you buy will generate a positive cash flow, you'll want to figure out the *cap rate,* or a property's net operating income as a percentage of its price. Some describe the cap rate as the real estate industry's version of a bond yield.

The formula looks like this:

Cap rate = Net income (Rent − Expenses) /purchase price

Sale Price

Assume you have a property that sold for $600,000 and it has generated a net income of $60,000. The cap rate would look something like this:

$$\frac{\$60,000}{\$600,000} = 10\%$$

The bottom line is that the lower the capitalization rate, the more you have to pay for each dollar of income. Most investors strive for a cap rate of 10 percent or higher, but since prices have skyrocketed, that rate has fallen for many investors. It is wise to research how rents in the building you are considering compare with those in other nearby properties. Also take into account when area leases generally come up for renewal. Property owners should provide this information as part of a fact sheet for prospective buyers. Take this information to a trusted advisor or lawyer who can further help you crunch numbers that best fit your financial situation.

Do the Math

To ensure that you're making the best investments possible, you'll want to figure cash flow projections on all properties you are considering for purchase. It will force you to examine market conditions in the area in which you want to buy and consider expenditures for the products and services your property will need. Remember the importance of seeking advice from financial and tax professionals.

Flipping in Action: How the Pros Do It

Flipping means different things to different people. For some investors, flipping is something you do in a weekend—or a few hours just for the adrenaline rush. For others, it can be a slower, longer process that involves purchasing a property and then turning it around for sale without doing much in terms of improvements or additions.

Everyone has heard stories about investors who never even walked into the property before they bought and sold it. Others have heard of many investors who spent the better part of a year living in and fixing up a property before finally deciding to sell it—they will tell you that they are flippers, too. Insiders like to use the term *wholesaling* rather than flipping because that is exactly what they are doing—buying wholesale from a seller with hopes of selling retail to a buyer. The gap between the two prices is the profit.

The Quick, No-Frills Flip

It might be worth reviewing the basic idea of how an actual flip might work. A flipper looks in a run-down neighborhood and finds a house that is vacant—there is nobody inside and no For Sale sign in the window. With a little checking around (that might require some time down at city hall), the flipper finds the owner and offers a contract to purchase the house at 50 percent of its after-repaired value with a low earnest-money deposit (maybe $50) and the rest of the deal in cash. The buyer then renovates the property. When the time comes to sell, the profit may be only several thousand dollars, but if he or she kept his or her costs as low as possible, he or she can make money by doing this over and over again.

When you begin investing in turnover property, be sure to consider exactly who your customer is. Often, you are dealing with people in trouble, perhaps even people who do not know they are in trouble. In a foreclosure situation, for example, it may be entirely possible you will show up at the owners' door and be the first person who tells them they are about to lose their property. The bottom line is that flippers often deal with people in financial distress who have nowhere to go. You will be both rescuer and profiteer. Just remember—you set the ethics of the transaction.

Spotting the Right Properties

As indicated previously, experienced flippers do more than just drive through distressed neighborhoods and knock on doors. They read everything they can to get a picture of a particular neighborhood, including the classified and legal ads in newspapers that most people overlook. They spend time studying public documents and considering which areas will gentrify next in their community. They start by watching prices, and then contact the owner—usually by mail to start. The National Association of Realtors (NAR) publishes median prices for many local markets every quarter. Visit www.realtor.org for more information.

To find the properties, buyers scan listings in print or online for key phrases, such as "Must Sell," "Needs Work," "Vacant," or "Motivated Seller." They will target damaged properties that are priced to sell; they also will try to develop relationships with real estate agents who call them first whenever they see distressed properties. People who do this for a full-time business might launch a series of direct-mail campaigns or billboard and newspaper ad campaigns promising cash for leads on inexpensive homes.

Flippers try to find the undiscovered neighborhoods, but they also keep a careful watch on established and up-and-coming areas. Real estate bargains can be found anywhere there is a distressed property or a highly motivated seller.

Your Team

Make it your goal to work with reasonably priced, skilled contractors, and rely heavily on trusted mortgage brokers (when financing is needed), lawyers, and tax professionals to help you close deals and save money.

It helps to focus on particular categories of properties until you learn all about them and create economies of scale in buying, renovating, and selling.

Need for Low Overhead

Smart flippers work on a cash basis because that keeps their property-holding costs to a minimum. They know how to inspect properties thoroughly and do only those renovations that provide the best returns on the dollar (see Chapters 8 and 16).

Keeping costs low is critical because in many cases flippers need to work with local agents to complete the transaction. High-volume flippers may be able to negotiate commissions lower than 6 percent, but consider this example: If an investor is trying to sell a home he or she has bought and renovated for $150,000, at 6 percent agent commission, that means he or she needs to clear at least $9,000 in profit just to cover those fees alone. As mentioned in previous chapters, that is only a small part of what is needed to close the buy-and-sell portion of the transaction.

Disaster Recovery—The Next Flipping Frontier

Flippers are always looking for the best real estate bargain, including those located in areas hit by natural disasters. For example, flippers headed down to the Gulf Coast to pick up bargain real estate in the aftermath of Hurricane Katrina. Though some investors are patient enough to buy, hold, and renovate property for sale when these communities stabilize and start planning for the future, others are going in for the quick kill.

A 2005 story in the *Wall Street Journal* reported that, "In places slammed directly by the storm, such as New Orleans and coastal Mississippi and Alabama, speculators are trying to grab damaged homes at discounts while owners of intact homes are listing their properties at premium prices; in Baton Rouge, LA, crowded with evacuees, nearly any house that comes on the market disappears instantly in a bidding war."

Whether flipping is right or wrong from a moral standpoint is open to discussion. But in 2005, a year that produced the worst natural disaster in America to date, it also produced the biggest move toward individual real estate investment in history.

Tighter Scrutiny

Chapter 8 mentioned that the FBI and other branches of law enforcement are taking a closer look at flipping and its potential for cheating homeowners. In 2008, communities and the federal government began to scrutinize real estate investment practices and limit predatory practices. Investors who wish to flip property need to stay abreast of these developments.

Flipping real estate is all about the timing and choreography. True flippers move property so fast—buying, selling, and closing in a matter of hours or days—that they are today's version of the day-traders who bought and sold stock in the late 1990s. Critics have lashed out at flippers for their contribution—or alleged contribution—to overheated markets. This has drawn the attention of lawmakers and housing-related agencies who are now trying to rein in the activities of flippers.

In 2003, HUD issued a rule that said only owners of record could sell properties that will be financed with FHA mortgages. The rule also stated that for resales that occur between 91 and 180 days where the new sales price exceeds the previous sales price by 100 percent or more, FHA would require additional documentation validating the property's value. In addition, the rule provides flexibility for FHA to examine and require additional evidence of appraised value when properties are resold within 12 months.

Flipping Ethics

Flipping is not a new development in real estate, but the sheer number of people who now become millionaires doing it indicate that there will be many people out there trying to profit by cutting corners. There are ethics to be followed in any kind of business dealing, and when ethics fail, there are victims.

In flipping, the frequent victim seems to be the seller who is duped into taking a lower price than he or she should. This happens often when the seller is older, when their language skills are poor, or if they generally are unaware of the true value of their property. But there are buyer victims out there, too.

Less-than-scrupulous flippers may align themselves with equally unscrupulous brokers, appraisers, and other people who falsely inflate the market value of the property they are flipping.

It makes sense to remember the 2000 stock market when considering a career in flipping. With large numbers of people hoping to get into the business, you need to be well-educated and honest about your dealings. That way, you might be one of those who succeeds if the market grinds to a halt.

It Is All about Margin of Error

When prices are rising in a market, it is easier for investors to cover up their mistakes. But as markets cool, faulty number-crunching and over-confidence start to erode the profitability of flipping. Chicago-based Real Estate Research Corporation recently published a market study showing that many top markets have become so successful that the tide has turned from buying to selling. If everyone is now looking to get out, who is going to buy?

Ready, Aim, Fire!

Although there are many different opinions on how to flip successfully, stick with a couple of guidelines in your planning. First, zero in on properties that can be bought for 30 to 50 percent below their market value after they are fixed up. At the same time, make sure you can extract at least a 20 percent profit margin after subtracting rehab expenses, taxes,

Ready, Aim, Fire! (*Continued*)

commissions, financing, and other costs. A 20 percent profit is something of a break-even point because most interest-only loans available to buy investment properties cover 80 percent of a home's expected market value. This undoubtedly will get tougher to do as the market gets more crowded with investors, but if you cannot meet these targets, do not do the deal—it is a good way to lose money.

In the previous chapter, you learned about the need for cash flow management in the real estate investment field. The need for such management becomes even more crucial when the market starts to turn against investors. Any overspending becomes lethal to profitability. Flippers have also faced another challenge in squeezing profits out of their holdings: The low-interest-rate environment over the past decade has made property owners out of many potential renters. So the fallback position of simply renting out real estate that does not immediately sell is no longer an automatic save unless that property is located in an area where many people tend to rent.

IMPORTANT TIP

There are professional investors who can afford to hire eyes and ears everywhere they own property. But that is because they have experience and the money to do it. This is another good reason why new investors should live close to the properties they own—within 15 minutes if possible. If you are close to your property, chances are that your knowledge of the neighborhood will prevent many problems down the road. For the problems that do crop up, it will be much easier dealing with them in person.

Cost of Contingencies

As most people learn when buying their first home, real estate is fraught with strange details and unexpected problems. Flipping adds speed to uncertainty, and that can often take all the financial incentive out of a transaction. Renovations might run into zoning or permit problems with attendant fees and lost time. You might find that the tenants you have inherited are nothing but trouble, and proceedings to evict them could take months. Property development around you could sharply change your investment picture for the property you have just bought.

No one can be all-seeing when it comes to investments, but with the amount of money at stake and the potential for small, consistent loss so great, it is hard to overstress the need for research in any real estate transaction.

Easier than It May Sound

Flipping in its most basic form is not terribly complicated. Its primary steps include researching the property, moving quickly to strike a deal, renovating, selling, and repeating. True flippers work on a cash basis and know from a legal and ethical standpoint the limitations of what they can and cannot do. Flipping may seem simple, but it is a risky business. The most successful flippers are well informed, very lucky, or a combination of the two.

 The time to anticipate potential tax, earning, or management problems in real estate is *before* you buy. That is why it is critical to lean on your team of investment advisors—from your tax attorney to your best contractor—to anticipate any potential problems in your investment that might occur at a later date. As with anything in life, you'll want to be prepared and well braced for both potential pitfalls and success.

25

Careers, Networking, and Continuing Education in Professional Residential Property Investing

Residential property investing is a full-time, primary career for some, a part-time hobby for others, and a good income generation tool for still others. Exactly where you stand in the scheme of things depends on how much time you have to put it into it, what other vocations you may be involved with, and how much income you need to generate from your real estate career.

Like most real estate investors, you're probably going to start out on a part-time basis with one or two properties. If and when the fever hits—and you realize that this could actually become a profitable venture for you—then you'll probably back off on the number of hours you put into your "real" job, and devote more time to property investment.

Or you may realize that real estate property investment is simply a bragging right and tax advantage that ends at those two multifamily properties you bought a few years ago, and that you've since rented out.

As you can see, the career choices in real estate investing are virtually limitless . . . and there is no right or wrong way to go about paving your way in this industry. The person who buys two properties and hangs on to them for 10 years can be just as successful as the one who buys a new property every year, builds a team of employees to run them, and flips them every year or two.

Within the real estate field, there are a number of career "titles" that you can have, including:

- *Property manager:* A company and/or individual who is responsible for the day-to-day operations of a building, such as cleaning and trash removal; ensuring that the various systems within the building, such as the elevators, HVAC, and electrical systems, are functioning properly; and possibly collecting rents and managing tenant relations.
- *Leasing agent:* The individual assigned the responsibility, usually by the building owner, to fill the property with qualified tenants.
- *Asset manager:* Someone who balances risk and reward in managing investment portfolios, including, but not limited to, real property and improvements. Asset managers either oversee property management activities, or manage the property them-selves.
- *Accounting and finance:* These professionals handle the taxes and financial matters associated with real property investment and property management.
- *Sales and marketing:* Individuals who take care of the sales and marketing functions associated with real property.
- *Owner:* The property owner himself or herself, who may handle some or all of the tasks associated with managing, leasing, and maintaining the property.

As you can see, you have a plethora of choices to select from, and not all of them require you to spend your own money to purchase real estate. You can still be involved with—and benefit from—both finan-cially and personally—the real estate field by taking on one or more of the jobs outlined.

Full Time or Part Time?

Whether you devote 12 hours a day or 10 hours a week to your real estate career depends on what else you have going on at the time, and just how much income you want to generate from your new venture. Here are a few advantages and disadvantages to consider:

Part-Time Advantages

◆ You won't have to spend too many hours on the job.
◆ You'll be able to continue with your primary career and/or hobbies.
◆ Your lifestyle will remain the same (or close) to its current state.

Part-Time Disadvantages

◆ You probably won't make as much money.
◆ You may not be taken as seriously in the field as you would if you were in it full time.
◆ You won't be able to devote the same number of hours to important functions like networking and tenant relations.

Full-Time Advantages

◆ The more hours you put into it, the more likely you are to achieve success quickly.
◆ You won't be burning the candle at both ends by holding down multiple jobs at once.
◆ You'll gain financial rewards faster because you are putting more hours per day into your new venture.

Full-Time Disadvantages

◆ The first two years (as with any business) could be challenging as you build your new business without the help of your prior income stream.
◆ You'll have to jump in feet first and start making money as quickly as possible.
◆ You may find that your personal time is invaded by calls from tenants and other pressing issues.

One of the best ways to ensure that you're maximizing your career as a real estate investor is to leverage continuing education. CompleteLandlord.com offers a host of educational opportunities for real estate investors, as do the many real estate schools (simply Google "real estate continuing education" for options in your area) and trade groups that are devoted to the advancement of investors, property managers, and landlords.

Groups offering formal educational programs and credentials include the National Association of Residential Property Managers (NARPM) online at www.narpm.org, National Apartment Association (NAA) at www.naahq.org, and Institute of Real Estate Management (IREM) at www.irem.org. Check out any or all of these associations online to see what options best meet your needs.

Appendixes

APPENDIX A

Summary of Icon Information in Appendix

Money Savers

These sections are designed to save you money. Use the information in them to make frugal decisions regarding your cash outlay when investing in and running your properties.

Money Makers

Here's where you'll learn how to make money in real estate. Ferret out the best possible tips and advice from these sections of the book and you'll be well braced to earn a living and more from your real estate investments.

Time Savers

We know there are only so many hours in a day, so use these areas of the book to shave precious time from your schedule and maximize the time spent on your landlording and real estate investment business.

Tour of the CompleteLandlord Site with Free Trial Membership Offer

CompleteLandlord.com·
Helping 59,899 Fellow Landlords be More Productive and Profitable

| Home | Landlord Tips | Q & A Forum | Products & Services | Memberships | Resources | My CompleteLandlord |

FREE Trial for 15 Days! Join Thousands of Other Landlords Who are Increasing Profits and Receive:

. 15 Days Access to CompleteLandlord.Com Lease Creation Pro^{SM} to build custom state-specific leases, as well as access to over 900 critical state-specific landlording forms ($149 annual value)

. BONUS Free Complete Tenant Screen with credit, criminal, background, terrorist checks and more ($24.95 value)

. Access to CompleteLandlord.com Property Management Solution^{SM} - easy to use Web-based property management tool organizes tenants, income / expenses, repairs, vacancies and generates reports all in one place! ($129 annual value)

. CompleteLandlord.com Landlord Profit Letter – packed with money making ideas($89 annual value)

. FREE 50-page Special Report –Rental Property Management Secrets for Landlords! ($19.95 value)

○ Read More   *We value your Privacy*

○ Start My Free Trial

Weekly Landlord Advisor ™ Tip of the Week

Is a Property Management Company Right For You?   Date:02/11/2008

If you're tired of the hassles of being a landlord but want to keep your investments, then a property management company may be the answer. There are three different types of property management companies, each with a varying degree of involvement.

Asset management companies focus solely on the property side of being a land Continued....

Browse Hundreds more FREE Landlord Tips by Topic

BROWSE TIPS NOW

› Real Estate Tax Planning for Landlords
› Rental Property Management Ideas
› Tenant Screening for Landlords

› Problem Tenants and Handling Eviction
› Property Maintenance and Repair
› Rental Property Investment Strategies

Property Management Solution^{SM}

The **Time** Saving Property Management Tool

A comprehensive, on-demand dashboard system for all your rental properties

Try It Now

Lease Creation Pro^{SM}

The **Money** Saving Forms Automation Tool

Customizable, legally valid, state-specific residential leases & related agreements

Try It Now

Press Coverage

Forbes
REALTOR MAGAZINE ONLINE
NEW YORK POST
Property Maven
RealEstateJournal.com
REAL ESTATE update

What Members Say

"Finally! A place I can go to get the help I need to run my buildings. Your tips are really helpful!"
  – **John Herman**
Montgomery, Ohio

"This is the place to find out what one did not know they needed to know. Thanks for looking out for the landlords of the world."
  – **Mariano Travino**
TX

"Great site! Keep up the good work!"
  – **Ted Warburton**
CA

more..

Claim your FREE Special Report *Rental Property Management Secrets for Landlords!*

Reduce aggravation and headaches, improve your cash flow and increase your profits from every investment property you own!

. The 9 points you should cover in every lease
. What your lawyer didn't tell you about Fair Housing
. Write an "apartment for rent" ad that gets your phone ringing
. A 7-step process for evicting problem tenants legally
. PLUS sign up for the weekly Landlord Advisor and receive
valuable weekly advice for landlords by la

Limited Time Offer 50-page $19.95 value IN NO OBLIGATION

| Enter Primary Email Address |

○ Send Me FREE Tips   *We value your Privacy*

BBB   CONFIRMED

250

CompleteLandlord.com
Helping 59,899 Fellow Landlords be More Productive
and Profitable

> Forms, Letters & Agreements   > Tenant Screens
> Online Property Management Software
> Need-to-Know Information and Landlord Community

| Home | Landlord Tips | Q & A Forum | Products & Services | Memberships | Resources | My CompleteLandlord |

CompleteLandlord.com Forum

Please click on a Category below to begin or view a Topic.

Categories	Topics covered in this Category	Topics
Buying property	Acquiring rental properties	23
Cash Flow	Maximizing your income	12
completelandlord.com	Completelandlord.com product line	10
Contractors	Vendors, contractors and other workers	8
Disclosures	Lead paint, asbestos and more	4
Discrimination	Rentals and fair housing	8
Eviction	Dealing with problem tenants	72
Insurance	Protecting your assets	3
Landscaping	Lawn and garden	10
Late Fees	Rent collection and fees	13
Leases	Signing the agreements and customized forms	45
Legal	Understanding the law	31
Maintenance & Repairs	Fixing issues and preventive work	27
Managing 1031 Exchanges	"Starker" transactions and trading up	2
Marketing	Getting the word out	2
Miscellaneous	Questions that don't fit into any category listed	46
New Landlords	Just starting	14
Non Payment	When things go south	13
Notices to Tenants	Communicating with residents	2
Pets	Dealing with animals	8
Property Management	The big picture	19
Rent collection	Getting residents to pay	7
Section 8	Public assistance programs	5
Security	Maintaining a safe place to live	3
Security Deposits	Handling the deposit	31
Selling Property	Disposing of rental properties	9
Software / Books	Resources	2
Students	Renting to college students	2
Taxes	Landlords and the government	15
Tenant Screening	Checking credit, employment, etc.	16
Tenants	Our customer	13
Utilities	Keeping the lights, electric, gas and cable on	7

Need Help?
Or first time?
CLICK HERE

Top Ten Topics

1. Withholding a Security/Damage Deposit (11 replies)

2. Failure to return a signed lease (10 replies)

3. What to do with my tenant (9 replies)

4. Management Company Fees (8 replies)

5. How much is enough? (8 replies)

6. Are Tenant Screenings Worth the Cost? (8 replies)

7. tenant breaking lease (7 replies)

8. DO I need to use a lawyer? (6 replies)

9. Newbie Question (6 replies)

10. When to pay a contractor (5 replies)

Add to Favorites ☆

251

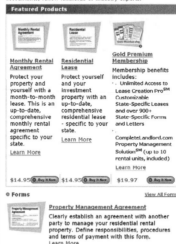

CompleteLandlord.com

Helping 59,899 Fellow Landlords be More Productive and Profitable

- Forms, Letters & Agreements
- Online Property Management Software
- Need-to-Know Information and Landlord Community
- Tenant Screens

| Home | Landlord Tips | Q & A Forum | Products & Services | Memberships | Resources | My CompleteLandlord |

Forms | Newsletters | Books | Kits & Software | Special Reports

Premium CompleteLandlord Memberships | News & Events | Legal Resources | Tenant Screen

CompleteLandlord Store

CompleteLandlord.com has brought together the products and services landlords need to be more profitable and productive. All forms have been reviewed and approved by attorneys, accountants, fellow landlords or industry experts.

Featured Products

Monthly Rental Agreement

Protect your property and yourself with a month-to-month lease. This is an up-to-date, comprehensive monthly rental agreement specific to your state.

Learn More

$14.95 Buy It Now

Residential Lease

Protect yourself and your investment property with an up-to-date, comprehensive residential lease - specific to your state.

Learn More

$14.95 Buy It Now

Gold Premium Membership

Membership benefits includes:
- Unlimited Access to Lease Creation Pro[SM] Customizable State-Specific Leases and over 900+ State-Specific Forms and Letters
- CompleteLandlord.com Property Management Solution[SM] (up to 10 rental units, included)

Learn More

$19.97 Buy It Now

⊙ **Forms**   View All Forms

Property Management Agreement

Clearly establish an agreement with another party to manage your residential rental property. Define responsibilities, procedures and terms of payment with this form.

Learn More

$9.95 Buy It Now

Monthly Rental Agreement

Protect your property and yourself with a month-to-month lease. This is an up-to-date, comprehensive monthly rental agreement specific to your state. Can be used to lease an apartment, condominium or house for a month to month lease term.

Learn More

$14.95 Buy It Now

Home | Landlord Tips | Q & A Forum | Products & Services | Memberships | Resources | My CompleteLandlord

About Us | Contact Us | Press Room | FAQs | Privacy Policy | Terms & Conditions | Site Map

Home | Landlord Tips | Q & A Forum | Products & Services | Memberships | Resources | My CompleteLandlord

Browse weekly Landlord Advisor Tips

[Search]

View All

Choose a Topic Below, and Read all the Tips in that Topic.

Real Estate Tax Planning for Landlords

The bad news about being a landlord is that all of the income that you earn from your rental units is subject to federal and state income taxes.

The good news is that tax planning for your rental property opens up many opportunities for sizable tax deductions. Although you may not actually file the taxes on your rental property yourself, as a landlord, it is very important to be familiar with tax deductions so you can keep the appropriate paper documentation for your tax records.

CompleteLandlord.com can help you with your tax planning to save you thousands of dollars and needless headaches with useful advice.

Rental Property Management Ideas

Whether you run your rental property business yourself or have a management team working with you, managing rental property has many legal facets every landlord should be knowledgeable about.

CompleteLandlord.com has put together the most important tips that will help you with your rental property management.

This section includes many topics of interest including official leases, tenant policies and special deposits. Remember, doing some of these activities yourself can end up decreasing your management costs.

Top Ten Tips

<Prev   1 2 3 4 5 6 7 8 9 10 ...   Next>

02/11/2008 **Is a Property Management Company Right For You?**
Topic: Property Management

02/04/2008 **Increase Your Bottom Line with Coin-Operated Laundry Machines**

<Prev   1 2 3 4 5 6 7 8 9 10 ...   Next>

Submit Your Tip and Earn $25

Submit a tip that gets published by CompleteLandlord.com and you will receive $25.

To learn more Click Here

Press Coverage

Forbes
REALTOR MAGAZINE ONLINE
NEW YORK POST
Property Maven
Real Estate Journal.com
REAL ESTATE WEEKLY

What Members Say

"I am a property manager and using CompleteLandlord.com has been very useful information for me. Found most of the answers I have been looking for all in one stop."
— Monica
FL

"This is the place to find out what one did not know they needed to know. Thanks for looking out for the landlords of the world."
— Mariano Travino
TX

"Great site! Keep up the good work!"
— Ted Warburton
CA

more..

CompleteLandlord.com
Premium Membership Benefits

9 Key Components	Silver	Gold	Platinum
1. Property Management SolutionSM	Up to 2 Units	Up to 10 Units	Up to 50 Units or more
Complete Tenant Tracking	Unlimited	Unlimited	Unlimited
General Ledger Accounting System	Unlimited	Unlimited	Unlimited
Management Reports	Unlimited	Unlimited	Unlimited
Dashboard	Unlimited	Unlimited	Unlimited
Resident Portal(Website)	Unlimited	Unlimited	Unlimited
2. Lease Creation ProSM **Customizable Documents**	Unlimited	Unlimited	Unlimited
Leases & Rental Agreement	Unlimited	Unlimited	Unlimited
Rental Credit Application	Unlimited	Unlimited	Unlimited
Pre-Lease and Post-Lease Inspection List	Unlimited	Unlimited	Unlimited
Garage and Parking Space Agreement	Unlimited	Unlimited	Unlimited
Pet Agreement Addendum	Unlimited	Unlimited	Unlimited
Leases, Agreements, Notices	☑	☑	☑
Applications	☑	☑	☑
Disclosures	☑	☑	☑
Letters	☑	☑	☑
Inspection Forms	☑	☑	☑
Addendums, Warnings, Surveys	☑	☑	☑
5. Archives of Landlord Profit Letter and Quarterly Issues	☑	☑	☑
6. Access to CompleteLandlord.com Library			
Special Reports			
Rental Property Management Secrets for Landlords	☑	☑	☑
Complete Guide to Conducting Tenant Screenings		☑	☑
Eviction Secrets for Landlords		☑	☑
How to Buy Foreclosure Property			☑
Understanding Rental Property 1031 Exchanges for Landlords			☑
Streaming Webinar/Audio Conferences hosted by Real Estate Experts			
Tax Planning Secrets for Landlords		☑	☑
Asset Protection Using LLCs			☑
7. Customer Care			
8. Content, Forms & Software Upgrades, Maintenance, Hosting, Storage, Multi-layer Security and Rental Unit Scaleablity	Unlimited	Unlimited	Unlimited
9. Incremental rental unit additions	$2.00/unit/mo	$1.00/unit/mo	$0.30/unit/mo
Premium Membership Monthly Price	$9.97/mo	$19.97/mo	$29.97/mo
Premium Membership Annual Price	$97/yr	$147/yr	$297/yr
Annual Membership Savings vs. Monthly Membership	(Save $22.64)	(Save $92.64)	(Save $62.64)
	Buy It Now	Buy It Now	Buy It Now

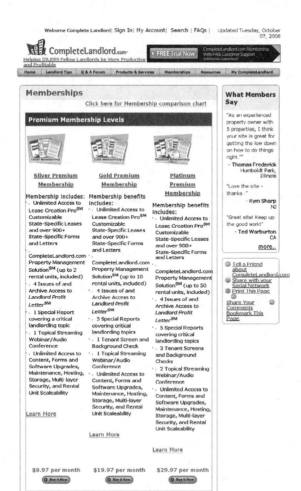

Home | Landlord Tips | Q & A Forum | Products & Services | Memberships | Resources | My CompleteLandlord

Memberships

Click here for Membership comparison chart

Premium Membership Levels

Silver Premium Membership

Membership includes:
- Unlimited Access to Lease Creation Pro℠ Customizable State-Specific Leases and over 900+ State-Specific Forms and Letters
- CompleteLandlord.com Property Management Solution℠ (up to 2 rental units, included)
- 4 Issues of and Archive Access to Landlord Profit Letter℠
- 1 Special Report covering a critical landlording topic
- 1 Topical Streaming Webinar/Audio Conference
- Unlimited Access to Content, Forms and Software Upgrades, Maintenance, Hosting, Storage, Multi-layer Security, and Rental Unit Scaleability

Learn More

$9.97 per month

Buy It Now

Gold Premium Membership

Membership benefits includes:
- Unlimited Access to Lease Creation Pro℠ Customizable State-Specific Leases and over 900+ State-Specific Forms and Letters
- CompleteLandlord.com Property Management Solution℠ (up to 10 rental units, included)
- 4 Issues of and Archive Access to Landlord Profit Letter℠
- 3 Special Reports covering critical landlording topics
- 1 Tenant Screen and Background Check
- 1 Topical Streaming Webinar/Audio Conference
- Unlimited Access to Content, Forms and Software Upgrades, Maintenance, Hosting, Storage, Multi-layer Security, and Rental Unit Scaleability

Learn More

$19.97 per month

Buy It Now

Platinum Premium Membership

Membership benefits includes:
- Unlimited Access to Lease Creation Pro℠ Customizable State-Specific Leases and over 900+ State-Specific Forms and Letters
- CompleteLandlord.com Property Management Solution℠ (up to 50 rental units, included)
- 4 Issues of and Archive Access to Landlord Profit Letter℠
- 5 Special Reports covering critical landlording topics
- 3 Tenant Screens and Background Checks
- 2 Topical Streaming Webinar/Audio Conference
- Unlimited Access to Content, Forms and Software Upgrades, Maintenance, Hosting, Storage, Multi-layer Security, and Rental Unit Scaleability

Learn More

$29.97 per month

Buy It Now

255

CompleteLandlord.com™

| Dashboard | Properties | Tenants | Accounting | Tasks | Documents | Reports |
| Admin |

| Properties || Units || Listings || Important Numbers || Announcements || Help |

Search Criteria

Properties [Add Property]

Property State:

ALL
Illinois
Idaho

Status:
Active

Sort by:
Name
Ascending

[Search]

Export data

Property	City	Status	Type		
Devonshire Bldg 1	Darien	Active	Rental		
Jay's Apartments	Chicago	Active	Rental		
K&C Apartments	Independence	Active	Rental		
sample	albama	Active	Rental		
Sample Property	Chicago	Active	Rental		
Socrates House 10	Chicago	Active	Rental		
staci	independence	Active	Rental		
Test property	Chicago	Active	Rental		
test123	chicago	Active	Rental		

Showing 1 - 9 of 9

Legend

Hover over the images for more information.

Resident statements on

Resident statements off

Update property images

Property set up for electronic payments

256

| Home | Landlord Tips | Q & A Forum | Products & Services | Memberships | Resources | My CompleteLandlord |

Welcome back, **Complete Landlord**

**Become More Productive and
Profitable Today!**

[Start My Membership Now]

Tuesday, October 07, 2008

○ Property Management Solution℠   What is this?

○ Forms   What's This?

Customizable Forms
Application & Screening Forms
Checklists
Leases, Rental Agreements & Addendums
Letters, Notices, & Disclosures
Miscellaneous
Receipts

[Browse All Forms]

Lease Creation Pro℠

Coming soon: Alaska, Delaware, Illinois and Ohio
(Standard Forms are currently available for these states).

○ Library

+ Special Reports

+ Streaming Webinar Conferences

+ Landlord Profit Letters

 Don't have Acrobat?
Click the image to the left to download.

○ Manage My Account

Personal Information
Order History
Forums
Change My Password

○ Tenant Screens   Read this First

You have 4 tenant screens available.

Tenant Screen
Tenant Screen
Tenant Screen
Tenant Screen

The link will deactivate & become gray to
allow time to process your tenant screen. If
you do not complete the process, the link will
reactivate in approximately 10 minutes.

View Reports

**Need more Tenant
Screens?**   [Click Here]

Home | Landlord Tips | Q & A Forum | Products & Services | Memberships | Resources | My
CompleteLandlord

About Us | Contact Us | Press Room | FAQs | Privacy Policy | Terms & Conditions | Site Map

Add A New Report

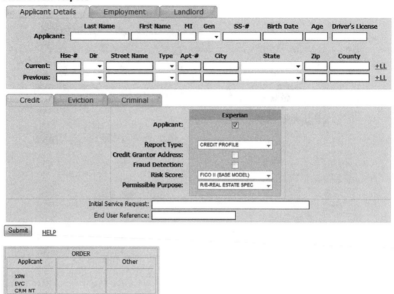

	Applicant Details	Employment	Landlord

	Last Name	First Name	MI	Gen	SS-#	Birth Date	Age	Driver's License
Applicant:								

	Hse-#	Dir	Street Name	Type	Apt-#	City	State	Zip	County	
Current:										+LL
Previous:										+LL

	Credit	Eviction	Criminal

	Experian
Applicant:	☑
Report Type:	CREDIT PROFILE
Credit Grantor Address:	☐
Fraud Detection:	☐
Risk Score:	FICO II (BASE MODEL)
Permissible Purpose:	R/E-REAL ESTATE SPEC

Initial Service Request:
End User Reference:

Submit   HELP

ORDER		
Applicant		Other
XPN		
EVC		
CRM NT		

258

Welcome

Welcome to the **CompleteLandlord.com Lease Creation Pro for Alabama**, which enables you to generate a lease and other related documents for you and your tenant.

What kind of agreement do you want to create?

○ Residential Lease (fixed-term, such as one year)

○ Monthly Rental Agreement (month-to-month)

○ Lease with Purchase Option (fixed-term with option to purchase)

Every lease package contains a variety of bonus forms that are optional for your use:

-- Rental & Credit Application
-- Pre-Lease & Post-Lease Inspections
-- Security Deposit Receipt
-- Receipt for Payment of Rent
-- Lead Paint Disclosure form & pamphlet (if required)
-- Garage & Parking Space Agreement
-- Pet Agreement Addendum & Pet Policy

Next ▌   Progress:8 %

5.4.2.1077

259

Welcome

Welcome to the **CompleteLandlord.com Lease Creation Pro for Alabama,** which enables you to generate a lease and other related documents for you and your tenant.

What kind of agreement do you want to create?

○ Residential Lease (fixed-term, such as one year)

○ Monthly Rental Agreement (month-to-month)

○ Lease with Purchase Option (fixed-term with option to purchase)

Every lease package contains a variety of bonus forms that are optional for your use:

-- Rental & Credit Application
-- Pre-Lease & Post-Lease Inspections
-- Security Deposit Receipt
-- Receipt for Payment of Rent
-- Lead Paint Disclosure form & pamphlet (if required)
-- Garage & Parking Space Agreement
-- Pet Agreement Addendum & Pet Policy

Next   Progress:8 %

5.4.2.1077

Residential Lease- Page 1 of 6

Complete a Residential Lease for Alabama.

What is the date of this lease agreement?

[10/6/2008] 🖩 ...

Hint: This is the date on which you are drafting the lease agreement, i.e. today's date.

What is the name of the landlord(s)?

Hint: Click on the "Add Row" button if there is more than one landlord.

[ ]   [Remove]

[Add Row]

What is the name of the tenant(s)?

Hint: Click on the "Add Row" button if more than one tenant is on the lease.

[ ]   [Remove]

[Add Row]

What is the street address of the rental unit?

[ ]

(e.g. 123 Main Street)

[ ]

(e.g. Clark Suites, Apt 1 G)

In what city?   [ ]

In what county?   [ ]

In what zip code?   [ ]

Describe the rental unit.

[ ]

(e.g. Front 3-bedroom unit on second floor of red brick 4-flat)

Is the rental unit furnished?

○ Yes ○ No

Hint: If the apartment is furnished, please attach a list of furnishings and appliances as an addendum to this lease.

On what date does the lease start?

[10/6/2008] 🖩 ...

How long is the lease term (in months)?

[12] month(s)
(e.g. 12)

☞ Back ☞ Next ■   [Progress:17 %]

5.4.2.1077

261

CompleteLandlord.com Lease Creation Pro™

● MY LEASES					Past	30 Da▾

STREET ADDRESS	TENANT	STATE	LEASE TYPE	DATE CREATED	EDIT	DELETE
123 Main Steet Clark Suites, Apt 1 G	Samantha Gates	Alabama	Residential Lease	10/6/2008	✎	○

📄 **Alabama Garage & Parking Space Agreement for Tenant Samantha Gates.rtf**
Distributed : 10/6/2008 3:58:03 PM

📄 **Alabama Receipt for Payment of Rent for Tenant Samantha Gates.rtf**
Distributed : 10/6/2008 4:05:30 PM

📄 **Alabama Residential Lease for Tenant Samantha Gates.rtf**
Distributed : 10/6/2008 3:52:15 PM

📄 **Alabama Security Deposit Receipt for Tenant Samantha Gates.rtf**
Distributed : 10/6/2008 4:05:30 PM

Create a New Lease

[Select a state ▾] (Start)

Coming soon:Alaska, Delaware, Illinois and Ohio,
(Standard Forms are currently available for these states).

262

CompleteLandlord.com™

| Dashboard | Properties | Tenants | Accounting | Tasks | Documents | Reports |
| Admin |

| Dashboard || My Info || Preferences || Support |

My Dashboard

Applications waiting to be accepted or rejected

Submitted	Ref #	Name	Property	Unit
11/08/07 02:46:46 PM EST	1486APP1292	sam tech123244	HYD	2

> **Tip**
> The dashboard serves as your command center, highlighting things that require your attention.

Leases ending within 90 days
You have no leases that are ending in the next 90 days.

Vacant Rental Units

Property	Unit	Since
Devonshire Bldg 1	B	
Devonshire Bldg 1	C	
Devonshire Bldg 1	D	
Jay's Apartments	101	
Jay's Apartments	102	
K&C Apartments	1001	
K&C Apartments	1003	
K&C Apartments	1004	
K&C Apartments	1005	
Sample Property	101	
Sample Property	102	
Sample Property	103	
Sample Property	104	
Sample Property	200	
Test property	401	
Test property	501	
Test property	601	
test123	1	
test123	2	
test123	3	
test123	4	
test123	5	

Tasks not yet assigned
You have no unassigned tasks.

My open tasks
You have no new or open tasks.

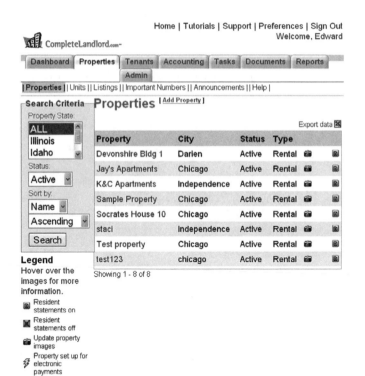

CompleteLandlord.com™

| Dashboard | Properties | Tenants | Accounting | Tasks | Documents | Reports |
| Admin |

| Properties | | Units | | Listings | | Important Numbers | | Announcements | | Help |

Search Criteria

Property State:

| ALL |
| Illinois |
| Idaho |

Status:

Active

Sort by:

Name

Ascending

[Search]

Legend

Hover over the images for more information.

📄 Resident statements on

📄 Resident statements off

📷 Update property images

⚡ Property set up for electronic payments

Properties [Add Property]

Export data 📊

Property	City	Status	Type		
Devonshire Bldg 1	Darien	Active	Rental	📷	📄
Jay's Apartments	Chicago	Active	Rental	📷	📄
K&C Apartments	Independence	Active	Rental	📷	📄
Sample Property	Chicago	Active	Rental	📷	📄
Socrates House 10	Chicago	Active	Rental	📷	📄
staci	Independence	Active	Rental	📷	📄
Test property	Chicago	Active	Rental	📷	📄
test123	chicago	Active	Rental	📷	📄

Showing 1 - 8 of 8

264

CompleteLandlord.com

| Dashboard | **Properties** | Tenants | Accounting | Tasks | Documents | Reports |
| Admin |

| Properties || Units || Listings || Important Numbers || Announcements || Help |

Search Criteria

Property State:

| ALL |
| Illinois |
| Idaho |

Status:

Active

Sort by:

Name

Ascending

[Search]

Legend

Hover over the images for more information.

Resident statements on

Resident statements off

Update property images

Property set up for electronic payments

Properties [Add Property]

Export data

Property	City	Status	Type
Devonshire Bldg 1	Darien	Active	Rental
Jay's Apartments	Chicago	Active	Rental
K&C Apartments	I
Sample Property	C
Socrates House 10	C
staci	i
Test property	C
test123	c

Showing 1 - 8 of 8

Add Property Wizard

* Required

Property Info

Property Name*	[ ]
Address*	[ ]
	[ ]
City*	[ ]
State/Province*	[v]
Zip*	[ ]
Type*	[Rental v]
Operating Account*	[ ]
Number of Units 0*	[1]

[Next]

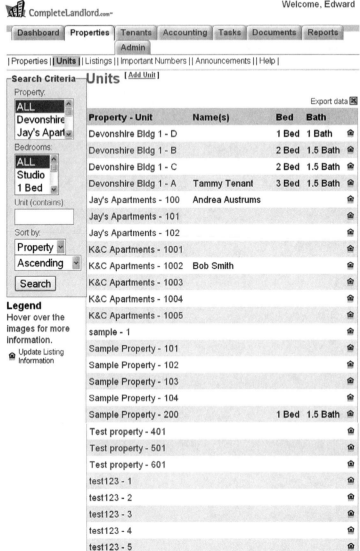

CompleteLandlord.com™

| Dashboard | **Properties** | Tenants | Accounting | Tasks | Documents | Reports |

| Admin |

| Properties || **Units** || Listings || Important Numbers || Announcements || Help |

Units [Add Unit]

Export data 📊

Property - Unit	Name(s)	Bed	Bath	
Devonshire Bldg 1 - D		1 Bed	1 Bath	🏠
Devonshire Bldg 1 - B		2 Bed	1.5 Bath	🏠
Devonshire Bldg 1 - C		2 Bed	1.5 Bath	🏠
Devonshire Bldg 1 - A	Tammy Tenant	3 Bed	1.5 Bath	🏠
Jay's Apartments - 100	Andrea Austrums			🏠
Jay's Apartments - 101				🏠
Jay's Apartments - 102				🏠
K&C Apartments - 1001				🏠
K&C Apartments - 1002	Bob Smith			🏠
K&C Apartments - 1003				🏠
K&C Apartments - 1004				🏠
K&C Apartments - 1005				🏠
sample - 1				🏠
Sample Property - 101				🏠
Sample Property - 102				🏠
Sample Property - 103				🏠
Sample Property - 104				🏠
Sample Property - 200		1 Bed	1.5 Bath	🏠
Test property - 401				🏠
Test property - 501				🏠
Test property - 601				🏠
test123 - 1				🏠
test123 - 2				🏠
test123 - 3				🏠
test123 - 4				🏠
test123 - 5				🏠

Showing 1 - 28 of 28

Search Criteria

Property:

| ALL |
| Devonshire |
| Jay's Apart |

Bedrooms:

| ALL |
| Studio |
| 1 Bed |

Unit (contains):

Sort by:

| Property ▾ |

| Ascending ▾ |

[Search]

Legend

Hover over the images for more information.

🏠 Update Listing Information

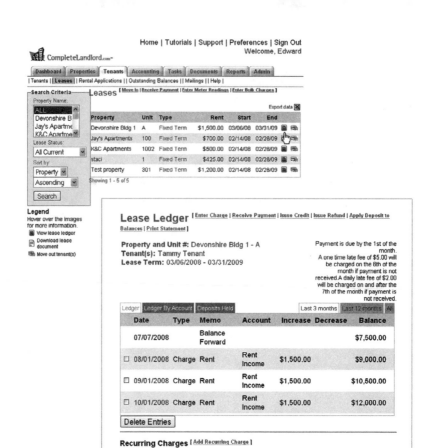

APPENDIX C

Essential CompleteLandlord Worksheets, Checklists, and Other Forms

Current Customizable Forms and Letters and Recently Revised Available for CompleteLandlord Members at CompleteLandlord.com:

Agreement to Amend Lease: Alabama

Agreement to Amend Lease: Arizona

Agreement to Amend Lease: Arkansas

Agreement to Amend Lease: Colorado

Agreement to Amend Lease: Kentucky

Agreement to Amend Lease: Louisiana

Agreement to Amend Lease: Maine

Agreement to Amend Lease: Maryland

Agreement to Amend Lease: Minnesota

Agreement to Amend Lease: Mississippi

Agreement to Amend Lease: Oklahoma

Agreement to Amend Lease: Oregon

Agreement to Amend Lease: South Carolina

Agreement to Amend Lease: Wisconsin

Agreement to Amend Lease Agreement: Washington

Apartment Lease: New York City

Changing the Locks Notice

Co-Signer Agreement

Collateral Assignment of Lease

Commercial Lease

Commercial Lease: Alabama

Commercial Lease: Alaska

Commercial Lease: Arizona

Commercial Lease: Arkansas

Commercial Lease: California

Commercial Lease: Colorado

Commercial Lease: Connecticut

Commercial Lease: Delaware

Commercial Lease: Florida

Commercial Lease: Georgia

Commercial Lease: Hawaii

Commercial Lease: Idaho

Commercial Lease: Illinois

Commercial Lease: Indiana

Commercial Lease: Iowa

Commercial Lease: Kansas

Disclosure of Information on Lead-Based Paint and/or Lead-Based Paint Hazards: Florida

Disclosure of Information on Lead-Based Paint and/or Lead-Based Paint Hazards: Georgia

Disclosure of Information on Lead-Based Paint and/or Lead-Based Paint Hazards: Hawaii

Disclosure of Information on Lead-Based Paint and/or Lead-Based Paint Hazards: Idaho

Disclosure of Information on Lead-Based Paint and/or Lead-Based Paint Hazards: Illinois

Disclosure of Information on Lead-Based Paint and/or Lead-Based Paint Hazards: Indiana

Disclosure of Information on Lead-Based Paint and/or Lead-Based Paint Hazards: Iowa

Disclosure of Information on Lead-Based Paint and/or Lead-Based Paint Hazards: Kansas

Disclosure of Information on Lead-Based Paint and/or Lead-Based Paint Hazards: Kentucky

Disclosure of Information on Lead-Based Paint and/or Lead-Based Paint Hazards: Louisiana

Disclosure of Information on Lead-Based Paint and/or Lead-Based Paint Hazards: Maine

Disclosure of Information on Lead-Based Paint and/or Lead-Based Paint Hazards: Maryland

Disclosure of Information on Lead-Based Paint and/or Lead-Based Paint Hazards: Massachusetts

Disclosure of Information on Lead-Based Paint and/or Lead-Based Paint Hazards: Michigan

Disclosure of Information on Lead-Based Paint and/or Lead-Based Paint Hazards: Minnesota

Disclosure of Information on Lead-Based Paint and/or Lead-Based Paint Hazards: Mississippi

Disclosure of Information on Lead-Based Paint and/or Lead-Based Paint Hazards: Missouri

Disclosure of Information on Lead-Based Paint and/or Lead-Based Paint Hazards: Montana

Disclosure of Information on Lead-Based Paint and/or Lead-Based Paint Hazards: Nebraska

Disclosure of Information on Lead-Based Paint and/or Lead-Based Paint Hazards: Nevada

Disclosure of Information on Lead-Based Paint and/or Lead-Based Paint Hazards: New Hampshire

Disclosure of Information on Lead-Based Paint and/or Lead-Based Paint Hazards: New Jersey

Disclosure of Information on Lead-Based Paint and/or Lead-Based Paint Hazards: New Mexico

Disclosure of Information on Lead-Based Paint and/or Lead-Based Paint Hazards: New York

Disclosure of Information on Lead-Based Paint and/or Lead-Based Paint Hazards: North Carolina

Disclosure of Information on Lead-Based Paint and/or Lead-Based Paint Hazards: North Dakota

Garage/Parking Space Lease
Agreement: Arizona

Garage/Parking Space Lease
Agreement: Arkansas

Garage/Parking Space Lease
Agreement: California

Garage/Parking Space Lease
Agreement: Colorado

Garage/Parking Space Lease
Agreement: Connecticut

Garage/Parking Space Lease
Agreement: Delaware

Garage/Parking Space Lease
Agreement: District of Columbia

Garage/Parking Space Lease
Agreement: Florida

Garage/Parking Space Lease
Agreement: Georgia

Garage/Parking Space Lease
Agreement: Hawaii

Garage/Parking Space Lease
Agreement: Idaho

Garage/Parking Space Lease
Agreement: Illinois

Garage/Parking Space Lease
Agreement: Indiana

Garage/Parking Space Lease
Agreement: Iowa

Garage/Parking Space Lease
Agreement: Kansas

Garage/Parking Space Lease
Agreement: Kentucky

Garage/Parking Space Lease
Agreement: Louisiana

Garage/Parking Space Lease
Agreement: Maine

Garage/Parking Space Lease
Agreement: Maryland

Garage/Parking Space Lease
Agreement: Massachusetts

Garage/Parking Space Lease
Agreement: Michigan

Garage/Parking Space Lease
Agreement: Minnesota

Garage/Parking Space Lease
Agreement: Mississippi

Garage/Parking Space Lease
Agreement: Missouri

Garage/Parking Space Lease
Agreement: Montana

Garage/Parking Space Lease
Agreement: Nebraska

Garage/Parking Space Lease
Agreement: Nevada

Garage/Parking Space Lease
Agreement: New Hampshire

Garage/Parking Space Lease
Agreement: New Jersey

Garage/Parking Space Lease
Agreement: New Mexico

Garage/Parking Space Lease
Agreement: New York

Garage/Parking Space Lease
Agreement: North Carolina

Garage/Parking Space Lease
Agreement: North Dakota

Garage/Parking Space Lease
Agreement: Ohio

Garage/Parking Space Lease
Agreement: Oklahoma

Garage/Parking Space Lease
Agreement: Oregon

Garage/Parking Space Lease
Agreement: Pennsylvania

Garage/Parking Space Lease
Agreement: Rhode Island

Notice of Initial Inspection: California

Notice of Intent to Enter

Notice of Lessee's Right and Opportunity to Purchase: District of Columbia

Notice of New Rules of Tenancy: Washington

Notice of Noncompliance: Ohio

Notice of Nonrefundable Deposit: Utah

Notice of Nonrefundable Deposit: Wyoming

Notice of Option to Request Inspection: California

Notice of Refund of Security Deposit: Kentucky

Notice of Reletting: California

Notice of Removal of Personal Property: Indiana

Notice of Renewal of Lease with Modifications: Delaware

Notice of Rent Arrears

Notice of Repairs/Construction

Notice of Sale of Abandoned Property: Minnesota

Notice of Sale of Personal Property: Wisconsin

Notice of Seizure Provision: Minnesota

Notice of Storage of Personal Property: Wisconsin

Notice of Suspected Abandonment: North Carolina

Notice of Temporary Shutoff

Notice of Termination: Iowa

Notice of Termination: New Jersey

Notice of Termination: Ohio

Notice of Termination: Oregon

Notice of Termination Due to Fire or Casualty: Kentucky

Notice of Termination of Lease

Notice of Time and Date of Inspection: Maryland

Notice of Time and Date of Inspection: Missouri

Notice That Eviction Will Be Filed in Court

Notice to Change Terms of Lease: Idaho

Notice to Change Terms of Lease: Indiana

Notice to Change Terms of Lease: Montana

Notice to Change Terms of Lease: North Dakota

Notice to Change Terms of Lease: South Dakota

Notice to Change Terms of Monthly Rental Agreement: California

Notice to Correct Violation or Vacate: District of Columbia

Notice to Landlord to Make Repairs

Notice to Lessee of Damages Exceeding Security Deposit: Virginia

Notice to Lessee to Reclaim Abandoned Property: California

Notice to Lessee to Reclaim Abandoned Property: Florida

Notice to Lessee to Reclaim Abandoned Property: Nebraska

Notice to Pay Rent or Quit

Notice to Pay Rent or Quit for Monthly Rental Agreement: Maine

Notice to Pay Rent or Quit for Monthly Rental Agreement: Massachusetts

Notice to Pay Rent or Quit for Monthly Rental Agreement: Minnesota

Notice to Pay Rent or Quit for Residential Lease: Maine

Notice to Pay Rent or Quit for Residential Lease: Massachusetts

Notice to Pay Rent or Quit for Residential Lease: Minnesota

Notice to Pay Rent or Quit for Residential Lease: Wisconsin

Notice to Pay Rent or Quit for Unpaid Check: Virginia

Notice to Pay Rent or Quit-MA

Notice to Pay Rent or Quit-OH

Notice to Pay Rent or Quit-Spanish

Notice to Pay Rent or Quit: Alaska

Notice to Pay Rent or Quit: Arizona

Notice to Pay Rent or Quit: California

Notice to Pay Rent or Quit: Colorado

Notice to Pay Rent or Quit: Delaware

Notice to Pay Rent or Quit: District of Columbia

Notice to Pay Rent or Quit: Florida

Notice to Pay Rent or Quit: Hawaii

Notice to Pay Rent or Quit: Idaho

Notice to Pay Rent or Quit: Illinois

Notice to Pay Rent or Quit: Indiana

Notice to Pay Rent or Quit: Iowa

Notice to Pay Rent or Quit: Kansas

Notice to Pay Rent or Quit: Kentucky

Notice to Pay Rent or Quit: Michigan

Notice to Pay Rent or Quit: Mississippi

Notice to Pay Rent or Quit: Missouri

Notice to Pay Rent or Quit: Montana

Notice to Pay Rent or Quit: Nebraska

Notice to Pay Rent or Quit: Nevada

Notice to Pay Rent or Quit: New Hampshire

Notice to Pay Rent or Quit: New York

Notice to Pay Rent or Quit: North Dakota

Notice to Pay Rent or Quit: Oklahoma

Notice to Pay Rent or Quit: South Dakota

Notice to Pay Rent or Quit: Tennessee

Notice to Pay Rent or Quit: Texas

Notice to Pay Rent or Quit: Utah

Notice to Pay Rent or Quit: Vermont

Notice to Pay Rent or Quit: Virginia

Notice to Pay Rent or Quit: Washington

Notice to Pay Rent or Quit: West Virginia

Notice to Pay Rent or Quit: Wyoming

Notice to Pay Rent Upon Abandonment: West Virginia

Notice to Quit: Connecticut

Notice to Quit: New Jersey

Notice to Quit for Breach: Alabama

Notice to Quit for Breach: Hawaii

Notice to Quit for Breach: Illinois

Notice to Quit for Breach: Minnesota

Notice to Quit for Breach for Monthly Rental Agreement: Pennsylvania

Notice to Quit for Breach for Monthly Rental Agreement: Wisconsin

Notice to Quit for Breach for Residential Lease: Pennsylvania

Notice to Quit for Failure to Pay for Utility Service: Alaska

Notice to Quit for Inflicting Substantial Damages to Premises: Alaska

Notice to Quit for Nonpayment of Rent: Arkansas

Notice to Quit for Nonpayment of Rent: Georgia

Notice to Quit for Nonpayment of Rent: Ohio

Notice to Quit for Nonpayment of Rent: Pennsylvania

Notice to Quit for Substantial Violation: Colorado

Notice to Quit for Violation Involving Controlled Substance: Michigan

Notice to Remedy Breach or Terminate: Hawaii

Notice to Remedy Default By Tenant

Notice to Remedy or Terminate for Noncompliance with Lease: South Carolina

Notice to Repair or Terminate for Noncompliance with Lease: Alaska

Notice to Repair or Terminate for Noncompliance with Lease: Arizona

Notice to Repair or Terminate for Noncompliance with Lease: Connecticut

Notice to Repair or Terminate for Noncompliance with Lease: Florida

Notice to Repair or Terminate for Noncompliance with Lease: Iowa

Notice to Repair or Terminate for Noncompliance with Lease: Kansas

Notice to Repair or Terminate for Noncompliance with Lease: Kentucky

Notice to Repair or Terminate for Noncompliance with Lease: Mississippi

Notice to Repair or Terminate for Noncompliance with Lease: Nebraska

Notice to Repair or Terminate for Noncompliance with Lease: Oklahoma

Notice to Repair or Terminate for Noncompliance with Lease: Oregon

Notice to Repair or Terminate for Noncompliance with Lease: Tennessee

Notice to Repair or Terminate for Noncompliance with Lease: Virginia

Notice to Repair or Terminate for Noncompliance with Residential Lease: Wisconsin

Notice to Tenant to Make Repairs

Notice to Terminate Due to Actions of Pet: Oregon

Notice to Terminate for Acts Relating to Illegal Drugs: Pennsylvania

Notice to Terminate for Breach: Virginia

Notice to Terminate for Illegal Activity: Arizona

Notice to Terminate for Noncompliance for Residential Lease: Wisconsin

Notice to Terminate for Re-entry of Offending Pet: Oregon

Notice to Terminate for Recurrence of Noncompliance: Alaska

Notice to Terminate for Recurrence of Noncompliance: Arizona

Notice to Terminate for Recurrence of Noncompliance: Connecticut

Notice to Terminate for Recurrence of Noncompliance: Iowa

Notice to Terminate for Recurrence of Noncompliance: Kansas

Notice to Terminate for Recurrence of Noncompliance: Kentucky

Sublease: Kansas

Sublease: Kentucky

Sublease: Louisiana

Sublease: Maine

Sublease: Maryland

Sublease: Massachusetts

Sublease: Michigan

Sublease: Minnesota

Sublease: Mississippi

Sublease: Missouri

Sublease: Montana

Sublease: Nebraska

Sublease: Nevada

Sublease: New Hampshire

Sublease: New Jersey

Sublease: New Mexico

Sublease: New York

Sublease: North Carolina

Sublease: North Dakota

Sublease: Ohio

Sublease: Oklahoma

Sublease: Oregon

Sublease: Pennsylvania

Sublease: Rhode Island

Sublease: South Carolina

Sublease: South Dakota

Sublease: Tennessee

Sublease: Texas

Sublease: Utah

Sublease: Vermont

Sublease: Virginia

Sublease: Washington

Sublease: West Virginia

Sublease: Wisconsin

Sublease: Wyoming

Tenant Employment Verification

Tenant Information Sheet

Tenant Move-Out Letter

Tenant Payment Record

Tenant Reference Check

Tenant's Notice to Terminate Tenancy

10-Day Notice to Quit: Arizona

10-Day Notice to Remedy Breach or Terminate: Arizona

10-Day Notice to Repair: Oklahoma

10-Day Notice to Vacate: Missouri

Termination Notice: Maine

3-Day Notice of Nonpayment of Rent: New Mexico

3-Day Notice of Substantial Violation of Rental Agreement: New Mexico

3-Day Notice to Quit: California

3-Day Notice to Quit: Idaho

3-Day Notice to Quit: Montana

3-Day Notice to Quit: Utah

3-Day Notice to Repair or Quit: California

3-Day Notice to Repair or Quit: Idaho

3-Day Notice to Repair or Quit: Montana

3-Day Notice to Repair or Quit: Utah

30-Day Notice of Violation: Maryland

30-Day Notice to Quit: New Hampshire

Unconditional Quit Notice

Unconditional Quit Second Notice

Violation of Pet Policy Letter

Waiver of Landlord's Claim to Annexed Fixtures

Waterbed Agreement-Addendum to Rental Agreement

$\mathbf{A}$PPENDIX D

Associations and Other Resources

Over the past decade, the world of information has changed considerably, particularly for real estate investors. Today, the Internet has created a wealth of property search and management resources that puts individuals in control of information as never before.

Web resources are spread throughout this book, but here is a summary of some of the most useful real estate investment sites you can find on the Web:

Associations

National Association of Realtors
www.realtor.org

National Association of Housing Cooperatives
www.coophousing.org

Construction Assistance

RS Means® Quick Cost Calculator
www.rsmeans.com/calculator/index.asp

Hanley Wood
(Provider of specialized paid reports on specific home renovation
and construction projects)
www.hanleywood.com

Credit Sites

FICO® Credit Score
www.myfico.com

Economic Information

UCLA Anderson Forecast
http://uclaforecast.com

U.S. Census Bureau Census of Housing
www.census.gov/hhes/www/housing/census/histcensushsg
.html

Financial/Tax Planning

The Financial Planning Association
www.fpanet.org

National Association of Fee-Only Financial Planners
www.napfa.org

U.S. Securities and Exchange Commission EDGAR database
www.sec.gov/edgar.shtml

Federation of Exchange Accommodators 1031 Exchange information
www.1031.org/

Foreclosure Information

RealtyTrac.com
www.realtytrac.com

Foreclosure.com
www.foreclosure.com

For Sale by Owner (FSBO) Information

ForSalebyOwner.com
www.forsalebyowner.com

BuyOwner.com
www.buyowner.com

HomeKeys.com
www.homekeys.com

Mortgage Trends

HSH Associates, Financial Publishers
www.hsh.com

Journals

CNNMoney.com
http://money.cnn.com/real_estate

Bankrate.com
www.bankrate.com

A PPENDIX E

Glossary of Real Estate Terms

A

Abatement A reduction or decrease in the value of a property that affects its market value or the amount of rent that may be charged to a tenant. Abatement usually occurs as the result of a discovery of something negative about the property (e.g., the roof must be replaced, the furnace will not make it through the winter, there is serious termite damage to the house) that decreases its worth and the price or rent it can command, or, in the case of a sale in progress, affects the price already agreed on by the buyer and seller. The term can also refer to a decrease in the local government's valuation of a property, which in turn leads to lower taxes.

Absentee Owner/Landlord An owner of a property who lives somewhere else and is not directly in control of that property. Tenants not only occupy the property but, if the owner has not appointed an agent, may also manage the property on the absentee owner's behalf on a day-to-day basis.

Absorption Rate The number of properties within a property development (e.g., a tract of land on which houses are being built, a building in which apartments are being converted to condominiums) that can be sold in a particular market within a particular time. Because the owner/buyer has probably borrowed money to fund the development and is paying interest on that money, he or she must factor in interest costs as part of the basic expenses.

Accelerated Depreciation Depreciation is a reduction in the value of a property resulting from the passage of time or changes in economic circumstances. Homeowners in recent years have come to think that property can only become more valuable (e.g., appreciate), but property does depreciate. For example, even though it may be well maintained, a property that is located in an area that becomes a hopeless slum or is beside the planned route for an expressway may depreciate. Depreciation may be used as a tax reduction. If a property loses its value quickly, this depreciation may be accelerated and claimed in the first few years of ownership; the depreciation deduction then decreases later in the property's life. Any income tax expert can provide details. Depreciation is also referred to as "writing down."

Acceleration Clause Most mortgages or loans include such a clause, which allows the lender to demand payment in full of the outstanding balance (e.g., to accelerate the loan) if the borrower fails to live up to the provisions of the agreement.

Actual Cash Value A term used in the insurance industry to describe the valuation of a building. It is determined by subtracting the decrease in value that is caused by such factors as age and wear and tear from the actual current cost of replacing the building.

Additional Principal Payment Making an additional payment on a mortgage. With a monthly mortgage payment of $2,000, the interest portion may be $1,750 and the principal portion may be $250. If the lender offers this sort of provision (and most do), the borrower may opt occasionally to pay an additional amount to reduce the principal (e.g., the amount owed) by more than the fixed amount of $250.

Adjustable-Rate Mortgage (ARM) Also called a variable-rate mortgage. This kind of loan has an interest rate that is determined by some outside index, such as the federal prime rate or the interest paid on government bonds. This kind of mortgage is most popular when this rate is lower, especially when it is much lower, than the interest on a fixed-rate mortgage would be. People who choose this kind of mortgage are hoping that the adjustable rate will remain below the fixed rate for a long time—or at least until their income improves. The savings in interest on an ARM, at least in the short term, can be substantial.

Affidavit of Title The seller's statement that the title (e.g., proof of ownership) is valid, can be sold, and is subject to no defects except those set out in the agreement of sale.

After-Tax Cash Flow The net profit of an income property after direct costs (e.g., interest on the mortgage, taxes, maintenance) have been subtracted.

After-Tax Proceeds The net proceeds from the sale of a property; that is, the sale price less the legal fees and expenses, the Realtor's commission, any taxes paid, and so on.

Agreement of Sale Also called purchase agreement, agreement of purchase and sale, land agreement, and so on. A legal contract in which the buyer agrees to buy and the seller agrees to sell a specific property. The agreement of sale contains all the terms and conditions of the transaction and is signed by both parties. These documents are essentially the same but differ slightly from state to state.

Amortization Schedule A statement of the payments to be made on an amortized mortgage loan. This statement generally shows the date and amount of each payment, the portions of each payment that will be applied to interest and to principal, and the balance (of principal) still outstanding on the loan after the payment has been made.

Annual Debt Service The amount that is required to service a loan in any given year; that is, the interest that must be paid to keep the loan current.

Appraiser A professional who is trained to assess the value of commercial or residential property.

Assumable Mortgage A mortgage that can be taken over (e.g., assumed) by the buyer from the seller when a property is sold. If interest rates are high, a low-rate assumable mortgage can be a great selling point for a property. However, this is not necessarily a common provision in mortgages. Buyers and sellers should always determine whether the mortgage contract contains such a clause.

Auction Selling property to the highest bidder at a public sale. Auctions are often used to sell property that has been foreclosed on or property that has failed to sell in the marketplace.

Auctioneer A professional who sells property at public auctions. Depending on local laws, this can be either a real estate agent or a licensed auctioneer. The auctioneer is usually paid a percentage of the final sale price of each property being auctioned.

B

Balloon Mortgage A mortgage loan that is repaid in fixed, periodic (probably monthly) payments until a given date. On that date, either the balance of the loan becomes due in one large payment or the amount of the payments rises significantly.

Balloon Payment The final payment that pays off a balloon mortgage.

Base Rent The set rent that is paid by a tenant and to which can be added additional fees as established in the lease (e.g., for upkeep, utilities).

Biweekly Mortgage A mortgage in which one half of the monthly payment is made every two weeks. With this kind of mortgage, 26 payments will be made in a year; the extra monthly payment that is made each year reduces the duration of the mortgage and the total amount of interest that the borrower will ultimately pay. Many people find such plans to be a fairly painless way to reduce the principal on a mortgage more quickly.

Blockbusting The unscrupulous practice of acquiring property (usually residential property) for less than market value by telling current residents that people of a different race or religion are moving into the area and that their property value will soon decline dramatically. This practice is illegal in the United States.

Boilerplate A slang term for a standard provision that usually appears in all similar contracts, such as the embargo against wild animals that is contained in virtually any lease for an apartment.

Bridge Loan/Financing A form of interim loan that is most commonly used when a buyer has bought a new house or condominium unit but has yet to sell his current residence. Thus, she may lack the funds necessary to make the down payment on the new residence or to pay two mortgages simultaneously. The bridge loan usually covers the down payment on the new premises and the monthly mortgage payment for a stated number of months. The bridge loan customarily ends when the buyer has sold the old premises and has the funds to pay off the lender.

Building Code Regulations that are established and enforced by a municipality to guarantee standards and quality of construction.

Buy Down The payment of extra money on a loan, such as the payment of additional principal when making a monthly mortgage payment, to reduce the interest rate and/or the life of the loan.

Buyer's Broker/Agent A real estate agent who represents the potential buyer. Agents commonly represent the seller, but potential buyers increasingly are engaging real estate agents to watch out for their interests also.

C

Capitalization Rate (Cap Rate) A way of calculating the value of income property by determining present income and multiplying it by a multiple that is universally acceptable to buyers of similar properties in the same area. For instance, if the net income of an apartment building is $200,000 a year and a multiple in common use in the area in which the apartment building is located is 10, the apartment building can be said to be worth $2 million.

Cash Flow Net earned income from an income property after all the expenses of holding and carrying the property are paid or factored in. Also called cash throw-off.

Certificate of Title A written opinion by a lawyer as to the validity of a person's claim to ownership of a particular property; such opinions may also be issued through a title.

Certified General Appraiser Someone who is licensed, after training, to appraise the value of property (qualification requirements can vary, depending on the particular jurisdiction).

Certified Home Inspector (CHI) Someone who is licensed, after training, to inspect and report on the physical condition of property (qualification requirements may vary, depending on the particular jurisdiction).

Certified Residential Appraiser (CRA) Someone who has met the licensing requirements to appraise the value of only and specifically residential property. See **certified general appraiser.**

Chain of Title A chronological listing of successive owners of a property, from the original owner to the present owner. Sometimes this kind of document also lists the particulars of each registration.

Chattel Articles of personal property such as household goods, furnishings, and fixtures that are not permanently affixed to a house.

Closing Costs Expenses, usually those of the buyer, that are over and above the cost (e.g., the sale price) of the property itself, such as legal fees, mortgage application fees, taxes, appraisal fees, and title registration fees.

Cloud (on title) Any unresolved claim of ownership against all or part of a property that affects the owner's title to that property and the marketability of that title. This kind of claim is usually resolved in court.

Commission The amount paid to a real estate agent or broker as compensation for services rendered in the purchase, sale, or rental of property. The amount is usually a percentage of the sales price or the total rental.

Commission Split The division of a commission when two or more real estate agents have been involved in the sale (or purchase) of property.

Comparables A way of establishing the market value of a particular property in which another property that has recently been sold, and is similar in location, size, condition, and amenities to the property in question is used as a guide to establishing the asking price.

Condominium A structure comprising two or more units in which the units are individually owned but the remainder of the property (e.g., the land, buildings, amenities) is owned in common. The maintenance of these common areas is supervised by the condominium corporation, in which each unit owner owns a share and has voting rights.

Contingency A condition that must be fulfilled before a contract can become firm and binding. For example, the sale of a house may depend on whether the potential buyer can obtain financing.

Conveyance The act of transferring title to (or other interest in) a property to someone else. Also, the document that effects that transfer; such documents include most instruments by which an interest in real estate is created, mortgaged, or assigned.

Covenant A promise contained in a contract or agreement. In real estate, this promise may be implied; that is, it may already be covered by local or national laws.

Credit History/Credit Report A statement of debts and obligations, both current and past, and of the record of payment of such debts. The lender obtains a credit history for an applicant to assess the risk in making a loan to that applicant. The lender is interested in determining whether a potential applicant is likely (and willing) to make the payments on a mortgage, and believes that her or his past behavior as a borrower will be a good indication of future behavior.

Custom Builder A builder who specializes in creating homes to the specifications of the landowner, as opposed to one who builds houses and then sells them after they are built, speculating that buyers can be found.

D

Debt-Equity Ratio A comparison of what is owed on a property with its equity (e.g., the current market value of the property less the amount owed on the mortgage or loan).

Decree of Foreclosure A court decree made when a borrower is seriously in default on a mortgage and the lender decides that the borrower will not (or cannot) pay. The decree declares the amount outstanding on the delinquent mortgage and orders the sale of the property to pay off the mortgage. The lender is then repaid to the extent possible (sales that result from foreclosure do not necessarily achieve full market value of the property).

Deed in Lieu of Foreclosure A document by which a borrower conveys property to a mortgage lender to avoid the expense of foreclosure.

Deed of Trust Used in many states in place of a mortgage. Property is transferred by the buyer or borrower to a trustee. The beneficiary is the lender, and the property is reconveyed to the buyer when the loan obligation is paid.

Defective Title Ownership that is not considered clean (e.g., that is subject to a competing claim or claims). Another meaning is ownership that is obtained by fraud.

Department of Veterans' Affairs (VA) The federal government agency that administers benefits for U.S. military veterans, including property loans and mortgage programs.

Depreciation The decrease in value of a property over time, which can also lead to a reduction in the owner's taxes (e.g., a capital loss).

Discount Real Estate Agent or Broker A real estate agent or broker who works for a commission that is less than that which is usual in a particular marketplace. Sometimes an agent who usually works for a standard commission (e.g., is not a discount real estate agent) accepts a reduced commission in order to secure a client or a listing.

Dual Agency In general, dual agency is a breach of real estate brokerage rules. If a single real estate agent is representing both the buyer and the seller in a particular transaction, the agent must disclose this fact to both sides. Otherwise, the agent is involved in a conflict of interest that is not allowed by most real estate brokerages.

E

Equal Credit Opportunity Act A U.S. law guaranteeing that people of all races, ages, genders, and religions must have an equal chance to borrow money.

Equity The market value of a property, less the debts of that property. Likely debts include the principal and accumulated interest on the mortgage, unpaid taxes, and a home equity loan.

Equity Loan A loan to a home or condominium owner that is secured by the lender against the equity the owner has built up in the property. Equity loans have become increasingly popular in recent years as a way of consolidating credit card debt (the interest rate on equity loans is usually far less than that charged by credit card companies) and tapping into what is often a large amount of money to use for home repairs and renovation or to fund some major expense such as an expensive vacation or a child's college education.

Escrow In real estate, the delivery of a deed by the seller to a third party (e.g., the escrow agent), to be delivered to the buyer at a certain time, usually the closing date. In some states, all instruments having to do with the sale (including the funds) are delivered to the escrow agent for dispersal on the closing date.

Eviction A court action to remove an individual from the possession of real property, most commonly the removal of a tenant.

F

Fair Market Value The price that is likely to be agreed on by a buyer and seller for a specific property at a specific time. This price is typically arrived at by considering the sales prices of comparable properties in the area, taking into consideration any special features of or upgrades to the property in question.

Fannie Mae (FNMA) A slang term for the U.S. Federal National Mortgage Association. This association purchases, sells, and guarantees both conventional and government (e.g., VA) mortgages. Fannie Mae is a corporation established by the U.S. Congress; it is the largest supplier in the country of mortgages to home buyers and owners.

Fixed-Rate Mortgage (FRM) A loan on which the interest rate does not change over the term (e.g., the life) of the mortgage. See **adjustable-rate mortgage.**

Flood Insurance Insurance that covers loss by water damage. Such insurance is required by lenders in regions known to be potential flood areas. The insurance is written by private insurance companies but is subsidized by the federal government.

For Rent by Owner (FRBO) The situation when a landlord tries to find a tenant without using an agent.

For Sale by Owner (FSBO) The situation when a seller tries to find a buyer without using a real estate agent or broker.

Foreclosure A proceeding that is usually instigated by a lender, in a court or not, to cancel all rights and title of an owner in a particular property when that owner has defaulted on payment of a mortgage. The purpose of the lender's action is to claim the title, so that the property can be sold to satisfy the debt still outstanding on the mortgage.

H

Handyman's Special A property that requires substantial work to bring it up to normal standards. Such a property is often sold at a lower price than it would be if it were in excellent repair.

High-Ratio Mortgage A mortgage in which the amount of money borrowed is 75 percent (or more) of the purchase price. The lender on such a mortgage usually requires the sort of insurance that is provided by various U.S. government agencies as a guarantee of the lender's risk in making the mortgage.

Home Equity Line of Credit A kind of loan that is increasingly popular. It is secured against the equity in a property. The borrower may borrow against that equity to a certain percentage of that equity's value and then, on a monthly basis, make payments of interest only or interest plus a portion of the equity borrowed, as desired. Many such loans have a time limit (e.g., the borrower must pay back the loan, if it is not already paid back, at some time in the future). Such a loan, which is in effect a second mortgage, must be paid back immediately if the property is sold. Also known as a revolving loan.

I

Income Property Any property that is developed (or purchased) specifically to produce income for its owner, such as an apartment building.

Independent Contractor A person who is hired to do building or renovation work for another person but is neither an employee nor an agent of that other person, such as a contractor who works for a fee.

Interest-Only Mortgage A type of mortgage that is increasingly popular in which the borrower pays only the interest and none of the principal during a certain period (e.g., 3 years, 5 years). After that, the borrower makes conventional payments containing both principal and interest for the remainder of the loan's term. Such mortgages are appealing to those who want initial payments on a mortgage to be as low as possible or those who expect the value of the property to rise very quickly, providing them with a profit without a substantial principal investment.

J

Joint Appraisal An appraisal that is conducted by more than one appraiser but states their common conclusions.

L

Lease A written agreement issued by an owner or landlord in renting a property (or part of a property) to another person. This agreement offers a description of the premises, the amount to be paid in rent, the rent payment due date (usually the first or last of the month), the agreed period that the rental will last, and the rights and obligations of both the landlord and the tenant.

Lease with Option to Purchase A kind of lease in which the tenant (e.g., lessee) has the right (but not the obligation) to purchase the property during the term of the lease. Payments made under the lease (sometimes wholly and sometimes in part, depending on the lease agreement) may be credited against the purchase price; that is, they may be used as a down payment. This is an ideal arrangement for any potential buyer who lacks the financial means to make a down payment.

Lis Pendens (Latin: Suit Pending) A recorded notice of a legal claim; it may affect ownership of a particular parcel of land.

Loan-to-Value Ratio The difference between the appraised value of a property and the amount being loaned on a mortgage.

M

Market Rent The amount that an owner can reasonably charge someone who wishes to lease a property. The determining factor is generally how much other landlords, in the same market, are charging for similar properties. Also known as economic rent.

Mortgage A loan that is usually granted for the purpose of allowing a borrower to purchase property. The loan is secured (e.g., guaranteed) by that property; in other words, the mortgage is registered on the title (e.g., the ownership record) as a claim on that property.

Mortgage Broker A middleman who brings borrowers together with potential lenders, thereby providing a service to borrowers who are not as informed about potential lending sources. Often, the broker collects a fee for this service from the chosen lender.

N

Negative Amortization The situation that exists when the principal amount of a mortgage increases because a payment is not sufficient to cover accumulated interest and the shortfall is therefore added to the principal.

Neighborhood Life Cycle The pattern of development and change that occurs in a neighborhood over a given period.

Net Leasable Area The area in a rental building that is available for rent to tenants. This is the area that is left after the exclusion of wasted space, such amenities as stairways and elevators, and the building's common areas.

Net Operating Income (NOI) The income from a property that is left after the costs of maintaining and servicing that property are subtracted.

O

Occupancy Rate The percentage of available rental space that is actually rented and in use in either a building or a community.

Offer A statement (either spoken or written) that informs one party of another's willingness to buy or sell a specific property on the terms set out in that statement. Once made, an offer usually must be accepted within a specific period (e.g., it is usually not open-ended). Once accepted, the offer by the one party and the acceptance by the other both are regarded as binding.

Open-Ended Mortgage A loan that allows the borrower to borrow further funds at a later date with the preparation (and registration) of an additional mortgage.

Operating Expenses The costs incurred on an income property that are directly caused by using that property to produce income, such as the expenses of heating the property, arranging for garbage removal, or advertising for tenants.

Owner-Occupied Any property in which the owner occupies all or part of the property.

Owner's Title Insurance A policy that protects a property owner from any defects in title that were not apparent at the time of purchase.

P

Payment Cap A condition of some adjustable-rate mortgages in which the level to which a monthly payment can rise is limited to a certain amount.

Percentage Lease A commercial rental agreement in which the tenant's monthly payment is a percentage of the gross sales of the tenant's business; usually, a minimum payment is also agreed upon. For example, a tenant might pay, as rental, 10 percent of sales, and sales might average $100,000 a month; tenant and landlord would agree, therefore, on a minimum payment each month of $10,000.

Permit A government body's written permission allowing changes to a particular property when such changes are regulated by that government body. For example, local municipalities normally require homeowners to apply for a permit if they wish to make substantial alterations to the outsides of their houses, so as to make sure that these changes are not at variance with the bylaws covering the area in which the houses are located.

PITI An acronym for principal, interest, taxes, and insurance, which are the most common components of a monthly mortgage payment.

Plat A map dividing a parcel of land into lots, as in a subdivision.

Potential Gross Income The amount of money that a commercial or rental property will generate if it is fully occupied and there are no unforeseen interruptions to that income (e.g., vacancies).

Preforeclosure Sale The sale of a property by a delinquent borrower that is agreed to by the lender. The sale may not produce enough money to settle the loan entirely, but the lender agrees to this kind of sale because it saves the costs of foreclosing and of the postforeclosure sale.

Prepayment Clause A statement in a mortgage that sets out the rules regarding extra payments toward principal (e.g., those in excess of what is required as part of the monthly mortgage payment).

Private Mortgage Insurance (PMI) Insurance that is required by a lender (and obtained from a nongovernment insurer) if the down payment on a property is less than 20 percent of its value.

Profit and Loss Statement Also called an income statement. A common form in accounting in which the components that result in net income are calculated. It is always a part of a company's annual report.

Public Auction A real estate auction that is open to the public at which properties are sold to pay mortgages that are in default. Such auctions are popular with potential buyers because properties being sold at a public auction often bring less than their market value.

Q

Quit-Claim Deed A conveyance in which the person doing the conveying is stating that he or she has no interest in a particular property.

R

Rate Cap The limit on how much an interest rate may change on an adjustable-rate mortgage, either for a given period or for the life of the loan.

Real Estate Agent An individual who is licensed to negotiate and arrange real estate sales; works for a real estate broker.

Real Estate Broker Someone licensed by the state in which he or she resides who works to engage in the real estate business in that state (e.g., to run or manage a real estate agency or brokerage). A broker may receive a commission for bringing a buyer and seller together to achieve a transfer of title; brokers may also be compensated for leasing property or for arranging an exchange of property. Brokers are responsible for the supervision of their company's associate brokers, Realtors, and agents.

Real Estate Investment Trust (REIT) A group investment in property that carries certain tax advantages for the participants. Both the federal and state governments regulate REITs.

Realtor The professional designation for a member of the National Association of Realtors (or an affiliated local group). A licensed real estate agent is not a Realtor unless that agent joins the association and agrees to abide by its code of ethics.

Refinance The situation when a borrower pays off one loan on a property and replaces it with another loan, often from the same lender. This is done most commonly when mortgage interest rates have decreased considerably from the rate the borrower is paying on the old mortgage. Thus, refinancing is a way for the borrower to reduce the amount of monthly mortgage payments.

Rehabilitation Tax Credit An income tax credit that is equal to as much as 20 percent of a person's costs for the refurbishing of historic properties.

Reserve Price The base price set before an auction that must be met in order for a particular property to sell during the auction process. For example, a house that is being auctioned with a set price (e.g., a reserve price) of \$200,000 may bring \$225,000 but would not be sold for \$195,000.

Riparian Rights The rights of the owner of land that borders water (e.g., a river, a lake, a creek) to use or control that body of water.

S

Second Mortgage A mortgage that ranks after a first mortgage in priority. A single property may have more than one mortgage; each is ranked by number to indicate the order in which it must be paid. In the event of a default and therefore sale of the property, second and subsequent mortgages are paid, in order, only if there are funds left after payment of the first mortgage.

Security Real or personal property that is pledged by a borrower as a guarantee or protection for the lender. With a mortgage, the borrower pledges the property that the borrower is actually buying; this security is registered on the title to the property and the lender may claim the property if the borrower defaults on (e.g., fails to pay) the loan.

Security Deposit Money that is paid by a tenant to a landlord, then held by the landlord to ensure that the tenant meets the obligations of the lease and does not damage the property. If the tenant damages the property, the landlord may use part (or all) of the money to make the necessary repairs. In many jurisdictions, the landlord is required to pay interest on a security deposit.

Sheriff's Sale The forced sale of a property to satisfy a debt or judgment.

Simple Interest Interest that is payable on just the principal of a loan and not on any accumulated interest.

Soft Market The situation that exists when there is more property for sale than there are buyers to buy it; as a result, prices decrease. Also known as buyer's market.

T

Tax Foreclosure The process leading up to the sale of property to cover unpaid taxes.

Tax Lien A registered claim for the nonpayment of property taxes.

Teaser Rate A low initial rate on an adjustable-rate mortgage, offered for a relatively short period as an inducement to potential borrowers.

Tenancy The right to use property under a rental agreement (e.g., a lease).

Tenant Fixtures Items that are added to rental property by a tenant. These normally might be considered fixtures (and therefore a part of the property), but, in a rental, the tenant can remove them at the end of the tenancy.

Termite Clause A term in a sale agreement that allows the buyer to inspect for termites. If any are found, the buyer may require the seller to fix the problem; otherwise, the buyer has the right to cancel the sale agreement. Termite infestation can be a serious problem, especially in the southern United States or California.

Title Company A corporation that sells insurance policies that guarantee the ownership of (and quality of title to) property. Also known as a title insurance company.

Title Search A review of all the recorded documents that affect a particular property. The purpose of this review is to determine the current state of title and usually also to establish whether the current owner has clear title (e.g., without liens, competing claims, mortgages).

Triple-Net Lease The sort of rental agreement that requires the tenant to pay all the operating costs of the premises.

Trust Deed An instrument of conveyance. A trustee may hold title to property on behalf of another person. For example, a court might appoint a trustee to hold property that a child has inherited because the child is not old enough to take legal responsibility for property ownership. On the child's coming of age, the trustee transfers title to the child.

Trustee Someone who is appointed by a court to execute any kind of trust arrangement. In real estate, a trustee may hold title to property under specific conditions and for a designated period.

U

Unsecured Loan A loan that is valid (e.g., the lender has given the borrower the requested funds) but is not secured by any asset. Such loans are virtually unknown; an exception would be a case in which the lender knows the borrower well, has had extensive business dealings with the borrower, and believes that the loan will be repaid.

Up-Rent Potential An estimate of how much the rent on a particular property is likely to be raised over a given period. Such an estimate might be offered to a potential tenant as an inducement to sign a lease.

Use A term mainly used in zoning bylaws or ordinances to indicate the purpose for which a property is occupied. Common types of use include residential, industrial, commercial, and retail.

V

Vacancy Rate A calculation, expressed as a percentage, of all the available rental units in a particular area and at a particular time that are not rented.

Variance An indulgence that is granted by a local government authority to allow an unconventional use of property. This could be an exception granted to a homeowner that allows him or her to create a basement apartment for a sick relative in an area in which zoning bylaws ordinarily allow for only single-family homes.

W

Walk-Through Inspection An examination, by the buyer, of the property he or she is purchasing. The walk-through inspection usually takes place immediately before closing and is intended to assure the buyer that no changes have taken place (and no damage has been done) to the property since the buyer agreed to buy. It also reassures the buyer that fixtures and chattels included in the sale actually remain on the property.

Warranty A legally binding promise that is usually given at the time of sale in which the seller gives the buyer certain assurances as to the condition of the property being sold.

Waste Allowing a property to suffer damage, or accelerated wear and tear, to the detriment of another person who has an interest in that property, thus diminishing the value of that person's asset.

Wraparound Mortgage A loan in which new debt is added to an existing first mortgage. The new money that is borrowed is blended with the money already owed and is registered on the title to the property (e.g., a second mortgage is registered as security for the new money). However, the old mortgage still also remains in effect. The interest rate is usually a blend of the old rate (on the first mortgage) and the new rate (on the second mortgage).

Z

Zone An area of a city (or county) that is set aside for a certain purpose, such as commercial, residential, industrial, or agricultural.

Zoning Rules and regulations controlling the use of land, which is broken down into districts, and determines how private property is to be used or what construction is allowed. Zoning may be commercial, residential, industrial, or agricultural. Zoning also restricts height limitations, noise, parking, and open space. Residential zoning may consist of single-family, two-family, or apartments.

Zoning Board of Appeals Local government board that resolves zoning disputes.

Zoning Laws Ordinances created by local government to cover real estate development, including structural and aesthetic points. They usually define usage classifications from agricultural to industry, building restrictions (such as minimum and maximum square footage requirements), and violations penalties and procedures.

Zoning Map Map that shows locality divided into districts and shows status and usage of each district.

Zoning Ordinances Regulations determined by each municipality to establish different zoning restrictions and classifications (e.g., building height and type of buildings). Penalties are assessed for violation of zoning ordinances. In some instances, variations to zoning ordinances are allowed and are called variances.

INDEX

CLL Catalog Taken from Online Store at 6/08

CompleteLandlord.com Premium Membership Benefits

9 Key Components	Silver	Gold	Platinum
1. Property Management Solution^{SM}	Up to 2 Units	Up to 10 Units	Up to 50 Units or more
Complete Tenant Tracking	Unlimited	Unlimited	Unlimited
General Ledger Accounting System	Unlimited	Unlimited	Unlimited
Management Reports	Unlimited	Unlimited	Unlimited
Dashboard	Unlimited	Unlimited	Unlimited
Resident Portal (Website)	Unlimited	Unlimited	Unlimited
2. Lease Creation Pro^{SM}			
Customizable Forms and Letters	Unlimited	Unlimited	Unlimited
Leases & Rental Agreement	Unlimited	Unlimited	Unlimited
Rental Credit Application	Unlimited	Unlimited	Unlimited
Pre-Lease and Post-Lease Inspection List	Unlimited	Unlimited	Unlimited
Garage and Parking Space Agreement	Unlimited	Unlimited	Unlimited
Pet Agreement Addendum	Unlimited	Unlimited	Unlimited
Leases, Agreements, Notices	✓	✓	✓
Applications	✓	✓	✓
Disclosures	✓	✓	✓
Letters	✓	✓	✓
Inspection Forms	✓	✓	✓
Addendums, Warnings, Surveys	✓	✓	✓
5. Archives of Landlord Profit Letter and Quarterly Issues	✓	✓	✓
6. Access to CompleteLandlord.com Library Special Reports			
Rental Property Management Secrets for Landlords	✓	✓	✓
Complete Guide to Conducting Tenant Screenings		✓	✓
Eviction Secrets for Landlords		✓	✓
How to Buy Foreclosure Property			✓
Understanding Rental Property 1031 Exchanges for Landlords			✓
Streaming Webinar/Audio Conferences Hosted by Real Estate Experts			
Tax Planning Secrets for Landlords		✓	✓
Asset Protection Using LLCs			✓
7. Customer Care	✓	✓	✓
8. Content, Forms & Software Upgrades, Maintenance, Hosting, Storage, Multi-layer Security and Rental Unit Scaleability	Unlimited	Unlimited	Unlimited
9. Incremental rental unit additions	$2.00/unit/mo	$1.00/unit/mo	$0.30/unit/mo
Premium Membership Monthly Price	$9.97/mo	$19.97/mo	$29.97/mo
Premium Membership Annual Price	$97/yr	$197/yr	$297/yr
Annual Membership Savings vs. Monthly Membership	(Save $22.64)	(Save $92.64)	(Save $62.64)
	⊙ Buy It Now	⊙ Buy It Now	⊙ Buy It Now

*Prices and terms subject to change without notice.

Save Time. Save Money. Make More Money. JOIN. TODAY!

CompleteLandlord.com Catalog (as of 12/31/08, Prices Subject to Change Without Notice.)

Landlord Profit Letter

The indispensable quarterly newsletter no landlord should be without, yours for just pennies a day!

Every month, important news breaks that can affect the world of landlording. Laws change. State rules and regulations change. And important real estate trends emerge that can affect your property, your tenants, your business — your future.

Where do you go for news, tips, updates, and detailed reports on the world of landlording? How do you know if you're following industry best practices? How can you save money … avoid common pitfalls … and maximize your rental returns?

The editorial team at CompleteLandlord.com has developed this newsletter to do what no other publication does: to go behind the scenes and bring all the news, ideas, tips, and statistics from the world of landlording together in one easy-to-read format. The CompleteLandlord.com team has more than 25 years of landlording, property investment, and rental management experience, and has helped hundreds of thousands of landlords save time and money since 1988.

Look what every issue of the Landlord Profit Letter delivers to you:
- How to Increase Profits — a different revenue generating idea each month, using examples provided by our seasoned and successful landlords!
- In the News — what's happening in laws, trends, markets, and headlines, and how they affect you. company (LLC) makes the most sense for you, your company, your employees, and your family.
- A Day in the Life of a Landlord — special regional accounts of landlord experiences, what they learned, and what they'll do differently next time.
- Time Saving Maintenance Repair Tips and Discounts — use just one of these tips and you have paid for your newsletter many times over!
- Landlord Landmines — the most common landlording pitfalls, and how to avoid them.
- Top 10 Lists — such as the Top 10 Ways to Save Money on Utility Bills … Top 10 Ways to Get Your Tenants to Like You.
- Landlord/Tenant Laws — legal updates from our expert staff of attorneys.
- Weekly Polls — we ask and you answer … listen to what your fellow landlords are doing across the nation.
- Vital Statistics — based on national and regional surveys of eviction rates, foreclosure rates, rent increases, and more.
- Questions and Answers — a review of the top concerns landlords are talking about in our Q&A Forum, along with useful advice.
- Plus Product Reviews, tips, cost-saving ideas, and more!

In landlording, you never know what you don't know. Learn how other landlords are boosting their cash flows in the landlording business or how selecting the wrong tenants can cost you thousands. You'll never know these secrets … UNLESS you subscribe to the Landlord Profit Letter.

Knowledge isn't just power. Knowledge is money! Order the Landlord Profit Letter today!

The Landlord Profit Letter and CompleteLandlord.com are part of the family of brands from Minotaur Media, LLC. All CompleteLandlord.com and Minotaur products and services are reviewed and approved by attorneys, accountants fellow landlords, or industry experts.

Profit Letter Subscription
Price: $89.00
Order Now!

Books

Ultimate Landlord Handbook

Maximize efficiency and revenues while reducing frustrating landlording problems using the essential legal and practical knowledge found in this book.

$19.95   **Buy It Now**

Ultimate Property Management Handbook

Some have made thousands … others have lost thousands. Don't be the latter. Information, insight and preparation are key when managing a rental property!

$19.95   **Buy It Now**

Ultimate Residential Investment Handbook

Don't make the BIGGEST investment of your life … without the BEST home buying guide ever written!

$19.95   **Buy It Now**

The Kit & The Software

Landlording Kit

Prepare yourself for higher profits and fewer headaches with step-by-step "real world" guidance on successful landlording. Includes important forms for your state. This landlord kit is essential for new or seasoned landlords.

$29.95   **Buy It Now**

Incorporation Kit

Protect your personal assets from operational risks and other business liabilities whether you're starting a new business or operating an existing one.

$49.95   **Buy It Now**

Attracting & Retaining Quality Tenants Kit

Discover the secrets smart landlords use to attract, screen, and choose quality tenants. Learn the easiest and most effective methods to find the best tenants.

$29.95   **Buy It Now**

Last Will & Testament Kit

Plan your estate responsibly and affordably with all the forms and instructions you need. Protect your loved ones, make your wishes known and award your assets as you desire with this kit.

$27.95   **Buy It Now**

Special Reports

Rental Property Management Secrets for Landlords

Rental Property Management Secrets for Landlords gives you tips from the pros on maximizing your income and minimizing your problems with the rental properties you own. You made a smart move becoming a landlord. Your portfolio of investment properties will ensure your financial future and a comfortable early retirement.

$19.95 **Buy It Now**

Tax Planning Secrets for Landlords

40+ page special report shows landlords how to maximize deductions on investment properties and save thousands of dollars a year at tax time! Now the editors and legal staff at CompleteLandlord.com have published a new Special Report, Tax Planning Secrets for Landlords, that can help you get every dime of tax savings you are entitled to as an investment property owner under current tax laws.

$19.95 **Buy It Now**

Eviction Secrets for Landlords

Evicting tenants is never fun. But whether it's the end of your problems — or the start of much bigger problems — depends on doing it right. When enough is enough — know your rights, know the law and protect your property!

$19.95 **Buy It Now**

Complete Guide to Conduct Tenant Screenings

How to avoid troublemakers, late-payers and deadbeats by using "tried-and-true" screening methods for your rental properties. Looking for Trouble-free Tenants? Stop dreaming … And start screening … With the Complete Guide to Conduct Tenant Screening from CompleteLandlord.com!

$19.95 **Buy It Now**

How to Buy Foreclosure Property

Interested in investing in foreclosed properties? Want to avoid the major pitfalls that can cost you thousands? The real estate experts and editors at CompleteLandlord.com tell you all you need to know! When it comes to foreclosed properties, the right information and preparation can make all the difference between finding great deals … and losing your shirt. Our experts deliver the crucial up-to-the-minute information YOU need!

$19.95 **Buy It Now**

Understanding Rental Property 1031 Exchanges for Landlords

Are you a landlord or real estate investor who wants to sell your investment property and avoid capital gains tax? A 1031 Exchange might be the answer you are looking for. This report will help you meet your real estate goals and provide you with the education necessary to complete a successful 1031 transaction.

$19.95 **Buy It Now**

Memberships

Silver Premium Membership

Membership includes:

- Unlimited Access to Lease Creation Pro[SM] Customizable State-Specific Leases and over 900+ State-Specific Forms and Letters
- CompleteLandlord.com Property Management Solution[SM] (up to 2 rental units, included)
- 4 Issues of and Archive Access to Landlord Profit Letter[SM]
- 1 Special Report covering a critical landlording topic
- 1 Topical Streaming Webinar/Audio Conference
- Unlimited Access to Content, Forms and Software Upgrades, Maintenance, Hosting, Storage, Multi-layer Security, and Rental Unit Scaleability

$9.97/mo - $97/yr   **Buy It Now**

Gold Premium Membership

Membership includes:

- Unlimited Access to Lease Creation Pro[SM] Customizable State-Specific Leases and over 900+ State-Specific Forms and Letters
- CompleteLandlord.com Property Management Solution[SM] (up to 10 rental units, included)
- 4 Issues of and Archive Access to Landlord Profit Letter[SM]
- 3 Special Reports covering critical landlording topics
- 1 Tenant Screen and Background Check
- 1 Topical Streaming Webinar/Audio Conference
- Unlimited Access to Content, Forms and Software Upgrades, Maintenance, Hosting, Storage, Multi-layer Security, and Rental Unit Scaleability

$19.97/mo - $197/yr   **Buy It Now**

Platinum Premium Membership

Membership includes:

- Unlimited Access to Lease Creation Pro[SM] Customizable State-Specific Leases and over 900+ State-Specific Forms and Letters
- CompleteLandlord.com Property Management Solution[SM] (up to 50 rental units, included)
- 4 Issues of and Archive Access to Landlord Profit Letter[SM]
- 5 Special Reports covering critical landlording topics
- 3 Tenant Screens and Background Checks
- 2 Topical Streaming Webinar/Audio Conference
- Unlimited Access to Content, Forms and Software Upgrades, Maintenance, Hosting, Storage, Multi-layer Security, and Rental Unit Scaleability

$29.97/mo - $297/yr   **Buy It Now**

News & Events

Tax Planning for Landlords: How to Save Thousands of Dollars On Your Taxes This Year – Webinar

Tax Planning for Landlords: How to Save Thousands of Dollars on Your Taxes This Year – Webinar

$99.00 **Buy It Now**

Series LLCs: How Landlords Can Maximize Their Asset Protection – Webinar

If you're a real estate investor, don't miss this CompleteLandlord.com Webinar where you'll learn how to reap the benefits of holding your real estate in a Series LLC.

$99.00 **Buy It Now**

The 10 Biggest Eviction Mistakes Landlords Make and How to Avoid Them – Webinar

If you've ever had to evict a tenant, you know what a nightmare it can be. If not, you should act now to prepare yourself – before costly problems arise.

$99.00 **Buy It Now**

Tips

- ▸ Real Estate Tax Planning for Landlords
- ▸ Rental Property Management Ideas
- ▸ Tenant Screening for Landlords
- ▸ Problem Tenants and Handling Eviction
- ▸ Property Maintenance and Repair
- ▸ Rental Property Investment Strategies
- ▸ How to Avoid Clogged Drains
- ▸ Beginning the Eviction Process: Termination Notices
- ▸ Is a Property Management Company Right For You?
- ▸ Increase Your Bottom Line with Coin-Operated Laundry Machines
- ▸ Greening Your Rental Property
- ▸ How to Avoid High-Risk Tenants
- ▸ Handling Tenant Move-Outs
- ▸ Rent Collection Procedures
- ▸ Freshen Up Your Rental Property
- ▸ Beware: Eminent Domain and more

Order Form

Please provide us with some basic information to begin your free trial.

First Name* _____

Last Name* _____

Address* _____

Address 2 _____

City* _____

State* _____

Zip Code* _____

Phone* _____

Best Time to Call _____

No. of Properties _____

No. of Units _____

Desired Website Address** : http://_____ . completelandlord.com

Company Name* _____

Primary Email Address* _____

I am a new customer _____

I am a returning customer and my password is _____

* Indicates a required field.
** Your Premium Membership includes CompleteLandlord.com's Property Management Solution.
For CompleteLandlord.com to set up the Website for your Property Management Solution you must provide a name to personalize the Website address. We recommend you use the company name of your rental business. Do not use blank spaces or special characters in the company name. For example, if your company name is Elm Properties you should submit "elmproperties" for the Website address. In this example the Website address would be: http://elmproperties.completelandlord.com

At CompleteLandlord.com, we're dedicated to helping you do more yourself. An important part of our service is providing you with the following support:

Call Customer Service at 866.931.9418. Our Customer Service hours are Monday through Friday, 9 a.m. to 5 p.m. Central time.
Contact us via email at customerservice@completelandlord.com

Tenant Screening

Irresponsible, destructive or criminal tenants can cost you thousands of dollars in property damage, missed rent, legal fees and court costs!

What secrets could your next applicant be hiding from you?

Your potential tenant won't let you know if he has a criminal record. She won't tell you if she's had prior evictions. But you'll find out — with a Tenant Screen from CompleteLandlord.com.

99% of the problems landlords face — from bounced checks to evictions — start with bad tenants. They don't respect you, they don't respect their lease, and they certainly don't respect your investment property.

But how can you know if the person who wants to rent your property is who he says he is? How can you know if she's responsible enough to make payments on time?

The answer is a Tenant Screen from CompleteLandlord.com

A CompleteLandlord.com Tenant Screen is the most advanced, most comprehensive way to screen prospective renters for your investment properties. Before you let prospects sign a lease, you'll run their identity through every relevant background check and search allowable by law, including:

Tenant Screen
Price: $24.95
Order Now!

- Credit Check
- Criminal Background Report
- Evictions Report
- Sex Offender List Search
- Terrorist List Search

The simple truth is, people will lie!

They'll forget, they'll falsify and they'll forge. Let a bad character into your rental property and, in the best case, you may lose a few hundred or thousand dollars … in the worst cases you may be liable for criminal activities that take place in property you own.

Don't let this happen. Get a Tenant Screen from CompleteLandlord.com today!

You wouldn't let a convicted felon into your home or allow a convicted sex offender to be around your children. Why would you let them into your rental property?

CompleteLandlord.com helps you be more profitable and productive in your landlording business. Landlording is stressful enough, even with great tenants. It's horrible with bad tenants.

What protected the landlords, their loved ones — and their expensive investment properties — can protect you, too. And the cost is far less than you might think — just $24.95 per Tenant Screen. A small price to pay for peace of mind!

Don't take chances with your property. The smiling face you see may not be who he or she claims to be! Protect your property and your security with a Tenant Screen from CompleteLandlord.com — the most comprehensive background check available without a private detective.

They may not tell you the whole truth. A Tenant Screen will. Order yours now!

Find these and other CompleteLandlord Products and Services at http://completelandlord.com/store.aspx

Be Sure to Read and Benefit from the **Entire**
The CompleteLandlord.com Ultimate Landlord Series

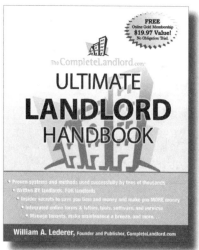

- Proven systems and methods used successfully by tens of thousands
- Written BY and FOR landlords
- Insider secrets to save you time and money
- Make MORE money
- Integrated online forms & letters, tools, software, and services
- Manage tenants, make maintenance a breeze, and more...
- Includes Free Online Gold Trial Membership

400+ pages $19.95/$23.95 CAN

- Insider Investment Strategies and Secrets from *the* Source
- Save Time & Money...Make *MORE* Money
- Find Properties that Will Increase Cash Flow and Work Best for *YOU*
- Streamline the Buy-Hold-Sell Process with Proven Online Tools
- Not a Get-Rich-Quick Guide--Get Rich the CompleteLandlord Way
- Includes Free Online Gold Trial Membership

350+ pages $19.95/$23.95 CAN

- 1 to 5,000 Rental Units - Know and Apply Industry "Best Practices"
- Avoid Legal Pitfalls & the Unexpected Managing Tenants, Vendors and Clients
- Sound Operating, Financial and Tax Advice from Experts
- Proven System and Methods Used Successfully by Tens of Thousands
- Integrated Online Forms & Letters, Tools, Software, and Services
- Includes Free Online Gold Trial Membership

250+ pages $19.95/$23.95 CAN